WITHDRAWN

Integral Books publishes today's finest writers and thinkers addressing the full spectrum of human activity—from business to psychology, spirituality to medicine, education to politics, art to ecology—with a comprehensive approach that encompasses body, mind, and spirit in self, culture, and nature. Rooted in the pioneering work of series editor Ken Wilber and his Integral Institute, these works of scholarship, nonfiction, and literature are designed to awaken, inspire, and liberate.

Soulfully Gay

How Harvard, Sex, Drugs, and
Integral Philosophy Drove Me Crazy
and Brought Me Back to God

Joe Perez

INTEGRAL BOOKS
Boston & London
2007

Integral Books
An imprint of Shambhala Publications, Inc.
Horticultural Hall
300 Massachusetts Avenue
Boston, Massachusetts 02115
www.shambhala.com

9 8 7 6 5 4 3 2 1

First Edition

Printed in the United States of America

♾ This edition is printed on acid-free paper that meets the
American National Standards Institute Z39.48 Standard.

Distributed in the United States by Random House, Inc.,
and in Canada by Random House of Canada Ltd

Designed by Jeff Baker at BookMechanics

Back cover photo by Robert Newell Photography

Library of Congress Cataloging-in-Publication Data

Perez, Joe.
Soulfully gay: how Harvard, sex, drugs, and integral philosophy drove
me crazy and brought me back to God / Joe Perez.—1st ed.
p.   cm.
Includes bibliographical references and index.
ISBN: 978-1-59030-418-1 (alk. paper)
1. Perez, Joe. 2. Christian biography—United States.
3. Gays—United States—Biography. I. Title.
BR1725.P445A3 2007
204.092—dc22
[B]
2006103064

Dedicated to the memory of
Bobby and Ray

He who would lead a Christlike life is he
who is perfectly and absolutely himself.
—OSCAR WILDE

Contents

Foreword by Ken Wilber

I am in the awkward situation of writing a foreword to a book by a gay person. This is an awkward situation not because Joe Perez is gay, but because I have to point it out. I feel the same damn irritation as having to refer to, say, Edmund White as a "gay writer." Nobody has to point out that I am heterosexual, although now I hear that I am not a heterosexual but a metrosexual, although, in fact, I have never had sex with a metro in my life. But I'm sure it is a wonderful experience.

Nevertheless, because I am going to have to include that information—culture today demands it, from those who are both for and against homosexuals—then let me say this. Joe Perez's book is perhaps the most astonishing, brilliant, and courageous look at the interface between individual belief and cultural values that has been written in our times. By a homosexual, or a heterosexual, or any other sexual I am aware of.

As it happens, this rather extraordinary chronicle unfolds around several conflict-inducing facts, one of which is that Joe is indeed gay; another of which is that Joe was raised Roman (homophobic) Catholic; another is that he often has authentic mystical states; and yet another is that Joe is, but only occasionally, clinically psychotic. It is the jolting collision of those items, held together by Joe's courage in the face of all of them, that makes this chronicle so extraordinary in so many ways.

The last item—the occasional trip into realms labeled madness—can mean, especially if you are a writer, that you are given to telling the unvarnished, brutal, searing truth, whether society likes it or not. And not the Sylvia Plath look-at-me kinds of truth, but the spiritual-seers and mad-shaman types of truth, the truths that really hurt, the truths that get into society's craw and stick there, causing festering metaphysical sores indicative of social cancers or worse—but also the types of truths that speak to you deeply, authentically, radiantly, if you have the courage to listen.

As it turns out, Joe is a writer, a rip-roaring wonder of a writer, and he had the courage to tell those truths, to endure them, to have them rip him apart, hospitalize him, brutalize him, kill and reassemble him, in one of the most astonishing tales of death and resurrection you are likely to find in today's literature.

There is one other reason this is an awkward foreword for me, which is that Joe's transformation, or at least its narrative, depends in part on my own writings. For those of you blessedly unfamiliar with my work, here's the *Reader's Digest* version, in one short paragraph, I promise.

In a series of over a dozen books, I have attempted to create a comprehensive map of human nature (which is a little less grandiose than it sounds). Everybody knows that you don't want to confuse the map with the territory, which is definitely true. But you don't want a totally fucked-up map, either. So in order to make as few mistakes as possible, I basically took over 100 of the best maps of human nature drawn by various cultures— East and West, premodern and modern and postmodern—and attempted to combine the enduring elements of each, along with whatever new insights I might add. The result is called "integral" because it attempts to be widely inclusive, combining the various truths into a view that is as coherent and comprehensive as possible.

What often happens if a person studies this integral map is that it begins to make room in your psyche, in your being, in your soul, for all the parts of you that were disowned, whether by society, your parents, your peers, whomever. An integral approach even makes room for those who did the disowning to you. And there, I believe, is part of the key to the extraordinary events that begin to unfold in Joe's awareness, his being, his life. In a remarkably short period chronicled in this book, as Joe takes up a more integral approach, there is a profound resolution and integration of an enormous number of seemingly contradictory items—anti-gay Catholic upbringing, life as a gay man, authentic mystical spirituality, psychotic delusions. I don't want to overplay the role of an integral approach, but it is part of this extraordinary journey of self-awakening and self-acceptance.

But having a map is one thing, traversing the real territory, quite another—especially if that territory is marked by the occasional straitjacket, brutal homophobia, drug addiction, a plummeting T-cell count, and deserting friends, all nonetheless cut with profound and authentic spiritual experiences, transcendental grace and glory, deep love and friendship where it counts, and insights that even shamans would envy, all in a bottle with a skull and crossbones on it.

Is it possible for a skull to smile, just out of spite? The anti-gay bias in most mainstream religions Joe is able not to *hate*, but to *integrate* by understanding that those aspects of religion are developmentally earlier, and, yes, lower, than the mystical elements of those religions, every single one of which agrees that homosexuality is perfectly acceptable to Spirit, which doesn't recognize those distinctions anyway. Such an integral approach acknowledges that all views have a degree of truth, but some views are more true than others—more evolved, more developed, more adequate. And so let's get that part out of the way right now: homophobia in any form, as far as I can tell, stems from a lower level of human development—but it is a level, it exists, and one has to make room in one's awareness for those lower levels as well, just as one has to include third grade in any school curriculum. Just don't, you know, put those people in charge of anything important.

As for the book you now hold in your hands, although this comparison is a cliché, allow me to run with it for a bit: this narrative begs comparison with Antonin Artaud, the critics' darling, who rescued his life from disaster by turning it into art. But I believe Artaud was poorly understood by both the Beats (who obsessed over his madness) and the professors (who obsessed over his art), because the point was not Artaud's art but his sincerity in his art—not his truth but his truthfulness. And Joe Perez is as truthful an artist as you are likely to find, certainly in today's atmosphere, where irony has replaced authenticity and surface veneer is valued over depth. Joe has followed his pain as it descends into madness and his ecstasy as it ascends into God, has refined sincerity itself as a way to understand his Christianity, his sexuality, his madness, his mysticism, and bundled them up in an integral embrace, and told the truth about them all.

I wouldn't report the following, if it weren't for that. As it happens, shortly after Joe had completed the first draft of the manuscript for this book, he had a relatively rare dip into madness—probably induced by his latest meds as T cells crashed under 100—during which period he sent me a copy of the draft, which was our first real contact. Curious, I began reading this riveting narrative, which reached at times a breathtaking beauty alternating with neuron-melting horror.

And then there it was, in the margin, and right next to a stunningly beautiful paragraph of prose: a series of paranoid scribbles, in magic marker, freshly written by the hand of someone gone briefly mad. Joe had gone through his manuscript, in that state, and written notes to me in the margins, and sometimes across the page itself, in circles, or squeezed between lines. Seeing the first scrawl, I burst into tears, sobbing at the sight of it all— exquisite beauty and crayon scribbles, all right there, all at once, the urgent messages splashed across the page like a hit-and-run driver splattering a body across the pavement—it was the *bothness* of those messages that tore my own heart in two, for they marked off the extremes between which Joe's life oscillates, soaring truths to torturing shadows—and yet some of the messages were so beautiful, touching, alive, yet not really there—still, on the page simultaneously, a screaming exclamation mark to a reality that was both beauty and betrayal, delusion and enlightenment—and only then did I begin to realize what an extraordinary, absolutely extraordinary, accomplishment Joe's narrative was—or rather, Joe's life was, a *life* as he has made it, fashioned it, forced it to be, with grace and glory and courage and surrender.

I don't want you to think Joe does that often—the trips into those states, that is. They are indeed rare. It's not merely or even especially the madness that makes this narrative, but the mystical states, deeply authentic, and the politics and the outreach and the bridge of light and the determination to see it all through. But how many times do you have to be in a straightjacket in the emergency room (it happened to Joe once) to get the point that reality is here to brutalize you, rape you, toss you on the side of the street and go its merry way? Start as a human being in this culture, then toss in madness, toss in mystical states, toss in being gay, toss in being HIV-positive, toss in a religion that assures you God hates you for all of that—and then look me in the eye and tell me you can feel okay about yourself. I dare you, I just dare you.

Well, friends, that is what Joe Perez manages to do. Read this book, and when finished, ask yourself, "I wonder if Joe can look me in the eye and tell me he feels okay about himself—deeply, deeply okay about himself?" And you will know the answer to that question is yes, a resounding, joyous, glorious, staggeringly beautiful *yes*.

It is that *yes* that has made Joe's life itself into a work of art, as beautiful an artwork as can be imagined, an artwork of the great perfection. And thus, for at least once that I am aware of nowadays, the cliché reveals the grain of truth that keeps clichés alive. The stuff of Joe's art, the raw materials, can be found in his essays, his blogs, this book, delivered with urgency and lust and luminosity, the best and the worst, the glorious and the degraded—there is room for all of it in that resounding *Yes!* for the secret is not that all of it is pretty, but that you tell the truth about it, converting even the grotesque into the sublime, if you tell the truth. Joe's life is being artfully lived in the very fact of its truthfulness, its deep embrace, shadows and warts and worms and all, woven unhesitatingly into the tapestry of a lustrous display, a deep peace, an abiding love . . . and therein, surely, a lesson for us all, this artwork that is a thing of beauty, this artwork that will never die, even when the frame around it perishes.

Acknowledgments

I am grateful to Ken Wilber for generously writing a foreword for an author he'd never met. Wilber, Jim Marion, Toby Johnson, Michael McCann, Ben Sharpe, David Fen, and David O'Neal read drafts of this manuscript and offered valuable feedback.

Fellow bloggers and other writers too numerous to mention gave me valuable feedback. I am especially grateful to everyone in the blogosphere whose words have been incorporated (with attribution) into the body of this book.

LoAnn Halden, editor at the *Weekly News,* and Bill Watson, publisher of *Contax Guide,* both gave important encouragement and support to my column.

Kendra Crossen Burroughs, editor at Shambhala Publications, and Jacob Morris have provided invaluable assistance in improving the manuscript for this book.

I want to thank the men of The ManKind Project, especially each man who has done his work with me in integration groups over the past several years. You have done much to teach me about being a man who connects his body, heart, and soul.

Finally and most especially, I am indebted to every member of my family for their love, support, and blessings over the years. Mom, you are the best. I love you.

Soulfully Gay

Introduction

By that which suffices the spirit, we can measure the extent of
its loss.
—HEGEL

This book focuses on the experiences and thoughts of one man, but the
journey depicted is the common quest to be soulfully, gaily human. Since
my childhood, I have struggled to grow in my understanding of life, God,
and everything else. Foremost among the questions with which I wrestled:
how shall I reconcile spirituality with sexuality? My explorations led to a
growth in consciousness that is tracked, step by step, in these pages.
Included is just over a year of journal entries written when I was 34 years
old. Not simply a memoir in the conventional sense, this is a look at how
religious beliefs and cultural values develop in stages of increasing validity
and truth. It is also an argument that some of the key problems that face
our society today—for example, the conflicts involving gays and religion—
stem from a lack of integral development. Finally, I also articulate a vision
for bringing about higher modes of awareness in the individual heart, trans-
mitting healing in our families and culture, and institutionalizing these
changes in our social and political structures.

What follows is a glimpse at a man's journey down two paths that can seem divergent or even antithetical but are ultimately united—self-discovery and mysticism. These two paths have a common aim: liberation. Liberation is initiation into our fullest humanity, including those aspects of our flawed self and crazy world that we would rather deny. This chronicle of faith and narcissism, mysticism and madness, brilliance and darkness, offers a vision of the possibilities of authentic freedom. This is a tale that insists there is value to deeply searching and baring our sufferings, no matter how disturbing, dangerous, or terrifying. Only then may we be carried beyond our limited selves into a greater, timeless, formless essence. Find your Self . . . if you dare.

I was born in September 1969 in Moses Lake, Washington, a farming town with a population of about ten thousand. My mother worked as a legal and executive secretary. My father was an Air Force veteran and potato farmer. He also worked at times as a barber and as a welder at a sugar-beet-processing factory. In the late seventies, Dad's plant closed and laid everyone off. A few years later, my parents split. Mom raised me almost single-handedly after the divorce. She was religious and faithfully transmitted her Roman Catholic tradition, but I was bored by mass and attended mostly out of a desire to please her. My father was nominally Baptist; but if he had any religious convictions, I never heard about them. My family rarely spoke about religious matters. However, my parents are second-generation Mexican-Americans, among whom piety is often considered respectable, just so long as it doesn't deviate too much from the respectable American forms.

My early religious education consisted in attending weekly catechism classes at Our Lady of Fatima called CCD (Confraternity of Christian Doctrine) each Wednesday after I finished my day at public school. Today I am grateful for the opportunity to have been exposed to such religious fundamentals as prayer, music, liturgy, and doctrine. From approximately 12 years of religious education, I have no horror stories involving domineering nuns or abusive priests. My teachers were good women and men who did the best they could. However, I detested attending CCD for many of those 12 years. When you're a boy in grade school, being religious just isn't cool. The more you take religion seriously, the more you are regarded with suspicion. I felt out of place and remote from my peers, especially most of the other boys. They upset me, because I thought they were rambunctious mischief makers who distracted serious students such as myself from our lessons. Unlike some other parishes, ours offered the sacrament of Confirmation not to children but to adolescents. The rite was a sort of initiation allowing students of high school age to officially commit themselves to the Roman Catholic faith. I eagerly looked forward to taking the sacrament, because thereafter I would be considered an adult. And as an adult, I would be free from all further religious obligations.

Although I frequently felt like an outcast in CCD, there was one boy whose companionship made the experience much more bearable. Keith was my closest friend from preschool to high school. Keith was as much a bad boy as any of the other boys in CCD, but we got along swimmingly nevertheless. His home was only a few blocks from mine, and both our houses were just a short distance from the church's school. We shared the walk home from CCD almost every week for many years, usually talking about frivolous and rebellious things, as boys do. We were both altar boys, and we arranged our schedules so we could often serve together at mass. We were even the altar servers at the funeral mass for Keith's older brother. After Kevin died from cancer, Moses Lake named a newly constructed street in his honor. As it happened, after Kevin Way was built, the street became the shortest route for our walks together. Hardly a week went by when we didn't go past the sign bearing his brother's name.

I had two older brothers of my own and an older sister. My relationship with Bobby, the elder of my brothers, was especially close, for we always seemed to have a natural sympathy with each other's feelings. Bobby was eight years my elder, a sensitive teenager with curly dark hair and brown eyes. With his friends, he could be altruistic to a fault; he would give whatever he had to please them. With me, Bobby was a mentor, caregiver, and protector. My brother taught me how to color with crayons so well that I won every supermarket coloring contest in my age bracket. I spent much of my playtime drawing mazes—hundreds and hundreds of them—and Bobby would always take the time to try to solve them. When I was younger, I would sometimes climb up to my brother's bunk to sleep. He sometimes begged me not to bother him, though, because I hogged the covers. Bobby was also a valuable ally when there was the occasional need for protection, whether it was from bullies on the playground or from Dad's angry outbursts.

In junior high school, I began to experience my first emotional and sexual attractions toward others. My attractions were primarily toward persons of my own sex, mostly boys who exuded a cool confidence and athletic prowess. As an adolescent, I had many friends who were girls, but I took little interest in female bodies. Instead, I grew aroused almost exclusively when seeing or thinking about attractive male bodies. My sexual feelings toward males came as naturally to me as feelings toward females came to the boys around me. When I masturbated to sexual fantasies involving boys, I experienced great pleasure and relief from sexual tension. I tried to fantasize about girls but rarely succeeded in reaching orgasm. American culture and society terribly stigmatized homosexuality (and still does to a large extent). Most religions claim that being a practicing homosexual is a one-way ticket to hell. Of course, today I recognize that there are many subtleties in religious views of homosexuality. But the message that I received as a youngster was clear: it was unsafe to acknowledge or express my same-sex attractions.

I succeeded in keeping my same-sex attractions a secret. When I eventually came out of the closet, nobody said, "I knew it all along." I told myself that my homoerotic longings would go away on their own if I didn't act on them. I told myself that if they didn't go away I could deal with the issue when I was older. I threw myself into many activities to divert my attention from sex: academics, piano lessons, fantasy role-playing games, video games, computers, and the high school newspaper and debate club. I answered "How are you?" with "Just fine, thank you very much." But "fine" was not my deeper truth. I kept family, friends, and everyone else from getting too close. Denial of my same-sex desires remained a source of inner conflict for many years.

When I was 13 years old, I had to recite a literary passage from memory in Mrs. Smith's Honors English class. I memorized the opening section of a Ray Bradbury short story about human colonists on Mars who find themselves mysteriously transforming into Martians. As I stood before the class, I tried hard to stand still enough to speak, but I couldn't. My feet were trembling so hard. I had to brace myself against something to keep from falling down. Taking pity on her shy pupil, Mrs. Smith invited me to give the speech sitting down. I gave the speech from a desk with my feet elevated. If my feet came into contact with the ground, their shaking created such vibrations that the entire desk would shake and rattle. The speech went just fine, thank you very much.

This recitation was hardly the first time I had spoken publicly. But in junior high, I lost the ability to communicate before groups without feeling a debilitating anxiety that stopped words dead in my throat. Perhaps it was tension created by the need to repress my homosexual feelings in order to stay in good standing with parents, church, and society. Or perhaps my debilitating shyness before groups was caused by something else. In any case, I began to realize that I would need to struggle to overcome my introversion.

I accepted without much questioning my church's teachings regarding God, Jesus Christ, the Holy Trinity, the Blessed Virgin, and so forth. The Church taught that God so loved the world that He sacrificed His only begotten son to die on a cross to redeem the world from sin. But I don't recall thinking too much about doctrine. As I grew older, some things about the world eventually began to strike me as perplexing. I had been taught that religion was supposed to be about things of great importance: the salvation of souls, the reason why we're all here, and so forth. But few people seemed to actually live their lives in ways that reflected the teachings of the religious authorities. My friends included Mormons, evangelical Christians, Pentecostals, Methodists, and Presbyterians. I got the firm impression that our churches taught a few different things but that one's denomination had more to do with accidents of birth than considered choices. Most people took on the religion they were given by their parents. Religion was just another label to wear, like being a doctor, a Latino, or an American. Others disagreed. They thought that religion offered nothing less than salvation from a soul's eternal damnation in hell.

Religion claims to address our ultimate concerns as humans; its success in that regard is debatable. Unquestionable, however, is its role as a contributor to conflict and violence in the world. Many terrible crimes have been committed in the name of God throughout history. If religion was just another part of one's identity, I began to wonder: why not shed it and end much strife in the world? What right did I have to believe my own religion was true, when other religions said that Roman Catholics were going to hell? Did I really believe that only Roman Catholics in good standing with the pope were going to heaven? The world could be a very confusing place.

When I was 16, I began to take a serious interest in religious faith. The key event was my attendance at a spiritual retreat as part of the CCD Confirmation class. The retreat was facilitated by other young adults from a national Catholic evangelical team. These were the first young people that I had ever met who struck me as actually filled with enthusiasm for the Roman Catholic Church. They spoke of their intimate relationship with Jesus and their love of the blessed sacraments. Most of all, they exuded warmth and joy and love, and I began to feel that I could trust them. I became more aware of how very little I actually trusted anybody. On this retreat, I saw other young people revealing their secrets, sharing their pain, and finding love and acceptance in return. I trembled inside with a desire to be purged of my secrets, but I kept quiet. As the retreat concluded, I remained in denial about my same-sex attractions but longed for the aliveness exuded by these passionate young people. I began to consider doing some sort of ministry later in life.

By this time, Keith and I were no longer walking to CCD. We had taken a driver's education class together the previous summer, and we both earned our licenses around the same time. Keith would pick me up each Wednesday and drive me to the Confirmation class. Sometimes he spoke about girls, beer, cutting class, and breaking rules. He gave me a pinch of snuff and laughed when I nearly gagged. One night he took me out for a joyride on a country road. It gave me such a fright, but I didn't say a word to stop him. Instead, we basked in the adrenaline rush. But after the religious retreat, Keith seemed more moody and introspective than I had ever seen him. I got the sense that we each wanted to say something to the other but were holding back. I wanted to tell Keith how painful it was to keep my secrets from the whole world. I wanted to tell him that I doubted my own worth and the teachings of religion. I wanted to tell him that the retreat stirred something deep within me, but I didn't quite know what it was. However, I said nothing. Even with my best friend, the fear of intimacy was simply too great.

One night, Keith pulled his car over to the side of the road and said that he had something to tell me. He said, "Thank you for being a good friend for so many years and for being such a good influence on me." That was all. But these tender words were difficult for Keith to express, and they showed a deeper bond than we had ever shared. In fact, I had never heard any man, save my father and brothers, speak to me with such kindness. Mushy sentiments aren't the sorts of things that boys usually say to each other, at least not in my experience. A man doesn't tell another man that he loves him; those are words for queers and faggots. Keith didn't use the word "love," but he might as well have. I wish I could remember what I said in reply to Keith that night, but the words elude my memory. I suspect that I didn't speak the one word that best described my deepest truth: love.

A short while after this conversation, Keith lost control of his car on an icy patch of highway. The car crashed into a semi-truck and Keith was killed instantly. Mom broke the news to me when she picked me up from school to take me to my piano lesson. We sat in the car as the last bell rang. I told her that there was no need to cancel my lesson. I told her not to worry about me. I told her that I would be fine. But a few minutes later I could no longer contain myself. She took me home, where I went to my room, shut the door, and cried. Crying alone was my familiar pattern for being with feelings of sadness.

I had some familiarity with death, but losing my best friend brought mortality closer to home than ever before. My visible grieving process was short. I felt bad and stayed home from school the next day. Then I said my goodbyes to Keith at his funeral mass. I sensed that something had changed for my friend on the retreat. There was something about him that wasn't there before. I didn't know what it was. I wondered if he may have healed an open wound related to his brother's death. I also began to wonder what spiritual perspective he may have found in his last days to have become willing to risk greater intimacy in our friendship.

In the months that followed Keith's funeral, I began to seek answers to questions about faith. The fact that two brothers in the same family had died so young was bewildering. Keith's father had a fatal heart attack the next year, adding to the incomprehensibility of the tragedy. What purpose could there possibly be for such madness in the world? Why does God permit suffering? Or is there no God? I also wondered about what had happened to my friend. He was gone, but was he in a better place called heaven? Should I pray for his soul? Should I even dare to consider the unspeakable possibility that Keith might be in hell, punished by a petty God for looking at *Playboy* or breaking a curfew?

Religion wasn't taught in public schools, and the official CCD textbooks weren't of much use, so I began to look for answers on my own. I read the New Testament for the first time and checked out a book from the library on Roman Catholic theology. The book claimed that the existence of God was known by reason alone and that modern philosophers beginning with Descartes and Kant committed a grave philosophical error in denying this basic truth. I didn't know what to think about these things. The book was far more philosophical and sophisticated in its approach to religion than anything I had encountered. Reading the book filled my head with more questions than answers.

As time passed, life continued much as it had before the accident. In the Catholic Church, I took the sacrament of Confirmation and occasionally went to the cemetery with my mother bearing flowers. She would visit the grave of her nephew Gabriel and others who were passed away. By this time, I was a member of the high school debate team. I had overcome much of my resistance to speaking in public, but everyone told me that my gestures were stiff and my tone of voice unnatural. I decided that I had to directly face my fear of public speaking, so I would practice in front of a mirror for hours at a time. I wanted very much to be a funny man, but my jokes were so bad that my friends dubbed them "Joe Jokes." By my senior year of high school, I became one of the state's top-ranked debaters and won second-prize trophies for two humorous speeches.

My friend and debate partner for two years was a Mormon whose parents were educated and well-to-do. Cannon shared the Mormon scriptures with me, and we once prayed together with his parents. I remember asking my friend why I should believe that his faith was the one true religion, as opposed to the teachings of the Roman Catholic Church. He said that according to the Book of Mormon, if I simply prayed with a sincere heart and asked God to reveal the truth, then He would speak the truth into my heart. That answer may have worked for Cannon, but it didn't satisfy me. How does anyone really know for sure that God is speaking to them? Cannon invited me to attend church with him, but I declined the invitation.

Cannon and I were both making plans for college. I had always pictured myself going to a university close to home, but when I learned that Cannon would be applying to Ivy League schools, I began to think twice. If Cannon was going to apply to prestigious schools, then why shouldn't I? I had been telling myself that nobody from Moses Lake ever goes anywhere like Harvard or Yale. Afraid of being perceived as arrogant, I was too timid to let anybody know that I considered myself worthy of the Ivy League. I applied to highly selective colleges and prayed that one of them would offer me lots of scholarship money. I wrote my college admissions essays on my attitude toward life, selecting a quote from the Stoic philosopher Marcus Aurelius as a jumping-off point. In my admissions essay to Harvard, I listed a speech on joke-telling techniques as my greatest scholastic achievement to date.

I enjoyed attending mass each week because it was an opportunity to take time away from my hectic school schedule to be with my mother. She spoke to me of the importance of faith and expressed her hope that I would learn to appreciate its value. She revealed the details of a near-death experience she had had as a child when she choked on a bone at the family dinner table. She had witnessed herself choking as if she were floating above her body, against the ceiling of the room. Then darkness enveloped her and a blue light came toward her. She believed that she saw a blue light on the other side of death that was the robe of the Blessed Virgin. She knew it was the Virgin Mary because the Mother of God is frequently depicted as wearing blue in Hispanic art. Mom didn't actually die, of course. She was saved from choking by one of her many brothers. She once told me: "You'll see how important faith is someday when you have children of your own." I replied that she was probably right.

Throughout my high school days, I remained in denial of my same-sex attractions and was sexually active with nobody other than myself. I wanted very much to be normal, so I dated a few girls. I enjoyed their friendship very much and found them attractive, even quite beautiful. However, kissing and caressing a girl inspired precious little romantic yearning or sexual arousal. At the same time, I longed deeply to kiss a handsome man. Dating girls didn't diminish my same-sex attractions in the least; in fact, my homoerotic fantasy life grew increasingly important to the point of obsession. My feelings toward men weren't going to disappear, and the dilemmas posed by my denial of them would follow me three thousand miles to Cambridge, Massachusetts.

My early childhood experiences were so sheltered that my airplane flight to Boston was my very first time east of Idaho. My freshman year at Harvard was an opportunity to expand my horizons in one of the most intellectually stimulating environments imaginable.

I originally planned to major in English but discovered a stronger interest in philosophy. Two classes fascinated me above all the others. Government professor Harvey C. Mansfield offered a course on ancient and medieval philosophers such as Plato, Aristotle, Augustine, and Aquinas. Reading Plato's *Republic* for the first time was an especially life-altering encounter, demanding that I go much deeper in my thinking than ever before. Philosopher Stanley Cavell offered a moral reasoning course that blew my mind wide open. He exposed me to insights from modern philosophers such as Locke, John Stuart Mill, Kant, Nietzsche, Emerson, Thoreau, Marx, Heidegger, and Wittgenstein. Simultaneously, he asked me to synthesize the moral ideas from these thinkers with literature and cinema. My term paper on feminism and moral perfectionism in Henrik Ibsen's *A Doll's House* earned me my first A at Harvard, a grade that built my confidence as a young scholar. However, it was exposure to Nietzsche's philosophy that most disturbed my mind. The German philosopher's vehement anti-Christian philosophy was gravely troubling and called me to question the beliefs and values of my sheltered Catholic upbringing. I soon adopted an open-minded attitude, as opposed to a rigid, defensive stance of doctrinaire agreement with the teachings of the Catholic Church. I declared my intention to major in philosophy. I hoped to spend my college days reading great books, probing the meaning of life, and encountering timeless wisdom.

I did not openly label myself agnostic. Instead, I struggled to articulate the meaning of my Christian faith amid many doubts. I confronted the fact that for many of the most educated members of society, religion is an irrational holdover from the distant past. Belief in God is regarded by many intellectuals as a sign of backwardness. Although the study of philosophy made me basically agnostic, I continued to search for truth and tried to do good. I attended the student mass at St. Paul's every week and tutored inner-city youth with other Christians. As an active member of the Catholic student association at Harvard, I found myself making friends with many young men and women who openly shared their doubts and faith. Together we questioned both the teachings of the Vatican and the dominant values of our liberal higher education. During this time, I remained in denial regarding my same-sex attractions. However, simply speaking my doubts about God and the teachings of the Catholic Church with as much candor as I could muster was a profoundly healing experience.

I returned home for the summer following my freshman year. The family broke terrible news: my brother Bobby was living with HIV, and he was very ill. And—by the way—he had attempted suicide nine months earlier. The reasons for his suicide attempt were said to be that he was gay, that he hated himself, and that he was angry with an ex-boyfriend. A psychologist told Mom that Bobby was gay because he had suffered emotional abuse from his father and that homosexuality is often a consequence of such abuse. My family decided to keep all of Bobby's troubles away from me because they didn't want me to be distracted from my studies. As it turned out, Bobby had recovered from his suicide attempt, found a committed partnership, and regained his will to live. However, he spent most of the summer in the hospital with a mysterious form of meningitis that the doctors thought would likely be fatal. I got a job doing manual labor for the Moses Lake parks department and spent most of my days weeding shrub beds to earn money for school. Mom and I drove three hours to Seattle every other weekend to visit Bobby in the hospital. My brother successfully fought the meningitis and returned to his home with Ray and their six dogs. My family accepted Ray into our family and visited the couple frequently. Although the news about Bobby's troubles came as quite a shock, I was emotionally unable to experience any deep feeling. I said comforting words to my brother and told him that I loved him, but I did not cry. I also seemed not to notice anything unusual about my absence of feeling.

That fall, I was glad to leave behind the heaviness of facing my brother's terminal illness. I looked forward to reuniting with my roommates and other friends. I had few friendships with women, a fact that I attribute to my inner sexual conflicts and low self-esteem. Most of all, I feared dating women because I didn't want them to discover my secret should I be unable to perform sexually. I was fortunate to have a wonderful group of male friends to hang out with, and over the years I grew increasingly comfortable opening up with them. Becoming emotionally vulnerable with men remained difficult work. It took me weeks to share the news about my brother's troubles with some of my closest male friends, and I did so only with the greatest anxiety. Declaring that I had a gay brother was especially difficult, because I didn't want my friends to associate me too closely with homosexuality. The most painful aspect of my friendships with my college friends was finding myself attracted to a few of them in ways that were confusing. I began to wonder if these were romantic feelings. I was troubled with secret emotional and sexual obsessions beyond my ability to control.

Harvard encouraged an atmosphere of acceptance for diversity, and the school strongly supported the meetings of a gay and lesbian student group. I met an openly gay man my age at a Catholic retreat. I marveled at Tom's openness about his homosexuality and the surprising amount of acceptance he found among so many people within the Catholic student group. I began to wonder what my life would be like if I were to discover that I was gay. Would I have the courage to come out of the closet, as Tom had done? Although I accepted Tom into my circle of friends, I also put up a wall against getting too close in the friendship. Tom was a constant mirror of the parts of myself about which I was most in denial. Distance from friends was the price I had to pay to keep my secrets.

Although I could not feel any strong emotions toward my brother, I spent much time thinking about his troubles. I spent my sophomore year of college divided between studies and brooding over the dramas of my family life. My favorite course was a science class taught by David Layzer called "Chance, Necessity, and Order." It tackled both evolutionary biology and quantum physics. I remember asking the professor if he believed that his theories about chaos and randomness demonstrated the impossibility of the existence of God, and he said yes they did. I also took a survey course on 19th-century German philosophy, a course on medieval literature, and an introduction to deductive logic. I spent months reading

Hegel's *Phenomenology of Spirit,* a remarkable book that for a short time in the early 1800s created a widespread sense that philosophy had achieved the ultimate synthesis of knowledge of all kinds. Whenever I tried to do my logic homework, I found myself totally blocked. I would just sit in the library, stare at the pages of the handouts for hours, and daydream endlessly. I stopped attending logic lectures because of my inability to study, and consequently I earned the first and only failing grade of my college career. I did well enough in my other courses, however, and even pulled an A in Professor Layzer's course.

At this time my interest began to shift from philosophy to psychology. My preoccupation with my brother's troubles led me to secretly read books regarding human psychosexual development. I studied a variety of psychological and psychoanalytical perspectives and found that there was little agreement regarding the etiology of homosexuality. Many theorists claimed that homosexuality and neurosis went hand in hand; however, others claimed that such theories were the result of unscientific prejudices. I wanted to believe the latter was true, but intellectual honesty required me to consider all possibilities. The medical establishment had gradually been won over to the view that homosexuality is normal, but critics dismissed the move as politically motivated.

The study of psychology led me to the conclusion that my lack of emotional response to my brother's troubles was neurotic. I made an appointment with a mental health counselor to discuss my neurosis but was too distraught to talk openly with her. I began to turn memories of my childhood over and over again in my mind, always with a focus on potential pathologies and possible explanations for my own homosexual feelings. I would go on long solitary walks along the Charles River in the early morning hours. These were the moments when I contemplated suicide. Perhaps only my desire to avoid adding to the burden carried by my mother prevented me from killing myself.

As my final exams approached, I found myself painfully blocked from studying. One night, after a full day of avoiding my work, I entered an unusual state of mind. I would describe the experience as trancelike, except that I was completely rational and lucid the whole time. I felt perfect bliss and happiness, but even the word "feel" seems inadequate. It was more like being Bliss, a state of being much stronger than a mere sensation or emotion. It had the intensity of the most powerful orgasm, but there was no sensation in my genitals or elsewhere in my body; rather, a state of euphoria seemed to permeate my entire body from head to toe. Not even that description seems right, for the joy was not located inside my body as opposed to outside it. It simply was.

In the midst of the Bliss, one image appeared in my mind's eye: a fist, in my head, uncoiling. When I envisioned the fist in the process of uncoiling, I immediately experienced a sense of lightness, serenity, and euphoria. After a while, the intensity of the experience began to fade; however, by simply picturing the fist in my mind and then seeing it uncoil, the Bliss returned as intensely as before.

The experience began immediately after I went to bed one night. I was basking in this state for a while, and then I decided to fill up a bathtub with warm water and get in. I felt so giddy, I wanted to laugh, sing, and dance around. However, I also wanted to be respectful of my sleeping roommate and neighbors in Winthrop House. At first, I expected that whatever was happening to me would be over at any moment. And yet it continued with no sign of abating. Hours passed. I had the feeling that if I didn't go to sleep, the Bliss could go on forever. Eventually I got out of the tub, dried myself off, and went to sleep. I slept great. In the morning, I felt calm and relaxed, but the experience was definitely over. I spent the next day in ecstasy. I couldn't stop thinking about the strange event. I spent much of the next day alone, and somehow the experience seemed so intensely personal that I didn't want to tell a soul.

In the days and weeks that followed, I felt a major emotional shift. Tears began to flow freely, and I welcomed their presence as a sign of emotional health. I began to enjoy life once again, getting back to the business of doing my neglected studies. After a few days passed, I told my roommate about the experience. I told him it felt like something I'd only vaguely heard about: a mystical experience of God. And then at dinner a short time later, I asked one of my chaplains if she had ever had a mystical experience. She said she had, and then she described it to me. I recognized elements of my own experience in what she shared; and although my experience had lasted much longer than hers I had no doubt that what I had experienced was an encounter with God. I knew virtually nothing about mysticism at the time, so I got hold of William James's *The Varieties of Religious Experience* and read the book from cover to cover. I recognized much of my experience in the reports of the mystics; however, I was surprised to learn that most mystical experiences are quite brief. The length of my experience seemed unusual.

My next load of courses in my sophomore year included psychological anthropology and biology. I lost interest in most of the philosophy courses but enjoyed the study of psychology immensely. I considered changing my major to psychology or anthropology. I struggled with one overarching question: what, if anything, did the mystical experience mean? Although I was certain that the experience matched the reports of mystics described by William James, I didn't quite know what else to think. There was no booming voice from heaven, no sights of angels or Jesus, no fiery conviction of the inerrancy of the Bible or the infallibility of the pope. Indeed, there was no cognitive content associated with the experience at all.

The best theory that I could come up with at the time was that, somehow, the experience was identical to directly encountering an Ultimate Reality. That is, an entity that the philosopher Hegel would have called Spirit. I imagined that perhaps I got a taste of the nature of the universe as it truly is and that somehow ordinary reality is less real. Perhaps Bliss is the only real thing, I supposed, and everything else is a mask over the true peace and joy at the core of the universe. I even imagined that when I die, my soul might return to that state, perhaps experiencing joy forever. Maybe, I figured, that's what heaven is.

This theory of what my experience might have been remained only that: a theory. I also considered another theory to be just about equally probable—namely, the idea that the experience was simply an explosion of serotonin or other chemicals in my brain intended by purely natural processes to restore my psychological equilibrium. I considered the possibility that there was no Ultimate Reality at all (none that I could know anything definite about, at least) and that mystical experience was merely a biochemical high created by firing synapses in the brain. According to this theory, there is no intrinsic value or purpose to my mystical experience, because there is no intrinsic meaning to anything. And when people die, all that they have ever been is simply annihilated; and that is all. All who have ever believed otherwise were terribly mistaken, were victims of delusion.

So it happened that as a young man I managed to have a direct mystical experience and yet remained for all practical purposes an agnostic. I was an open-minded agnostic, to be sure—and a man who still continued to struggle with religious beliefs. But an agnostic I was nonetheless. I refused to give the mystical experience a final, or even provisional, interpretation. I held a variety of possibilities in tension but simply didn't know what to believe about them. The memory of the Bliss became ever more irrelevant to my life with each passing year.

I continued to attend mass and Catholic student functions, but in my inner life a gulf grew between my sense of identity and the religion of my childhood. In this space of freedom from fear of the religion's condemnations, I discovered that I had the courage to look at my homosexuality for the first time. What I saw was a mess of conflicting feelings and beliefs. Nothing in my experience gave me any hope that my attractions could be changed. Yes, I had internalized shame, but was there any good reason to be ashamed of my body and its innate attractions to other men? There is something innate about sex that self-evidently affirms the goodness of the body and of erotic pleasure. I thought that the phobic attitude of religions toward pleasure and sexuality was surely wrongheaded. Orthodox Christian doctrine links pleasure with Satan, holding that pleasure was suggested to Adam and Eve by the wickedness of the serpent. Essentially, Christian tradition teaches that pleasure is bad because a talking snake told us so. How ridiculous is that!

One question seemed inescapable in my mind: if homosexuality is a natural and good thing, and gay sex is morally okay, then what does it mean that every major world religion (that is, Christianity, Buddhism, Hinduism, Judaism, Islam, and Confucianism) has condemned homosexuality to one degree or another? The hypothesis of the atheists that God does not exist and that religion is an illusion seemed to offer the most plausible explanation for this generalization. Religion is almost certainly the fruit of the herd's unconscious resentments and prejudices, the future of an illusion, the will of priestly classes to dominate and control others, and the projection of humanity's attributes onto a nonexistent mythic realm. Nietzsche,

Freud, Marx, and Feuerbach were right, and the Christian theologians were wrong. When I looked at the world in this way, I began to acknowledge for the first time the buried anger and resentments I felt toward religions. How dare they condemn homosexuality or any other natural thing such as pleasure! Such condemnations are surely the source of the only true evil in the world, I imagined.

I spent the summer following my sophomore year working once again in the parks of my hometown. Mostly I weeded and trimmed trees, but sometimes I picked up litter or hauled things around in the city truck. At this time, another possibility about religion occurred to me: "What if God exists but the ways in which I am thinking about God are inadequate?" Every chance I could get, I devoured the 800-page book by Roman Catholic theologian Hans Küng called *Does God Exist?* and his 700-page book called *On Being a Christian.* The theologian actually argues that all of the traditional philosophical arguments for the existence of God fail. However, he later performs a meta-analysis of the arguments and shows that when taken as a whole, they reveal a probability for the existence of a God, if one is properly conceived. For Küng, God is not to be conceived of as a supreme being, above the clouds, in a physical or metaphysical heaven. He advocates a concept of God erected on the best aspects of the philosophies and theologies of Hegel, Teilhard de Chardin, and Alfred North Whitehead. Küng offered a panentheistic conception: God is in this world, and this world is in God; God is the infinite in the finite, the transcendent in the immanent, and the absolute in the relative. Küng approvingly quotes Dietrich Bonhoeffer as saying "God is the beyond in the midst of our life."

The next fall, I changed my major from philosophy to comparative religion. For the next two years, my schedule was filled with comparative religion courses, and I often studied alongside the students at Harvard Divinity School. I wrote my senior thesis on the concept of human nature in the work of two thinkers, the American political theologian Reinhold Niebuhr and the Peruvian priest Gustavo Gutierrez. My focus was liberation theology, a branch of religious thought that claims that theology must be done from the purview of the poor and the oppressed. The notion of God as liberator from suffering was intellectually interesting, but it didn't really fit my experience of the world. I could write about political and liberation theology from a detached perspective, but my beliefs were simply not well formed. If there were a God who brought about liberation from suffering in history, then surely it would look something like the force described by these theologians. But Christianity's tale of a God who loved each person, brought liberation to the oppressed, and offered every soul an opportunity to spend eternity in paradise seemed far too optimistic and fairy-tale hopeful to possibly be true. I didn't buy it. And Christianity's condemnation of homosexuality began to seem all too ignorant and increasingly detestable with every passing month of study.

By my senior year of college, I grew comfortable expressing my sexuality. I came out of the closet and had my first sexual experiences. I struggled with picking a single label and deemed myself too inexperienced to know for sure what to call myself. I chose the bisexual label, deciding that it was best to keep my options open. However, in conversations with friends, I acknowledged that I considered it quite possible that I was actually homosexual. Although I was capable of performing sexually with either gender, my preference was definitely for emotional and sexual relationships with men. As I came out of the closet, the need to try to reconcile my homosexual desires with Christianity faded, for the religion of my upbringing no longer seemed credible enough to warrant the effort. Nevertheless, as graduation approached, I decided to continue my study of religion, if not as a theologian then perhaps as a psychologist or sociologist.

After graduation from college, I attended the Divinity School at the University of Chicago. My course of study was focused on the sociology and psychology of religion. My courses with sociologist Martin Reisbrodt included the history of social theory and an elective on fundamentalism in the modern world. I also attended lectures by Peter Homans, a professor of religion and psychological studies in the Divinity School. His book, *The Ability to Mourn: Disillusionment and the Social Origins of Psychoanalysis*, had a profound impact on my thinking. Homans argues that psychoanalysis originated as a creative response to the disillusionment of traditional communities and their religious symbols following the industrial revolution. For Homans, the ability to mourn is closely related to the ability to make meaning from, and grow in psychological complexity as a result of, personal, political, and religious losses. Losing religious attachments was vital to the lives of the founders of psychoanalysis, especially Freud. I came to appreciate the changes in my psychological depth that may have been occasioned by my own loss of religious attachments.

Although the focus of my work was on the scientific study of religion, I continued to be perplexed by issues that seemed to require philosophical or theological meditations. I felt a palpable sense of inner confusion, restlessness, and fragmentation. The world still didn't make much sense, but I had grown numb to the incoherence. I formed a reasonably comfortable identity as an urban, young gay man, but underneath it all was a profound lack of conviction about the meaningfulness of life.

If I was fragmented inside, it surely was not for lack of knowledge of philosophies contending for my adherence. I was acquainted with numerous intellectual currents that might have become the basis for a healthy sense of self-esteem as a queer man, but each philosophy seemed only to have part of the truth. Secular postmodern academic queer theorists claimed that all antigay attitudes are ignorant prejudices and brutish power grabs by bad heterosexuals seeking to hold on to the privileges inherent in something called compulsory heterosexuality. Liberal religious thinkers offered liberation and feminist theologies that draped familiar religious language over intellectual edifices derived from Marxism, feminism, and queer theory. That's what they called giving "fresh interpretations" to traditional religious beliefs. They talked about heterosexism and homophobia as sins, and they claimed that homosexuality is a purely natural biological variation and, as such, morally neutral. Although I found much to agree with in academic queer theory and liberal theology, I had little peace of mind after reading these books. My self-esteem did not improve as a result of a pessimistic worldview that said everything is meaningless and, by the way, the evil bigots and the wicked homophobes are in charge. Nor did I find the feel-good liberal theologies convincing on a deep, emotional level, because it seemed as if there were some unpleasant truths about both religion and homosexuality that they were avoiding.

The most subtle of the conservative Christian theologians gave voice to some of my secret fears about the truth about same-sex desires. They frequently wrote about the dignity and common humanity of gay men and lesbians. Some even said efforts by gays to find love and committed relationships were of sacred worth, and that these expressions should be viewed with compassion. However, they also spoke about homosexuality as if it were a disorder, a condition like alcoholism or kleptomania that was itself morally neutral. God didn't make people gay; homosexuality was the by-product of a broken universe of suffering and sin. God wills happiness for all people, they said. The best route for gays to find happiness is to take up their same-sex desires as a cross of suffering and to commit themselves to abstinence or, if possible, monogamous heterosexual marriage. This sort of conservative religious perspective, spoken sincerely with the intention of love, was frustratingly difficult to dismiss out of hand as merely the product of ignorance, hate, or callous efforts to shore up heterosexual privilege. I sensed intuitively that it was wrong (and strangely disturbing) but remained unable for many years to articulate a coherent and completely persuasive response. Gradually, I came to realize that the allure of these conservative religious beliefs was not what they said about homosexuality's meaning but that they were able to talk about homosexuality as something that had a rightful purpose in a meaningful and ultimately good universe. That's more than could be said for most varieties of secular thought, including queer theory.

Unshakable certainties in my life were few and far between, and these included the righteousness of my own anger toward religion and deepening awareness of the inevitability of mortality. In 1991, Bobby died from AIDS after a four-year battle with the disease. While I attended divinity school in Chicago, more tragedies continued to strike at home. A cousin died, then my grandmother, and then my brother's partner. At the time, I didn't have the money to fly to Washington for the funerals. I had read books on death, but nobody really taught me wisdom about how to grieve. I isolated myself, grew remote from my feelings, and was sometimes wary of answering the telephone. I felt certain there would be more bad news on the other end of the line.

Dark moods made it very difficult for me to study, and I dropped out of divinity school and took a variety of jobs in the financial industry. Later I would work for Internet start-ups and software companies as a researcher, writer, and project coordinator. Several more deaths of friends and in my extended family followed, including the loss of a favorite aunt and uncle who were my godparents. Just when the days didn't seem like they could get any bleaker, I tested HIV-positive at the age of 24.

I was sitting in my doctor's office and asking what it meant that my baseline T-cell count was 232. The doctor explained that the numbers seemed to indicate that my HIV infection was progressing very rapidly. I pressed my doctor to tell me how long I had to live. I felt out of control in the situation, so being able to peg a deadline on my death sentence seemed the one thing that could help restore a sense of order to my life. Reluctantly, my doctor prognosticated: "If you don't do anything, and I'm not recommending that, then you would probably live another two years. However, if you immediately start a combination therapy involving AZT and one other drug, probably 3TC, then you could live longer."

I asked, "If I do, how much longer could I live?"

My doctor wouldn't give me an exact answer, but I surmised that I could arrive at a ballpark figure by taking the two-year figure and doubling or tripling it at best. I began to plan for life as if I were going to be dead by the time I was 30.

It is altogether humbling to report that learning that I had a terminal illness did not immediately turn me into a saint, or even a deeply "spiritual" person. In fact, I went through an initial period of shock, followed by mourning and confusion. Then life mostly seemed to go back to normal. Except that it was now colored by a deeper anxiousness, bitterness, and sense of futility than I had ever before experienced. Far from giving me a positive attitude on life, my HIV diagnosis seemed nothing if not a curse. In fact, hearing other HIV-positive people speak about how they saw the disease as a "gift" or "blessing" was enough to make me want to puke.

I had too much integrity to adopt some sort of Pollyanna attitude. Facing the prospect of death at a young age, I wanted so much to experience everything that I hadn't yet. I wanted to find true love. I wanted to do great things. I wanted to be somebody. Yet a cross of resentment and despair hung around my neck, seemingly making it impossible to get enthusiastic about life.

The religious right is fond of preaching that AIDS is a punishment for the sins of homosexuals. Despite my lack of faith in a god, I was more inclined to believe something quite contrary. So far as I was concerned, it was religion itself that was to blame for AIDS. Religion, it seemed to me, taught homophobia and prejudice that inflicted deep and shaming wounds on all gay people everywhere. The result of religion-fueled homophobia was shame and a lack of social support for gay marriage. The fruits of religion's hostility toward gay people: illegal sex, sex in secret places among people with identities hidden out of fear, the flourishing of anonymous sex and compulsive sex among people with battered self-esteem, and the development of a culture of shame where AIDS could spread.

It wasn't just orthodox religion that I found suspect. I blamed New Age dogmas for making matters worse. These soft-minded beliefs proclaimed that sickness is all a creation of the mind, so the first thing to ask someone with a terminal illness is: what is it that's so fucked up about you that led you to cause your own illness? Upon learning of my HIV diagnosis, a well-intentioned friend sent me an audiotape by New Age spiritualist Louise L. Hay. I had no reason to doubt that there were subtle connections between mind and body. However, the way that New Agers seemed to oversimplify such connections struck me as horrifyingly uncompassionate. Blaming victims of AIDS and cancer for causing their own illness was one of the stupidest ideas that I'd ever heard. There was no reason to listen to the audiotape, unless I also had a mind to don a hair shirt or put a loaded revolver to my head. I never did listen to it.

On top of all these crimes of religionists and spiritualists, there was, above all, simply the unfairness of life. AIDS is a bitch. That's true for anyone, and I saw my own diagnosis as an especially rotten piece of bad luck. At the time I was infected, I was almost still a virgin, at least when it came to intercourse. I contacted my past sexual partners, and they both confirmed that they had recently tested HIV-negative. I concluded that I'd been infected with HIV through oral sex, a feat that some of the "safe-sex" activists at that time claimed was impossible. A few gays even to this day still deny that it's really possible to become infected through unprotected oral sex. Research later confirmed that unprotected oral sex is less risky than unprotected anal sex but that it's possible for HIV to be transmitted through oral-genital contact. I recall reading that the odds of transmission in performing a single act of "giving head" are probably about 1 in 200, provided there are no open sores on either partner. The odds for acquiring HIV by "getting head" are thought to be even lower.

Since I had taken precautions and played by the safer-sex rules as best I understood them, becoming HIV-positive seemed all the more infuriating. I refused to accept responsibility for becoming HIV infected, so it seemed I had nobody to blame except Ronald Reagan, society, fundamentalists, and the God I didn't believe in. I even blamed an ex-boyfriend, a seminarian living in Chicago. We dated for a year until he ended the relationship abruptly and immediately began to date other men. I was so filled with anger and jealousy that I began to hook up with anonymous partners in an effort to keep up with him and to prove my sex appeal. Although my ex-boyfriend stayed HIV-negative, I tested HIV-positive only months after the breakup. Far from being a doorway to deeper spirituality, the HIV diagnosis seemed to open the door only to cynicism, despair, and resentment. I lived as if a God that didn't exist hated me. I felt powerless to do anything except lash out and strike back at anything real that could serve as a suitable proxy for God.

I soon found myself plunging headlong into a culture where sex and drugs promised to take away the deep pain that I carried. I searched in vain for a steady boyfriend, but seldom managed to make a relationship last more than a few months. After being rejected several times for disclosing my HIV-positive status, I stayed away from approaching HIV-negative men. Support groups for gay men with AIDS brought additional friendships into my life, but no prospective life partners (at least none who were also attracted to me). The gay male subculture of porn theaters, bathhouses, phone chat lines, and other places for casual sex soon helped me to cope with feelings of loneliness. They were sleazy options, but they were also the easiest way to get what I wanted when I wanted it and in plentiful supply. I even learned how to party on weekends with recreational drugs, something I had never previously done. The drugs helped me to relax into feelings of connection, light-heartedness, and euphoria. They also temporarily obliterated feelings I didn't want in my life, especially the grief and shame. I wasn't much concerned about side-effects and long-term consequences such as addiction because I didn't expect to live long enough to suffer from them.

Unlike the God that I no longer believed in, at least the drugs and sex were real. And that was one value that I could cling to, even in my darkest hour: being genuine, being true to what is, and being real.

At this time, I also began to take medications to treat the HIV. Despite the drugs, my immune system continued to lose the battle. Soon I had exhausted all the available drug treatments. My hope for survival seemed to hinge on the arrival of a new class of drugs called protease inhibitors. I began to take the new drugs in 1996, just as they became available, but my immune system showed little sign of improvement. The AIDS miracle drugs that were extending the lives of many others seemed to offer little hope for me. I doubted that I would live to see my 30th birthday. The emotional pain in my life grew nearly unbearable, and only sex and drugs seemed to offer relief from a largely joyless existence. Eventually even these escapes began to show their limitations, and the struggles and insanity of addiction followed just as surely in time.

I moved to Seattle, where I expected to die. By the eve of my 30th birthday, I had almost entirely forgotten about my mystical experience as a Harvard sophomore. My addictions took me to temporary states of euphoria nearly as magnificent as the bliss of mystical joy, but it had been a long while since life seemed enjoyable in itself. My experience as an addict was short and unglamorous. When the rocket ship came back to earth, I found myself just a little more emotionally numb, a little more jaded, and a little more self-hating. My physical body grew ever weaker, uglier, more brain damaged, and closer to death. Very soon my hedonistic self-absorption was nearly absolute, and I cared about nothing as much as my next high. I couldn't imagine life without my addictions, and there was nothing that I wouldn't do, say, or become to feed them. If I couldn't have the Bliss that I had once tasted, then drugs and sex would just have to do.

Something unusual happened in the summer of 1999. I had not taken drugs in several weeks, but my ordinary state of mind dissolved. In its place was an enduring and magnificent high that I enjoyed day and night for many days. Even weeks, I think. This exuberant mood was punctuated by visions that were alternately awe-inspiring and deeply disturbing. My sense of self, life, and God had profoundly shifted. But something wasn't quite right. Madness followed.

• • •

As a result of erratic behavior on my 30th birthday, I was involuntarily committed to a psychiatric ward. The doctors gave me psychotropic drugs that eventually returned me to ordinary reality. No longer considered a danger to myself or others, I was released from Harborview Hospital three weeks later.

In the five years following my hospitalization, I gradually came to find myself on a path of healing. I consulted psychiatrists, psychologists, astrologers, shamans, psychics, philosophers, and theologians. I broke long-standing communion with one religious organization and discovered new bonds of fellowship in others. I came to learn how to acknowledge and embrace my shadow. And I developed a more profound respect for the innate beauty, awe, and wonder of life and the preciousness of my own gifts. Perhaps most important, I found new depths of peace in relation to all aspects of myself, including joy and delight in my own sexuality as a man who loves men. I came to experience as a genuinely spiritual attitude certain theological ideas that I had dismissed for years as interesting but irrelevant theories.

What follows is a chronicle of my efforts to clear away the fog of the mind and calm the storms that have haunted and blessed my soul. As the story begins, I find myself on a quest to understand what it means to be gay. I wasn't satisfied with the simplistic, one-dimensional answers of some biologists, historians, and other intellectuals. I was seeking the clarity of mind to grasp the deep underlying connections among sex, politics, culture, and spirituality. There's a mystery to be unraveled, and the solution to the puzzle gradually leads me to the conclusion that ideas about homosexuality evolve in levels of increasing truth and adequacy. As this understanding emerges, my own level of awareness leaps forward to higher levels. The culmination is a theory that locates something that I call "homophilia" at the root of all existence and the heart of Christian revelation.

As part of my process of healing and growth, I also began to write. These writings included a private journal, two weblogs, and a biweekly newspaper column. A weblog, or blog, is simply an online journal containing dated posts or entries. This book is based on these short writings, most of which were done between November 2003 and December 2004. The writings are presented in chronological order. Most dates are generally accurate within a few days; however, I have taken liberties with the chronology of some journal entries. I have made other changes to content in order to enhance readability or for literary effect. Overall, I have tried not to let a strict adherence to facts get in the way of truth or beauty.

Over the months tracked by this journal, my perspective on a great many things evolved. By reading the journal entries in the order in which they are presented, you may follow along as my perspective shifts and notice the twists and turns in the plot along the way. Be aware that each entry builds on the preceding ones, and so skipping around or reading ahead is not recommended.

My integral development brought with it a perilous burden and an unexpected gift. As my health deteriorated, I tunneled into buried memories for a forgotten secret. Dreams offered clues to a riddle so threatening that I had even repressed awareness of the question itself. Nevertheless, I was compelled to reconnect with a missing piece of my life's puzzle, even as I feared that doing so would drive me mad. In the final days of this chronicle, I grasped the forgotten secret. Predictable and yet unanticipated, the truth was still more awesome and terrifying than I had imagined. But the knowledge fit like the waxen wings of Icarus, the Greek god who flew too close to the sun.

1 God Is Gay

It's my conviction that slight shifts in imagination have more impact on living than major efforts at change . . . deep changes in life follow movements in imagination.
—THOMAS MOORE

Friday, November 7 (Teotihuacán, Mexico)

The Aztecs gave Teotihuacán a name that means the place where men become gods. If anyone is going to become a god today, it sure isn't me. After spraining my ankle on the first day of the pilgrimage, I'm grounded.

I'm here on the Street of the Dead standing in the middle between two pyramids: the Temple of the Sun and the Temple of the Moon. Mom's here with me and together we're watching the tourists go up and down. I've been looking forward to being at the pyramids for a week; but after being here for a few minutes, I just want to go home.

Is this all there is? This was supposed to be the big climax. I saw the Virgin of Guadalupe, the famous statue of Christ the King, cathedrals, mummies, and now these pagan temples. This is Mexico—birthplace of my ancestors, land where my great-uncles (men with the surname of Lara) painted the ceilings of cathedrals—but I don't feel the holiness.

I know that I walk on sacred ground, but I don't feel connected to anything that I can call God or Spirit or Higher Power. The Christian sites remind me of the homophobia and sexism of the Roman Catholic Church. And the ancient temples remind me of human sacrifices for pagan cultures that were probably every bit as homophobic and oppressive. Thinking about all that religion just gives me the creeps.

Two days ago the tour bus was cruising outside of Guadalajara, and I was drifting in and out of sleep. I caught a bit of a conversation that has stuck with me:

A woman asked, "Father, your arm . . . How did you get that scar?"

The Mexican priest traveling with us on this segment of the tour replied, "When I was a boy, one day I was going to school and I spilled something on my uniform. I ran home to change clothes, but there was no clean shirt. Nobody was home, so I couldn't ask anyone to wash a shirt for me. So I started washing it myself. My father came home and caught me. He beat me and took the hot iron to my wrist."

"But father, I don't understand. Why did he do that to you?" the American woman asked.

"He did it because laundry is women's work, and he believed nothing is more shameful for a man than to do the work of a woman. He meant to teach me a lesson about how to be a man."

All my life, I've had teachers offer lessons about how to be a man. They usually start something like this: You must be strong. You must get out of bed in the morning. You must do things that you don't want to do. And above all else, you must hate everything within you that is weak or feminine or unmanly. Religion has often been the teacher of such lessons.

An elderly Mexican man shoved a box of hand-carved turtles in my face and quoted an unbelievably low price. I saw one turtle that reminded me of something I made out of clay when I was a child, and it made me smile. I pointed to the green one and pulled out a 20-peso coin.

"No," he said. "Twenty *American* dollars."

I should have known. I waved him away, but he continued to pester me. Mom also tried to get rid of him.

"He likes the green one, señora!"

"No, he doesn't. The green one is ugly. *Feo. Muy feo!* Get it away from us!"

As I limped back to the tour bus, I resigned myself to the feeling of being unfulfilled. I don't know what I came here to find, but I'm walking away empty.

In the evening, I left my crutch in the hotel and caught a cab. I found my way to a gay leather bar in Zona Rosa. I had barely arrived when I made eye contact with a good-looking man in his late twenties. He wore a white shirt and a gold cross around his neck. I thought he looked like a young Spanish movie star. Feeling uncharacteristically assertive, I introduced myself.

"*Voy en la mañana por los Estados Unidos. Este es mi noche final en México. Hablas inglés?*"

Unfortunately, the man's English was as poor as my Spanish. Soon we ran out of things to say, and then I took his hand and we walked up a staircase and through a series of dark rooms. We found some privacy.

Afterward, I left feeling empty and returned to my hotel room for a shower. There was a thrill in the moment, for sure, but where was the holiness? Is this all there is?

There's something missing in my life: a spirituality that is fully alive and rich, body and soul. But part of me refuses to go there. If I do, I fear that I could lose . . . What? I don't know.

If ever there was a part of me whole and shiny and green, then it will need to stay away for now. I'm afraid it will cost too much.

Saturday, November 8 (Seattle, Washington)

In a few minutes, the airplane is going to land at Sea-Tac Airport. I just finished reading a book by Mark Thompson called *Gay Soul: Finding the Heart of Gay Spirit and Nature*. It's a collection of in-depth interviews with sixteen elders who are sharing the fruits of their wisdom, men like Joseph Kramer, Andrew Ramer, Clyde Hall, and Harry Hay. Each of these men has put their stamp on spirituality in the gay community in a profound way.

There are plenty of areas of disagreement among the men interviewed.

One point of dispute is whether there is a specifically gay spiritual sensibility. Ram Dass is one who doesn't think that there is. He said in his interview: "The deeper your spiritual practice, the more you are aware that everybody is androgynous." In other words, spirituality erases distinctions such as gender and sexuality. That's why he said in the same interview that the very term "gay soul" seemed so jarring to him.

However, as some of the other writers suggest, I think there must be something valuable, distinctive, or unique about the experience of being gay. Otherwise, why would there be homosexuality at all, if we live in a meaningful universe and the Bible-beating fundamentalists are wrong? There must be something that Spirit had to achieve through gayness that could not have been done in another way. I'm inclined to think so, but it's hard to say exactly what that something is.

The final chapter, an interview with Jungian psychologist Mitch Walker, is one of the best in the book. Unlike Ram Dass, Walker suggests in no uncertain terms that the psychological and spiritual development of gays is not the same as for straights. I keep turning again and again to a paragraph where Walker discusses the mythic archetype of the Double, or the Same:

> The archetype of the Same is an image of reflecting selfness, but a paradox of similarities and differences together in an erotically yearning, intense way that's hard for us to talk about, especially if we're raised in male/female ways of thinking. There are many facets of duality. One alternative tradition to the man/woman, king/queen duality is that of the two brothers, which can be found in ancient myths like the Mesopotamian story of Gilgamesh and Enkidu and Egyptian legends about Horus and Seth.

If Walker is correct, then the spiritual paths of gays and straights are separate, because they are shaped by radically different orientations to fundamental mythological archetypes. I think that he's saying that straights are drawn to connect to the divine through otherness, and gays through sameness. There's a certain elegant beauty in this idea.

I sense that there's something here that can help me to unravel the question of whether there is a distinctively gay perspective on spirituality. Yet something about how it's formulated seems not quite right. There seems to be truth both in the idea that spirituality erases distinctions such as gayness and also in the idea that gayness is in some sense spiritually important. I'm not sure how to put these two apparently conflicting views together, but I think that's what I need to do.

Sunday, November 9

Welcome to my online journal, *The Soulful Blogger!*

This is a blog about spirituality, not just religion. Spirituality is one of those words for which it seems everyone has a different definition. I view spirituality as involving everything that brings wholeness and healing to our bodies, minds, and spirits. Therefore, my journal will encompass topics that may not seem obviously spiritual at first glance . . .

Tuesday, November 11

Recently I've been studying astrology two nights a week with Seattle astrologer Laura Gerking. The other night in class a few of us began to joke that someone should invent magical astrology trading cards. Then people could trade karma.

"Don't like Saturn square to your Sun? No problem. I'll take it, if you'll take my Pluto / South Node / Sun conjunction in Virgo."

"What, no takers? Why doesn't that surprise me!" (The Pluto / South Node / Sun conjunction in my horoscope is an unusual configuration. Some astrologers call it a "past life repeat" and claim it represents a virtual replay of an old and troublesome karmic pattern.)

"No way! I'm not giving up my Uranus / Mercury / Jupiter conjunction in Libra, not for your Venus / Mars trine."

Joking aside, I asked myself this question: Given the choice, would I want to exchange my life for someone else's? Would I trade being gay for being heterosexual, if I could? The notion of getting rid of all the painful lessons of my life was momentarily appealing, but then reality started to sink in. Maybe in another lifetime I would have children of my own and maybe I wouldn't get AIDS. On the other hand, if I swapped lives, I could end up a Christian fundamentalist . . . or worse. Is the grass really greener in someone else's yard? I doubt it.

In the end, the entire class decided that as bad as our shit was, nobody wanted to trade karma even if we had the option. The devil that you don't know is always worse than the one that you do.

Thursday, November 13

The intellectual openness and liberalism of the Unitarian Universalist religion has long held a strong intellectual appeal for me. There are no dogmatic creeds. Not even belief in God is required. UU congregations include self-identified Christians, Jews, Buddhists, and pagans.

Unitarianism is also perhaps the most gay-friendly religion in the world. Gays are welcome at the highest levels of leadership, and same-sex marital unions are blessed. The thought of worshiping in a place where I am welcomed and accepted as a gay man is very appealing.

I attended services a few weeks ago at the University Unitarian Church but haven't made it back yet. While the UU theology appeals to my intellect, my heart is slow to warm to the actual services. They strike me as "Christian lite," like a shell of a formerly more vibrant tradition that has been hollowed out by rationalism and doubt. Since the religion doesn't seem to believe in anything in particular, it's hard for me to get excited about what they offer.

I'll eventually be back in some sort of religious community, but I'm not in a rush. Now that I've stepped away from the Roman Catholic Church, I feel a need for some breathing room.

Today many former Catholics are turning to the Episcopal Church. That's an option I haven't ruled out entirely. However, my problems with Christianity go deeper than simply wanting the Church to change its teachings about homosexuality. I'm not one of those gays who's completely happy with Christianity in all aspects except that I want the Church to approve of my sex life. I'm afraid I just don't believe the core teachings of the faith anymore, at least not in the way that I think most other Christians still do.

I've been following a discussion on the blog of a UU divinity student named Matthew Gatheringwater. He describes himself as both UU and atheist, and he's asking good, tough questions. For instance, he asks whether UU is an interfaith experience within each congregation, a distinct religious perspective, or both. If it's an interfaith experience, then what incentives do Buddhists, Wiccans, and others have for being Unitarian Universalists? Why not just be Buddhist or Wiccan? In short, what is the essence of religious community when you take away a common creed?

I, for one, don't have answers to these questions. Not yet. I am asking similar questions in my own life, and it is not clear to me what benefit, if any, I could receive by joining a UU church. Wrestling with these sorts of questions is part of my ongoing soul work, as it seems that Matthew's questions are for him. I wish him well.

Friday, November 14

Breaking Up with God Is Hard to Do

When I was a boy in grade school, belief in a loving God came easily to me. God was the answer to my question, Where does everything come from? I prayed with confidence that my prayers were always heard.

I sometimes envisioned God as a benevolent teacher and humans as His dutiful pupils. Follow the rules, do your homework, learn your lessons, and when class is dismissed you can frolic forever in the divine playground. The classroom was sometimes stifling, but usually it was a nurturing place of joy and enchanted mysteries.

Being Roman Catholic was an important part of life during my teenage years and early adulthood. The church was where I learned to experience my spirituality—how to pray, how to celebrate the sacred moments of life, and how to cope with death.

As I became aware of my homosexuality, my faith was often a source of internal conflict. Like many others, I saw the Vatican as full of closed-minded hypocrites, and I suspected that many church leaders were themselves closeted, self-hating homosexuals. I had no desire to worship in such a church.

When I was 20 years old, I began to come out of the sexual closet. As a result, continuing to worship in the Catholic Church suddenly became very uncomfortable. However, leaving the church altogether was more than I felt I could handle, so I decided to take a break.

I called the break a "sabbatical," and it lasted for about 13 years. From time to time, I'd attend mass. But worship always left me feeling fragmented and frustrated, never spiritually whole. When I did connect to authentic feelings, it was usually anger (at the Catholic Church) or sadness, not joy.

Religion was an integral aspect of my life, just as my hands and feet are part of my body. Remember Aron Ralston? He was the 27-year-old hiker who, after being pinned beneath an 800-pound boulder for five days, used a pocketknife to free himself by amputating his own arm. He told rescuers that he had run out of water and his very survival had depended upon breaking free.

For many religious people, leaving their religion behind can be as challenging a decision as cutting off one's own arm. It's not something one does lightly, and many people will avoid the break at all costs. For example, 70 percent of queer Catholics don't practice their religion but still call themselves Catholic, according to the Gay/Lesbian Consumer Online Census.

That's an astounding number when you think about it. Imagine if seven Republicans in ten didn't like most of the policies of George W. Bush but stayed in the party anyway. Or what if seven out of ten members of People for the Ethical Treatment of Animals didn't like animals but refused to give up their PETA membership cards?

What's this about? According to Robert Fuller's book *Spiritual, but Not Religious: Understanding Unchurched America*, there are three main reasons why people maintain an ambiguous relationship with their religion despite "falling away." First, they might be motivated to continue a nominal connection to an organized religion because of their family background. Second, they may be concerned that disaffiliating with their religion could harm their social standing. Third, they simply may be timid about making a final break from religion.

It's primarily this third motivation that stood in my way of leaving the

Catholic Church, because for many years I identified my religion with my spirituality. This meant that leaving the Church was almost like breaking up with God.

After over a decade of being lapsed, or "on sabbatical," this year I finally said goodbye to the Catholic Church. I issued no press releases. I nailed no bulletins on church doors. For the most part I went quietly.

And I began the coming out process all over again. This time it meant telling people that I'm no longer Roman Catholic. The Vatican's continual attacks on the dignity of gay people were simply more than I wanted to bear.

I respect that there are a number of gays who are staying in the Catholic Church and will continue to work for change. God bless them. I honor the difficult choices they have made, even as I know that my spiritual path is taking me in another direction.

What did leaving the Catholic Church mean to me? I finally realized that I could go no further in my spiritual growth by staying put, one foot in a hostile church and one outside. I wanted a spiritual path that I could step into with both feet. Like the hiker trapped by the boulder, I knew something invaluable was at stake: my survival. My spiritual survival.

Today I don't have a church, but I envision the universe itself as a loving, nurturing Higher Power and benevolent teacher. And I see myself as a continuing student of spirituality. My faith hasn't been lost so much as it has gradually grown into something new and more mature.

Monday, November 17

Sacred Encounters and Profane Sex

The following is a poem by Timothy Liu entitled "Survivors":

> Some mornings I do not hear
> the alarm go off. The lightest
> touch will startle me awake,
> filling our bedroom with cries
> of birds. It's not the hours

spent in therapy, nor self-
help books stacked beside our bed,
that keep me up until four
each night—it's your body
reeking of alcohol. Hold me
like a dream that will dissolve,
a childhood you never had.
Go on sleeping while I count
fifty dollar bills floating
up the chimney, black sheep
without a shepherd. It's not God
we trust, but ash, spindled
faces that never cracked a smile.

When I first read this poem, I immediately felt uncomfortable. A memory came to me like an unwelcome houseguest. I remembered a time about eight years ago . . .

I was lying naked in a darkened cube of a bathhouse at four in the morning, pressed against the soft, brown flesh of a stranger who reeked of alcohol. I felt disgusted with the pathos of the situation, and part of me wanted to leave; but something led me to stay and simply rest for a while.

Timothy Liu's poem invites us to reflect on the sometimes unseemly, pathetic side of sexuality. Timothy Liu is a gay, Asian-American, Mormon poet who is noted for exploring the intersections of sexuality and spirituality.

"Survivors" can be found in his 1995 collection, Burnt Offerings. The image of a "black sheep without a shepherd" is fitting for the spiritual condition of gay men in a world where religion is often hostile to our sexuality. (Christ is often depicted as a shepherd and the faithful as sheep.)

I am struck by the poem's powerful ending: "It's not God / we trust, but ash . . ." American poet Robert Bly tells us about ash. Ash is a code word for dark, depressed time. Ashes connote death.

In Iron John, Bly writes that young men in Viking times were allowed two or three years of ashes; during this time they would lie down in the communal house in a sooty place between the fire and the ash pile, doing nothing useful and refusing to clean themselves. It was a sort of ritual hibernation.

After spending time among the ashes, young men found themselves transformed. Bly tells of this legend: "Starkad . . . remained in the ashes several years, until his foster father invited him to go on an expedition. At that point he stood up, shaved, and dressed and became one of the best warriors on the expedition, and later became a distinguished poet as well, remembered in the sagas." Out of time spent in ashes comes awakeness and aliveness, more unsettling than the shrill cries of an alarm clock.

The road of the ashes is the way of descent into deep grief. Ashes diminish the inflated ego. Spiritual work is dangerous, says Bly, because it often produces men who seek to "ascend" to spiritual realms without first feeling their grief. One sign of this ascension is emotional numbness (that is, a sense of being disconnected from feelings). Another sign of ascension is that our psyche may unconsciously begin to arrange our life in ways that force us into painful crises where we have to do our grief work.

Liu's poem suggests that there is nourishment he gets from his partner that talk therapy and self-help books (that is, the ways of ascension) do not supply. What is this soul food? The poem's title suggests that the poet and his companion enjoy the commiseration of survivors. I imagine that the poet connects to his own pain by seeing it mirrored by his lover.

In another poem, Liu writes: "men who were never loved, I love."

Shared suffering can bring men together who otherwise seem to have little in common. Indeed, it is the experience of surviving homophobia that creates the powerful sense of brotherhood that all gay men share. When we hear of another gay man who is attacked by bashers or rejected by his family, we instinctively feel a connection.

Liu's poetry in *Burnt Offerings* does not renounce the profane, ugly, brutal face sometimes worn by gay sexuality in an antigay society. He affirms sex in public toilets, even in an outhouse. Liu affirms sex with strangers. In another poem, he pleads: "Love me / not as a wife but as the stray cat / who sleeps on your chest each night."

Liu's affirmation is not a moral judgment. Instead he invites us to descend to the murky depths of soul, soot, and ash. From this perspective, judgment is simply a way of ascending up the chimney like 50 dollar bills. The poem may stir uncomfortable feelings and buried memories, but we are called to simply stay and rest for a while.

"Survivors" is an affirmation of the profound sacredness available to gay men even in seemingly profane sexual encounters. But this sacredness doesn't come cheap. We may think that what we long for is God in the form of a gorgeous lover or the delights of the flesh. But what we may really want is to see our own long face covered in ashes.

Tuesday, November 18

I believe the world has reached a point in the evolution of consciousness where people are outgrowing Christianity's hostility and hatred toward the body, sexuality, women, and homosexuals. Many of those who reject the worst of Christian tradition are people who still consider themselves Christian. Christianity's success or failure in adapting to the evolving state of humanity with fresh vision will determine whether the religion survives the centuries ahead or continues to decline and wither away.

Sometimes I find myself struggling with feelings of bitterness, anger, and resentment toward conservative Christians. In these moments, I try to stay attuned to the better insights of my spiritual awareness. I seek to accept the world as it is and to cultivate an appreciation that somehow conservative religion, with all its defects, is serving the aims of Spirit.

I don't have to like the conservatives' religion, but I can still respect that somehow it is playing a role in Spirit's plans. Perhaps conservative religion is simply a dialectical stage in some future Hegelian synthesis. Maybe in the course of time, we will discover that all forms of religion that are limited, defensive, and rigid will die . . . and forms of religion more attuned to a holistic, expansive Spirit will thrive. My spirituality gives me reason for hope and optimism in the future spiritual evolution of humanity.

Is my faith in spiritual evolution naive? I don't think so. I know something about suffering and the possibility of self-delusion. I have read history and know that it's a bloodthirsty tale filled with atrocities and inhumanity. In spite of these painful truths, I still think spiritual evolution of some sort must be real. But when I'm honest with myself, some days I think maybe I'm deluded and there really is no reason to hope.

Wednesday, November 19

I've been exploring dozens of weblogs on religion and spirituality for the past few weeks. Is there a clue in these blogs to the zeitgeist of the age? It is striking that most of the journals are written by Christians who are over-whelmingly socially, politically, and theologically conservative. Moreover, the tone of writing is vicious and defensive nearly to the point of paranoia. Don't these guys (and most of them are men) have anything better to do than to trash and demonize gays, feminists, and "godless liberals"?

These Christian bloggers seem to carry a painfully unpeaceful sort of energy. I don't have the stomach to spend much time reading what they say. I am saddened by all the nastiness, negativity, and fear among them.

The Christian tradition has such treasures as Thomas Merton and saints with a real dedication to social justice for the poor. Where are those Christians, and why aren't they blogging about their spirituality? Where are the Christians who write with a tone of love and compassion rather than shrill condemnations? Why is there such a rush to judgment among these bloggers, rather than to understanding?

I think I've pissed off some of these religious conservatives, because I've called their religious views "heterosexual supremacy." Heterosexual supremacy doesn't necessarily advocate the hatred of gay people, but it always advocates heterosexism. Heterosexism is the belief in the superior-ity of heterosexuality over homosexuality. It generally calls for the mainte-nance of "special rights" for heterosexual people only, such as legally sanc-tioned civil marriages that are restricted to parties of the opposite sex.

I don't want to be unfair to these conservatives or unkind in discourse, but I just don't see a more accurate way of describing them than calling them heterosexual supremacists. I've told them: if the pointy white hat fits, wear it.

Thursday, November 20

This is a historic day. The Massachusetts Supreme Court has overturned the oppressive law that denies gays the right to marry, and ordered the state to legalize gay marriage within six months.

I've read the court's decision and concur with the reasoning of the majority. They observe the plain fact that the history of constitutional law is the story of the extension of constitutional rights and protections to people once ignored or excluded. Conservatives call this the "invention of rights" and "judicial activism." But I don't think that view does justice to the evolving nature of our collective social understanding of rights and responsibilities.

As an American, I love my country. Yet as a gay man, I am accustomed to being in a group that is attacked, persecuted, and marginalized by the laws and our elected leaders. The law of my country makes me a second-class citizen. Today I am glad to be an American and grateful for the courageous judges in Massachusetts.

Friday, November 21

Earlier today I met with my counselor, Harry (not his real name). His approach to counseling is informed by Jungian psychology, shamanism, astrology, and a variety of other influences. We spent much of our session today talking about issues involving my daily routines.

I'm a night owl. My typical schedule for years has kept me up past midnight (going to sleep between 1:00 and 4:00 a.m. isn't uncommon) and sleeping in as late as humanly possible. Erratic sleep behavior has made it virtually impossible to actually create stable and healthy morning routines. Working out? Fat chance. Meditation? A pipe dream. Better to leave such things for late night, if they're going to happen at all. On days when I'm not feeling well, I find myself running late, rushing for a meeting at work, running to an appointment, sprinting for a bus, or trying to avoid the rush-hour traffic.

Having a seriously compromised immune system exacerbates my erratic energy flows. Research has shown that people living with HIV experience greater fatigue, lower energy levels, and a greater need for sleep than non–HIV-infected people. HIV is known to disturb the body's circadian rhythms (that is, our biological clock). But it's hard to say for sure exactly what impact HIV has had on my energy. I'm hesitant to blame every ache or pain on the virus. All I can say with certainty is that my sleep and energy patterns were somewhat erratic before HIV, and they've been even more erratic since.

I know that having a regular meditation practice would be a good thing, but I can never seem to find time in the morning for the 20 or 30 minutes it would take. Today, Harry suggested that I start the routine by simply reserving a few minutes each morning for quiet time and then taking it from there. In other words, I could short-circuit my perfectionist impulse by setting more realistic goals. That's a plan just simple enough that it might work.

Saturday, November 22

Sagittarius

The sun has entered the part of the sky associated with Sagittarius. During this time of year, our spirit encounters the energy of the Archer. The Archer's arrow is always in motion, perpetually in an optimistic, adventurous quest. Sagittarius calls us to move beyond all fragmented, partial visions of reality and to assemble the fragments into a big picture of The Way Things Are. The Archer's aim is Truth.

Tuesday, November 25

Mark Shea is a Seattle-based writer responsible for a weblog called Catholic and Enjoying It! His website is currently ranked in the top 50 in popularity, according to The Truth Laid Bear, a weblog that ranks the popularity of weblogs. That probably makes Shea's blog the most widely read religion blog on the Internet.

Today, Shea linked to *The Soulful Blogger*. I suppose I should be grateful for the exposure. However, I'm not sure this is what you would call "good publicity."

Apparently, Shea finds my site to be a fine example of a dangerous trend called the New Religious Synthesis. The term is coined by James Herrick, a conservative Christian who believes that the main enemy of Christianity today is not secularism but New Age spiritualism. How can Christians spot the enemy? According to Herrick, there are telltale signs that can alert you to their presence: an interest in "mysticism," attempts to "de-historicize the Bible," the "deification of Reason," and the idea of "spiritual perfection through evolution."

Menacingly, Herrick calls the New Religious Synthesis the "Other Spirituality." It is dangerous because it has no place for traditional Christian dogmas. Instead, the synthesis understands belief in "fixed revelations" as an "early stage in religious development" and thus as an impediment to the coming age of religious unity. Belief in dogmas is important, presumably, because failure to submit to the authority of religious dogma may result in one's soul perishing in hell for eternity.

Well, what can I say? It looks like Shea's got me pegged! ;-) I'm not sure what more to say.

Perhaps it would serve me to note for Shea's readers that I am no foreigner to Roman Catholicism. My spiritual journey has led down the path from practicing liberal Catholic to lapsed Catholic and now a happily former Roman Catholic. The way I describe myself today is catholic in the truest sense of the word: open to truth wherever it appears, including the world's great wisdom traditions, science, nature, or direct mystical experience. Christianity remains an enduring positive influence, as it is my belief that Christianity includes much that is good, true, holy, and worthy of my continued adherence (even while I reject the notion that somehow its mythology supersedes or is in some sense superior to every other mythology).

One of Shea's readers followed the link to my website and wrote: "There is so much evil in that website, it is truly palpable. I have never been there before, and I intend never to return."

It's not every day that I'm called evil by total strangers, so I must admit that this makes me uncomfortable. I sense a great deal of fear and hostility among many on the religious right. I don't want to get caught up in a game of "I know you are, but what am I?" Still, I can't help but wonder what disowned parts of himself—shadow projections, as the Jungians say—this man is attributing to me. I pity a man so insecure as to write what he did.

Wednesday, November 26

A prediction: in centuries to come, historians will debate the question of the most influential Roman Catholic intellectual of the 20th century. They will eventually realize that a certain Oxford professor of Anglo-Saxon will have had the most lasting consequence for the Roman Catholic religion.

As fans of his books are well aware, J. R. R. Tolkien wrote *The Lord of the Rings* epic as only one small part of an elaborate mythology that tells of God's (Ilúvatar's) actions of redemption in history (the War of the Ring) and victory over evil (Sauron). Tolkien has succeeded fantastically in the task where so many thinkers have tried and failed: reimagining and reinvigorating the Roman Catholic mythology into new modes of expression that are compatible with the postmodern mind, responsive to the demands of religious pluralism, and bursting with ecological sensitivity.

With all the attention paid to Tolkien's Roman Catholic faith, it's quite common to regard his works as virtually a Christian allegory. Tolkien himself detested allegory and rejected the notion that his works should be read in such a fashion. However, he acknowledged having discovered himself writing *The Lord of the Rings* from an implicitly Catholic theology at first and later revising the book to make its parallels to Catholicism more consistent.

To the best of my knowledge, nobody seems to have noticed that along with the absence of religion in Middle Earth there is also a deafening silence concerning the institution of marriage. If marriage is as central to the tenets of the Catholic Church as theological conservatives insist, this seems an awfully glaring omission for a so-called Catholic epic.

The wedding of Aragorn and Arwen is the book's only serious look at marriage, and much of the Aragorn/Arwen story is told only in the Appendices. In contrast, Tolkien portrays deep, loving, and affectionate friendships between men, particularly in the relationship between Frodo and Samwise. Friendship, not marriage, is the dominant leitmotif for relationship in *The Lord of the Rings*.

I suspect the absence of any particular stigma associated with homosexuality in the mythology is probably attributable to the absence of a sociocultural imperative for reproduction to enhance the survival of any particular race in Middle Earth. Middle Earth may be regarded as a vision of what earth might have become, if forces of evolution had not produced cultures in which the necessity for biological reproduction to enhance cultural survival became linked to a moral imperative for procreative sex.

According to most reliable accounts, J. R. R. Tolkien was a fairly orthodox Catholic; and if there's any evidence that his views on sexuality departed from those of the Vatican, I don't know of it. Nevertheless, Tolkien's books are remarkably silent regarding the sexuality of their characters. Sex doesn't seem to have been of much interest to Tolkien the writer, and the same can be said of his characters, most of whom are men who seem to prefer the company of other men. This, along with the absence of religion in Middle Earth, is quite interesting and generally ignored by the religiously orthodox.

Of course, it's always tricky to make an argument based on the silence of a text. To say that the text of *The Lord of the Rings* is silent with regards to homosexuality is not the same as saying that the text is pro-gay. By the same token, it's not fair to read homophobia into the text when it's plainly not there.

This crucial point is lost on orthodox admirers of Tolkien, because they are so eager to find in Middle Earth a mirror of their own traditionalist dogma. Tolkien's world does mirror the Catholic Church's mythology in many ways, but not with regard to homosexuality. Its silence creates an opening for viewing Tolkien's mythology as I do, as an essentially Roman Catholic worldview purified of its archaic prohibitions against same-sex sexual expressions. The silence of the texts is important, because it allows for a plurality of readings.

Thursday, November 27

Some of the conservative religious visitors to my blog have been poking fun at my interest in astrology. Apparently they feel my immortal soul is in jeopardy because of my "dabbling in the occult."

Although I am studying astrology, I am neither pro- nor anti-astrology as such. Traditional astrological beliefs that planets influence human affairs don't seem rationally defensible to me. Newspaper horoscopes are merely entertainment. I don't even read them. As with any spiritual tool, astrology is only as useful as the consciousness of the person who applies it. In the hands of a skilled and conscious astrologer, I believe astrology can be a profoundly useful tool. But in the hands of an unskillful astrologer, astrology can be an instrument of delusion, superstition, and fatalism.

Truly conscious astrologers do not claim that planets "influence" or "cause" human affairs. The claim is rather that astrological symbolism describes human affairs on a mythopoetic, "archetypal level." Astrology can be a tool for introspection and accessing the subconscious mind. In some cases, astrology may also become a tool for mysticism and enhancing one's sense of connectedness to nature.

Saturday, November 29

Prologue to T.I.O.B.G.

Homosexuality is a mystery. It's a puzzle that invites reflection without predetermined answers and openness to discovering knowledge that we can't predict in advance. What's the purpose of homosexuality? What's the point of being gay, if having a same-sex orientation is not mere aberration or random chance?

I believe there are answers to these questions beyond those that we've been taught by psychology, biology, and conventional religion. I believe that the search for the meaning of homosexuality is ultimately a spiritual quest.

In this journal, I propose to explore The Importance of Being Gay (T.I.O.B.G.). I'll be asking: For what special purpose, if any, are gays here? What is homosexuality for? In short, how can we unravel the mystery? I will begin to assemble a vision of how homosexuality fits into a big picture of everything in the cosmos.

You can think of this vision as a metaphysics, cosmology, or worldview. You can even call it a mythology if you like. I will. However, by "myth" I don't mean to imply that I think this vision is untrue. On the contrary, I very much believe that the story that I will be telling is accurate. I just don't expect to necessarily be able to prove the truth as fact.

Before I get started, there's something I want to say that may help you to follow the story that I will be telling about homosexuality: I believe that human beings are souls on a spiritual journey. God (or Spirit, or Higher Power, or whatever you call it) is at the beginning and end of that journey, and is the force or process of evolution along the way. Our souls have two archetypal desires: the desire for reunion with God and the desire for separation from God. The desire for union with God is the stronger of the two, but they are both strong desires. These desires play out in the course of an individual's spiritual journey (some say this journey lasts more than one lifetime). Based on these desires, we perceive our needs, make choices with free will, perform actions, experience consequences based on those actions, and ultimately experience reactions. Following Eastern traditions, I call this dynamic of action and reaction karma, which basically means that we reap what we sow. Our soul manifests with certain personality traits or characteristics because we're at a particular point in our spiritual journey and have to find our way back to God. In other words, babies are not born *tabula rasa*, empty containers to which the substance of personality is added. Their innate characteristics seem to come from somewhere; that place is the origin of karma. This is true regardless of whether you believe in reincarnation, souls that preexist in the mind of God, the legacy of ancestors passed down through DNA, or some admixture of these possibilities.

Some brief notes regarding terminology are in order. I regard a homosexual as a person who has affectional, emotional, and sexual attractions predominantly to members of the same sex. A bisexual has similar attractions to members of both sexes. Most commonly, I use gay as a term referring to all persons who have adopted a sexual identity as a homosexual person. For variety, I will sometimes speak of gay men and lesbians. I use transgender as an umbrella term to refer to all persons who don't fit neatly into the narrow boxes of gender identity widely accepted in our society. I also frequently use gay in an inclusive sense that embraces in its definition all homosexual, bisexual, and transgender persons. Queer is another frequently used umbrella term; however, many gay people feel excluded by it. Along with the vast majority of individuals of my generation and younger, I am comfortable with the term "queer" and will use it interchangeably with gay or GLBT (an acronym for gay, lesbian, bisexual, and transgender).

One more thing: I'm a gay man and I write from that perspective. Much of what I say may be relevant for heterosexuals, lesbians, bisexuals, and transgender folks. But then again, it may not be. I do not claim to speak for anyone but myself. In these posts, I am speaking primarily to an audience of gay men. If you are not a gay man, you will have to make the necessary adjustments for you. And I wouldn't dream of speaking on behalf of any group, especially one to which I don't belong.

Sunday, November 30

T. I. O. B. G. 1 of 6: God Is Gay

Human nature teaches us about the nature of God, the Source of All and the Destiny of Everything. Human beings include male and female. God is like a man and God is like a woman. There is beauty in mankind and in womankind, and God is so beautiful that God's beauty includes all the beauty of women and men.

We can try to express what these aspects of human nature teach us about God with words, but only poorly. We could say, for instance: God is male. God is not male. God is female. God is not female. These are all fine (but limited) ways of talking about God.

Human nature teaches us about the nature of God. We include gay people and straight people. Gay people love in gay ways and straight people love in straight ways. We can try to express what human nature reveals about God with words, but only poorly. We could say, for instance: God is gay. God is not gay. God is straight. God is not straight. These are fine (but limited) ways of talking about God.

God is like a gay person and God is like a straight person. There is beauty in gay people and in straight people, and God is so beautiful that God's beauty includes all the beauty of gays and straights. There is beauty in gay ways of loving and in straight ways of loving, and God's ways of loving are so beautiful that they include all the beauty of gay and straight ways of loving.

God made some men gay, because He made them in His image. God made gay men to love in gay ways, because God loves in gay ways. The beauty of gay men reflects the beauty of God. The beauty of gay ways of loving reflects the beauty of God's gay ways of loving. When someone fears and hates a gay man, he or she fears and hates God. When someone denigrates, despises, loathes, and harms a gay man, he or she denigrates, despises, loathes, and harms God.

Some people have repressed the truth about God's gayness, because they have hated and feared God. Some who have repressed the truth about God are straight and others are gay. The truth about God's gayness has been revealed to those whose eyes are open.

Monday, December 1

T.I.O.B.G. 2 of 6: The Soul Is Gay

The deepest truth about human beings is that we are the perfect reflection of God, and that perfection is evident in our soul. In life, every soul manifests or incarnates in particular forms of gender and sexuality, such as man or woman, straight or gay. Every soul necessarily takes a particular form, because it has specific things to learn about reuniting with God that cannot happen in any other way.

The soul's sense of being an independent, distinct entity (that is, a particular form of God's manifestation) is called a self. While on the surface a soul appears as a self, at a deeper level, every soul contains within its nature the potential for the qualities of all forms (for example, a gay man possesses the potential to exhibit both masculine and feminine qualities).

We can try to express these truths with words, but poorly. We could say, for instance: The soul is male. The soul is not male. The soul is female. The soul is not female. The soul is straight. The soul is not straight. The soul is gay. The soul is not gay. These are all fine (but limited) ways of talking about the soul.

Human beings seek to experience reunion with God by encountering God in relationship to one another. We can speak of the persons who so reveal God to us as our soul mates. Every soul knows the qualities of its soul mates, because every soul knows the qualities of God that it feels separated from. God has placed the knowledge of the soul mates in our intuition.

Straight persons seek soul mates especially in souls manifesting as persons of the opposite sex. God has placed knowledge of the opposite-sex qualities of the soul mate in the intuition of every straight person. Gay persons seek soul mates especially in souls manifesting as persons of the same sex. God has placed knowledge of the same-sex qualities of the soul mates in the intuition of every gay person.

Some people have repressed the truth that some souls may be said to be essentially gay and that all souls have gay qualities at their deepest levels, because they have also denied the truth about the gayness of their own soul and God's own gayness.

Tuesday, December 2

T.I.O.B.G. 3 of 6: The Two Prime Forms and Directions

All manifestations of God manifest with yin and yang qualities and directions. Traditionally, yin forms are said to be feminine and yang forms are said to be masculine. All persons contain both yin and yang qualities in different measures; it's not always true that men contain more yang qualities than women and vice versa. Furthermore, the qualities considered masculine and feminine vary in different times and places.

It is not simply the case that some manifestations of God are yin while others are yang. Instead, all manifestations contain both yin and yang qualities at their deepest levels. For example, masculine men and butch women may be said, perhaps, to have a greater proportion of yang than feminine persons. But all persons contain both yin and yang. Feminine women and effeminate men may be said, perhaps, to have a greater proportion of yin than masculine persons. However, yin and yang qualities are universally present.

According to tradition, yin is said to be associated with darkness, the moon, femininity, passivity, receptivity, relationship, connection, and love. Tradition says yang is associated with light, the sun, masculinity, activity, penetration, the self, independence, and freedom. While these are fine ways of talking about yin and yang at a very general level, yin and yang are more than the sum of our associations with them. Yin and yang are also the two archetypal directions of the movement of all souls toward reunion with God. Yang is always directed outward and yin is always directed inward.

In other words, yang forms seek reunion with God in otherness, or that which is beyond the self, and yin forms seek to join with God in sameness, or that which is contained within the self. This duality describes the two prime directions for the soul's fundamental desire to be reunited with God. There are actually an infinite number of directions that this desire may take, but it's helpful to start by talking about just these two.

Having established the two prime qualities and directions of reality, let's talk about gayness. The soul manifests in both gay and straight forms. The gay forms are yin, in the sense that they seek union with God in sameness. The straight forms are yang, in that they seek union with God in otherness. In other words, the contrast between gay and straight is a manifestation of the universal duality between yin and yang directions.

Gayness and straightness are not accidents of social conditions or biological functioning; rather, they are expressions of the principles of unity and duality at deep levels of reality. Gayness happens because all manifestations seek throughout history to achieve unity with God through the principle of unity. The gay self-sense of persons who identify as homosexual is an expression of this deep spiritual truth.

So far we have only been talking about gayness and straightness. Keep in mind also that the qualities considered gay and straight (or queer, bisexual, two spirited, active/passive, top/bottom, butch/femme, and so forth) vary in different times and places, according to historical, cultural, and social conventions. There are actually an infinite variety of ways of loving, and we have been talking about just gayness and straightness as a convenience.

Homosexuality is a particular form of sexual expression in which the soul seeks reunion with God by merging with a similar soul. The true value of homosexuality is that through homosexual forms, souls are seeking reunion with God by embracing through Love that which is a reflection of the self. Gay people teach us about the principle of sameness. It is through all patterns of gay or same-directed forms that humankind can come to know about the unitary patterns of God.

Heterosexuality is a particular form of sexual expression in which the soul seeks reunion with God by merging with a different soul. The true value of heterosexuality is that the soul is seeking reunion with God by manifesting in forms that are embracing through Love that which goes beyond the self. Straight people teach us about the principle of otherness, for it is through duality that humankind can come to know about the dualistic patterns of God.

Some people have repressed the truth that gayness is a valuable and essential way of seeking God, because they have also denied the truth about God's gayness and the soul's gayness. It is impossible to properly understand God without properly understanding gayness.

Wednesday, December 3

T.I.O.B.G. 4 of 6: The Four Prime Patterns

All things are manifestations of the principles of unity (God or Spirit) and duality (yin and yang). Yang describes masculine, outer-directed, and other-directed things. Yin describes feminine, inner-directed, and same-directed things. The natural order of human beings reflects these divine principles in an infinite variety of combinations. However, it is useful to start talking about the natural order of things by talking about just four prime patterns.

There are four archetypal patterns manifest in all human beings and other forms of reality. Although this belief is not widely recognized or understood, people talk about manifestations of these patterns all the time as if they knew what they were talking about. And it is common for people to say that only two of these patterns are proper (that is, the forms that correspond to heterosexuality) and the others are defective or distorted (that is, the patterns that correspond to homosexuality). This is an inaccurate belief, because it misunderstands that these are the four universal patterns underlying all of reality, and it is impossible to properly imagine reality without seeing all four patterns in harmony.

The natural order of things includes a great diversity of combinations of yin and yang. Many people intuit through a variety of philosophies the conviction that yin and yang are fundamental principles of reality. However, these same people have often failed to recognize that yin and yang actually appear as both qualities and directions in precisely four archetypal patterns (see figure 1):

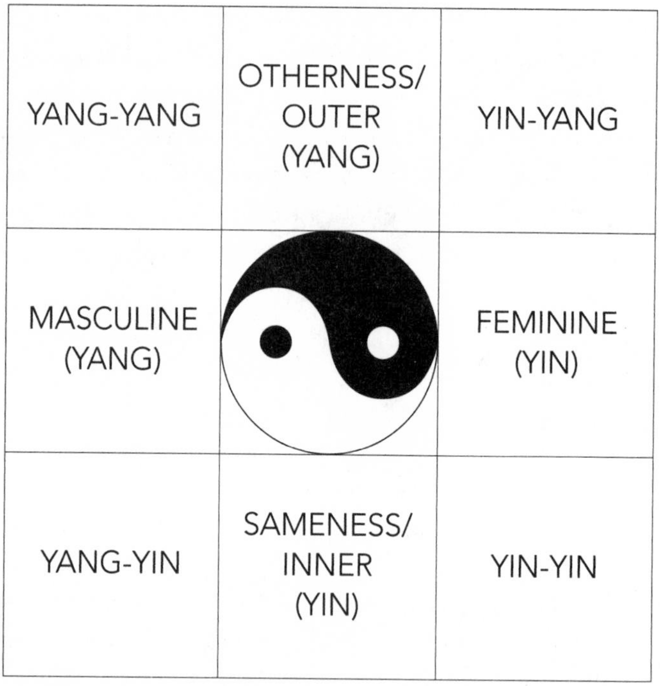

YANG-YANG	OTHERNESS/ OUTER (YANG)	YIN-YANG
MASCULINE (YANG)		FEMININE (YIN)
YANG-YIN	SAMENESS/ INNER (YIN)	YIN-YIN

Figure 1. Yin, yang, and the four prime patterns.

- Yang-Yang. Masculine and other directed (straight men uniquely teach us about this pattern).
- Yin-Yin. Feminine and same directed (lesbians uniquely teach us about this pattern).
- Yang-Yin. Masculine and same directed (gay men uniquely teach us about this pattern).
- Yin-Yang. Feminine and other directed (straight women uniquely teach us about this pattern).

A common mistaken belief is that the natural order of human beings includes only yang-yang and yin-yang combinations (straight men and straight women) and that all other combinations are, to borrow a phrase commonly applied to homosexuality by Roman Catholic theologians, "intrinsically disordered." This belief's most common manifestation is heterosexism. Heterosexism is usually defined as a belief in the superiority of heterosexuality over homosexuality, or a belief about the immorality of sexual behavior among gays. All formulations of heterosexism share a common insistence that heterosexuality is natural, ordered, and righteous while homosexuality is unnatural, disordered, and/or sinful. Although heterosexism is posited as a belief about sexuality, it is also implicitly a belief about the natural order of all things in the universe.

Once the truth about the natural order of things is understood, it becomes clear that heterosexism reflects a biased overvaluation of yang (the masculine aspect of reality) and undervaluation of yin (the feminine aspect of reality). This belief is understandable in a culture that is heavily prejudiced against the feminine in all its forms, yet it is manifestly not a true reflection of the inherent, balanced nature of the universe.

Although it is useful to talk about these four archetypal patterns among human beings, it is important not to make unwarranted analogies. All persons contain within themselves, at their deepest levels, the two archetypal qualities and the two archetypal directions.

In sum, there is a connection, but no exact correlation, between these four deep patterns and the personal identities that today we call straight men, gay men, straight women, and lesbians. Gay and straight identities give visible surface expression to deep underlying structures of reality. Persons of all sexual and gender identities give rise to the exact same deep structures, but they do so in different ways.

Thursday, December 4

T.I.O.B.G. 5 of 6: The Two Directions of Love

What is love? Love is not merely an emotion. Love is another name for the soul's archetypal desire to be reunited with God, the Source of All, and the actions that are manifested as a result of that desire. In other words, love is another name for the two archetypal directions that describe all reality. Love describes the very process by which all reality is reunited in history with God. In this sense, it can be said that God is Love.

There are two archetypal ways of loving—yin and yang. Yin ways of loving seek to be reunited with God in inner-directed or same-directed ways.

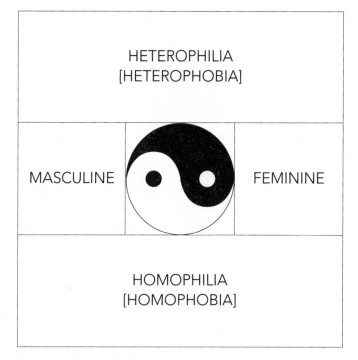

Figure 2. Heterophilia and homophilia.

Yang ways of loving seek to be reunited with God in outer-directed or other-directed ways. There are actually an infinite variety of ways of loving, but it's helpful to start by talking about just two (see figure 2).

Gayness and straightness are each, in their purest forms, expressions of the two archetypal ways of loving. Gayness is another name for the yin form of loving: the desire to love in inner-directed or same-directed ways, and the actions that spring from that desire. Another name for gayness is homophilia, or love of the same. Straightness is the yang form of loving: the desire to love in outer-directed or other-directed ways, and the actions that spring from that desire. Another name for straightness is heterophilia, or love of the other.

It is a common misconception that gayness and straightness are essentially about sex, but this is a mistaken belief held by those who have gotten hung up on sex. Heterophilia is the love of God in otherness, and homophilia is self-love, or receptivity to the love of God in sameness. All specific manifestations of love between two beings reveal a peculiar combination of both heterophilia and homophilia.

Some people have repressed the truth that homophilia is a valuable and essential way of loving, because they have also denied the true nature of love and the nature of gayness.

Friday, December 5

Today I picked up all but one of my HIV medications from the drug store. I asked the woman behind the counter if she could tell me the actual cost of the drugs, not just what my insurance co-pay is. Here's the data: $13.79 for a drug that inhibits chronic nerve pain from peripheral neuropathy, $363.79 for an antiretroviral, $487.59 for another antiretroviral, $806.49 for another antiretroviral, and $39.99 for a drug that treats a side effect of the antiretrovirals. Grand total for the month: $1,701.65.

My monthly cost after insurance: $103.79. This doesn't include several hundred dollars that I'll pay out of pocket this month for insurance premiums, doctor and hospital visits, and various other health-related expenses.

Saturday, December 6

The concept that human beings, including gay people, are made in the image of God, is hardly new or original. But utter the words "God is gay," as I did recently on my blog, and you better believe that some people's buttons will get pushed. One of the great things about blogging is the ability to immediately get feedback from the world.

Kathy Shaidle, a conservative Roman Catholic blogger, was kind enough to share her views with me in an e-mail. It seems that she saw my post not as an attempt to express the truth about reality as I see it, but primarily as an attempt to shock and offend the orthodox:

There are no new heresies under the sun, and many a fool has wasted his ink trying to make a name for himself by cooking up a new one with which to shock the orthodox. We are not as shockable as you might think, because, being orthodox, we're well aware of man's twisted fallen nature.

A progressive Baptist preacher who blogs under the pseudonym of Real Live Preacher wrote that the world may not be ready to hear what I have to say:

> It's hard enough for the Christian community to accept where things seem to be inevitably going with the issue of homosexuality. What you wrote would blow the top off a lot of people's heads, further entrench them with anger and their belief that homosexuals have some kind of evil agenda to dismantle all they hold true and fair about God.

My response: I am not particularly worried about offending the religious right or being called a heretic. While I honor the best of Christianity, I do not call myself a member of the Roman Catholic Church or any other denomination. I am writing down my thoughts about the true connections among homosexuality, God, and the universe not to shock fundamentalists but to share my vision with all who are seekers of Truth. And to get clear, for myself, about what I really believe.

My post, "God Is Gay," was not intended to be shocking (except perhaps to folks deep in denial). Rather, my aim was to radically affirm the true value and dignity of gay people and, in the process, that of all people.

Not all of the feedback was critical. Indeed, a woman named Marissa wrote: "This is so beautiful it gave me chills." And a Unitarian Universalist minister read my post and then responded on his own weblog. He wrote, "I knew it all along!"

I couldn't agree more. I only wrote the words a few days ago, but in a sense I feel I was simply putting down for the first time some core ideas that I have secretly carried my whole life within me.

Sunday, December 7

T.I.O.B.G. 6 of 6: The Two Directions of Fear

What is fear? When I speak of fear, I have in mind more than a feeling. Fear is another name for the soul's archetypal desire to be separate from God, the Source of All, and the actions that are manifested as a result of that desire. In this sense, there are two archetypal expressions of Fear—yin and yang. Yin ways of fearing are frightened by being reunited with God in inner-directed or same-directed ways. Yang ways of fearing are frightened by being reunited with God in outer-directed or other-directed ways. There are actually an infinite variety of ways of fearing, but it's helpful to start by talking about just two.

Homophobia and heterophobia are, in their purest forms, the two archetypal forms of Fear. Homophobia is the yin form of Fear: the resistance to experiencing God in inner-directed or same-directed ways. Heterophobia is the yang form of Fear: the resistance to experiencing God in outer-directed or other-directed ways. It is a common error to think that homophobia and heterophobia are essentially about fear of gays or straights, but this is a mistaken belief held by those who have gotten hung up on sex.

Some people have repressed the truth that homophobia is a harmful and unnecessary way of being, because they have also denied the true nature of Fear and the nature of gayness. The truth has been revealed to those whose eyes are open.

Monday, December 8

Healing Homophobia, One Man at a Time

Gay or straight, every man needs sexual healing. But fewer have the courage it takes to heal.

Meet Steve Tracy. Steve is a heterosexual, married man who recently turned 50. About four years ago, he began to do personal-growth work in a men's group. Some of those men were homosexuals. Steve soon became aware that he felt afraid in the company of gay men. He was troubled by his homophobic reactions and wanted to overcome them.

When Steve was four years old, a man in a park raped him. It was so traumatic that his mind repressed the memory. Steve didn't even learn about it until he was in his thirties.

But Steve suspected that his homophobia might have another origin. When he was nine, Steve's parents divorced. At that time, he was befriended by a married man I'll call Gary. Gary and his wife took Steve skiing, fishing, hunting, and on vacations. And when Steve was 11 and 12 years old, Gary molested him.

For more than 30 years, Steve carried the experience of these traumas with him in his body—partly in the form of homophobia. Unconsciously, he reacted to all gay men as if they were sexual perpetrators. Intellectually, Steve knew better than that. But the homophobia was a reaction seemingly outside his ability to control.

Steve came to understand that to overcome his homophobia he would need to confront his childhood perpetrator. He tracked Gary down using the Internet and verified his identity. After seeking the guidance of a close friend, a gay man whom Steve trusted, he began to write a letter to Gary.

Steve wrote that that he was doing spiritual work that involved bringing his own shadows into the light. He asked Gary how many other young boys he had seduced and whether he had ever been caught or received treatment. He explained that Gary's response would dictate what his own would be. He put the letter in the mail and prepared himself emotionally to "go to war with this man."

Only five days later, he received a reply. Gary wrote, in part:

Dear Steve,

Your letter came about an hour ago. For eleven years I have wished I could write to you and make amends for the sick behavior I displayed when you were a young boy. Today is my eleventh Alcoholics Anonymous birthday. In AA the Ninth step is to make amends to anyone we have wronged during our lives. For this reason, and personal reasons, I have wanted for years to tell you how terribly sorry I am for the behavior I displayed when I molested you. As a young adult (mentally very sick adult) I should never have acted out in the manner I did. Steve, you must realize that it was totally my fault and that you had nothing to do with what happened.

Steve couldn't believe it. His hard-as-nails anger began to soften into compassion. Steve continued reading . . . Gary went on to say that at the time he had molested Steve, he had been secretly bisexual. He claimed a new victim every few years.

Then Gary was caught and spent three years in prison. Gary lost everything: his career as a school principal, his wife of 25 years, and his health (he was infected with hepatitis B). But he didn't give up on life.

Gary entered therapy, found sobriety, came out of the closet, and found a committed relationship with another man. He also became active in 12-step work of carrying the message of recovery to his community. His doctor came to his tenth AA birthday party and was so impressed with what he saw that he put Gary on the list to receive a liver transplant.

Shortly afterward, Gary went into liver failure. He was placed in a care facility to die. By a small miracle, a liver became available and he recovered.

Gary told Steve that forgiveness would be too much to expect, but he wanted him to know that he had really loved him. He just wishes he hadn't carried it too far. He ended the letter with, "God bless you Steve, [signed] Gary."

As Steve read the letter, he began to cry. He read it over again and marveled at the healing ways of the Higher Power he calls "Great Spirit." By a coincidence, Steve's letter to Gary arrived on Gary's 12-step birthday, and Gary's reply to Steve arrived almost exactly on Steve's own 12-step birthday. Steve remembered the slogan in his recovery fellowship that coincidences are God's way of remaining anonymous.

Steve immediately called Gary and forgave him. And then they cried together. After forgiving Gary, Steve's homophobia began to fade, and he was soon able to form closer friendships with gay men.

Steve shared his spiritual work with the men's group, and the men were overjoyed at Steve's healing. Today Steve continues to facilitate emotional healing through his work as a counselor in Olympia, Washington, and with The ManKind Project, an international men's organization devoted to reclaiming the sacred masculine in our time.

It takes great courage for a man to combat his sexual shadows. It takes even more courage to forgive.

Wednesday, December 10

When religious officials recite scripture passages from the Bible or Koran that advocate the murder of gays, will they be held accountable for inciting violence? That seems to be the issue raised in Australia, according to a news report today.

An Islamic cleric there stands accused of making derogatory comments about homosexuals as he read from the Koran at a prayer service, saying that they should "have their heads chopped off." One thousand people were in attendance at the service.

What happened in Australia could happen elsewhere with Christian, Islamic, or other clerics. Fundamentalist Christians commonly cite purportedly antigay Bible passages without critically examining their full context, in order to justify their hatred and fear of gays.

I wonder how long it will be before a Christian cleric will stand accused of a crime for reciting Leviticus 20:13 ("If a man lies with a man as one lies with a woman, both of them have done what is detestable. They must be put to death; their blood will be on their own heads.")? Perhaps it will take a hate crime perpetrated in response to a Bible-thumping preacher's sermon to put this thorny issue to the test. I hope I'm wrong.

Friday, December 12

A Man and a Virus and a Blackbird

For the longest time, one of my pet peeves was HIV-positive people who call themselves "HIV." That's right, as in "I'm HIV" or "I've been HIV for three years."

When I would hear a guy say words like these, I'd want to give the dude a reality slap and say, "You are not your disease!"

Of course, I never did. I understood that the guy probably meant nothing at all by it, except perhaps that he was too lazy to utter the adjective "positive" after "HIV."

But a voice inside me nevertheless wanted to shout: "I AM NOT HIV. I AM NOT A VIRUS. I AM NOT MY DISEASE. I WILL NOT BE DEFINED BY A DISEASE. BEING HIV-POSITIVE IS A PART OF ME, BUT NOT THE SUM. I AM MORE. I AM ME. HIV IS NOT ME."

Because I had all this emotional energy around the subject, I knew this was about something more than just a missing adjective. I sensed that I held beliefs about HIV in shadow, and I wanted to gain clarity about what they were. I became willing to look at the risks that I might face if I changed my beliefs about HIV.

The human immunodeficiency virus has long ago infected my T cells. This Trickster had fooled my cells into becoming a breeding factory for more HIV. If the virus was one sick practical joker, was I nothing more than its hapless stooge? As I reflected on my resistance to being HIV, part of a famous poem by Wallace Stevens came to mind. But the words that came to me were a little different than I remembered . . .

A man and a virus
Are one.
A man and a virus and a blackbird
Are one.

I sighed and laughed. In a manner of speaking, I am HIV. I have merged with this viral life form more intimately and completely than I have joined with the living bags of carbon, hydrogen, and oxygen that I call friends and family. When we speak of the strength of family ties, we say that the connection to our relations is "in my blood." By that score, HIV was closer to me than family.

Yet the voice of resistance remained: "I am me. HIV is not me." By looking at my shadow, I came to understand that being HIV threatened my self-image. If I believed that I was HIV, then perhaps I was not who or what I thought I was. Perhaps I was not Joe Perez. Perhaps I was something else entirely: a deeper reality that we may call the soul. Part of me already believed this intellectually, but it's a belief that takes a while to really sink in.

I began to accept the idea that I was not who I took myself to be. This brought about a taste of death to my ego (that is, my self-image). There was no bolt of lightning as I sat under a bodhi tree, but I felt lighter . . . as if I had just reclaimed a piece of my soul.

The Buddha taught that life is characterized by *samsara,* a word that is often translated as "suffering." Birth, decay, death, sorrow, pain, grief, despair, not getting what you desire: these are all forms of suffering. He also taught that liberation from suffering is made possible by letting go of our attachments. Enlightenment is the state of being free of all attachments, or liberated from all suffering.

The granddaddy of all attachments is the sense of being a separate individual, an ego or self. In practice, this is a stubbornly hard attachment to be rid of, and there aren't many folks who can claim to have reached Enlightenment. Looking at the shadow around my disease helped me to lighten my tight grip on that attachment, at least for periods of time.

Today, I can finally utter the words, "I am HIV." And I can also say: "I am not HIV." Those are both fine ways of speaking, because both notions helped me to see the emptiness of my self-image. Finding an empty space within helped to make room in my soul for God.

Monday, December 22

Capricorn

The sun is moving into the territory of sky known as Capricorn. The Goat is constantly climbing to higher ground, gaining greater perspective on its place in the whole scheme of earthly things. Sign of the archetypal masculine, it seeks a union of the inner self with social realities. It depicts the human need for integration into conventional morality, institutions, religious communities, and society as a whole. The Goat strives for integrity with the objective order of reality.

Tuesday, December 23

The Roman Catholic Church's ongoing obsession with homosexuality continues to make news on an almost daily basis. Today, the *Chicago Sun-Times* reported that a group of clergy denounced what they say is "vile and toxic" language from the Vatican aimed at gays and lesbians.

Two dozen priests sent an unusually strongly worded letter to church officials blasting recent church statements as divisive, exclusionary, violent, and abusive. They wrote: "As priests and pastors we are speaking out to make clear that our gay and lesbian brothers and sisters are all members of

God's family, brothers and sisters in the Lord Jesus and deserving of the same dignity and respect owed any human being."

The letter falls short of saying the full truth: it's not just the language but the very moral theology of Catholicism itself that is "vile and toxic." I call it a theology of heterosexual supremacy. According to the news report, Cardinal Francis George received a copy of the letter and issued a response: "The church speaks, in moral and doctrinal issues, a philosophical and theological language in a society that understands, at best, only psychological and political terms. Our language is exact, but it does not help us in welcoming men and women of homosexual orientation. It can seem lacking in respect."

This is a terribly patronizing response. Cardinal, there are plenty of intelligent people who understand philosophical and theological language, and we still believe that your edicts are vile and abusive. Making antigay language friendlier will not cut out the cancer at the heart of the Church's moral teachings.

Some gays are praising the Catholic pastors for their courage in speaking out, but I think they're too cowardly. They assuage their liberal guilt by attacking the Church's rhetoric while giving silent assent to the actual beliefs in question. Nothing will stop the cancer in the Church short of a radical rethinking of the Church's regressive sexual theology, including acknowledging a divine purpose and end to homosexual orientation, and articulating a moral theological framework within which that end may be responsibly realized, including a sacramental context of holy union.

Thursday, December 25

Hey, Jesus

Hey, Jesus, it's me, Joe Perez. I'm writing to say happy birthday. I'm feeling blue because this is the first Christmas where I'm no longer a part of your Church.

Not that I was ever one of your faithful servants. As the Indigo Girls sing in "Hey, Jesus," I've been nothing if not one of your black sheep. Back when I used to call myself a Catholic, there was always a nagging sense that I didn't belong with the others. Now I don't even know whether to call myself Christian anymore.

I always felt different. This troubled me, because for a lot of my life, especially my childhood, I thought that being a good Christian was the best possible thing anyone could be. It's like good, holy, sacred, and Christian all meant the same thing. There simply was no other way to look at the world.

Being gay and all, I guess I'm one of the undesirables that your church leaders rarely miss an opportunity to heap abuse upon. Anyway, I decided I'd save the Catholic Church some trouble, so I checked out on my own. There's a longer story, but you don't want to get me started, because then I'd be talking your ear off.

Jesus, I guess the reason I'm writing you this letter is to say thank you. Now that I have more of an outsider's perspective on your followers, I've begun to see just how important your life really was. I believe you were a true child of God; and your life, teachings, and death have shown me much about just how divine human beings have the potential to be.

You have shown me much truth about the divinity of love, the blessedness of the poor and the oppressed, and the eternity of hope. Thank you for being a revelation of God to me. I could go on, but I'm afraid if I keep going you might get a big head.

If you were walking the earth today, my heart tells me that you wouldn't be part of the Christian Church either. I know you had some run-ins with the religious authorities of your time—self-righteous religious leaders who had all the answers down pat, who did crazy things like shunning and publicly shaming the sinners. You preferred the company of the outcasts and the sinners. And thinking about that, I feel closer to you than ever.

Friday, December 26

Why "Hate the Sin, Love the Sinner" Is a Lie

The other day, I was shopping at the local drug store when I bumped into my friend and former housemate, Steve (not the Steve who is involved with the ManKind Project). I saw that he had a black eye and a bruised face. He told me that he and another friend, a lesbian, had just returned from a vacation where they'd been attacked on a cruise ship by a group of homophobes.

The bashers hurt him so badly that he sustained broken facial bones, but he's healing now. As the bashers bore down on him, he realized that he'd never seen hatred before in such a pure form. Hatred. I can only imagine what my friend went through, and I get angry just thinking about it.

I was in an angry sort of mood recently when I found an op-ed in the *New York Press* called "Bring Back Hate." The author's name is Mark Gavreau Judge, and he announced that hate is "a lost virtue in lost times." Hate, a lost virtue? This guy must be nuts, I thought. Here's a taste of what he said:

> It's time to bring back hate. To be sure, as a Christian it is important that I try to separate my hate for evil from the person pushing evil, whether it's a morally kneecapped woman screaming for abortion, a rapist or a thief. Hate the sin and love the sinner and all that. But increasingly in our culture, the rule is, psychoanalyze the sinner and explain away the sin through socioeconomics—either that or it spills vats of hate on silly targets, like the president. We are in desperate need of the real thing, saved for an appropriate target.

And what is the appropriate target? Judge wrote: "Liberals can't abide the idea that some acts are in and of themselves intrinsically evil, in every situation, and must be met with pure hate."

Ah, I see now. Hatred is okay so long as you only hate things that deserve to be hated. Like homosexual sexual expressions and artificial birth control, for example, two things the Roman Catholic Church teaches are "intrinsically evil."

Judge is absolutely wrong about hatred. But as with many wrongs, there's a tiny kernel of truth. That truth is that the feelings of righteous indignation, anger, and rage are neither right nor wrong. Those feelings, painful as they may be, are not to be judged. We feel them, and it is good not to deny them or to pretend they're not there.

But hatred is not the same as anger, although Judge appears clueless regarding the difference. *Merriam-Webster's Dictionary* defines hatred as "prejudiced hostility or animosity." Hatred requires prejudice or prejudgment. You might say that the equation of hatred is the feeling of anger plus a judgment about the innate badness or evilness of the hated thing.

I believe strongly that no soul is evil. Someone may be so bad that all I can see is evil, but from God's point of view, there is still a beautiful soul. I think that when we judge something as evil, this is really a projection of some dark truth about ourselves that we haven't come to grips with yet, a shadow buried in our unconscious.

As I see it, to hate is to fall into delusion and shadow projection, no matter who or what the target is. Hating is a very human (and therefore forgivable) thing to do, but it is neither necessary nor virtuous. No amount of sophistry can turn hatred into a virtue. Calling hatred a virtue and advocating more of it for any reason is disturbing, dangerous, and irresponsible.

But what about Judge's "Christian disclaimer"? He did write, after all, "Hate the sin and love the sinner and all that." Very sincere. It's worth pointing out that "Hate the sin and love the sinner" is not a Bible verse (you can go to bible.gospelcom.net and search for the words—they're not there). While those words appear nowhere in the Bible, there are plenty of instances where Jesus tells us to love our enemy. "Hate the sin and love the sinner" is nothing more than a made-up phrase used by some people to justify their prejudice and hatred.

I wonder what Judge or other right-wingers would think if the shoe were on the other foot. Imagine, if you will, that there is a new and mythical religion that told its followers that belief in Christ was an intrinsic evil and an abomination that merited death, just as the Bible teaches is true of homosexual acts. Now imagine that this religion also claimed to be a religion of peace and love, so its self-righteous believers were told they have a duty to hate the Christian religion, but love the Christian.

Furthermore, imagine that the believers in this hypothetical religion were told that Christians were acceptable in society, just so long as they did not act on their religious beliefs. In fact, imagine that believers were told that Christians should be welcome in the U.S. military, but only if they didn't reveal or act upon their Christianity. The government might even issue a policy and call it, "Don't tell us about Jesus Christ, and we won't ask."

Such a religion, if it existed, would easily be seen as simply a thin veil over repugnant anti-Christian bigotry. Well, when Christians like Judge invoke "Hate the sin and love the sinner" to promote hatred of gays while cloaking their intent with a biblical-sounding fallacy, I think that's more or less the same thing.

When some average Joes and Janes see headlines like "Bring Back Hate" by writers like Mark Judge, I think they begin to feel it's okay to bash a few gays now and then. It is never necessary to hate. Respectfully, Mr. Judge can keep his hate.

Wednesday, December 31

David Morrison is a writer, chastity advocate, Internet blogger, and founder of Courage Online, a group for Catholics struggling with same-sex attraction. David and I have been exchanging friendly notes of disagreement to each other on our weblogs.

David criticized a gay Buddhist who wrote, "I cannot help but feel reconvinced that [gays] must build our own spiritual organizations and cosmologies, because [homosexuality] will never be the priority of the rest of the human race. So—Buddha, Jesus, a little of this, a little of that—but yes, let us make it in our own image."

David called his reply, "Why Bother?" Here's a taste:

If the option is to worship a God we create in our own image and who does not exist outside of our own system of creating it, why bother? I am led to recall the story about the seminarians who were subjected to a lecture from a modernist "scripture scholar" who tried to tell the seminarians that it didn't really matter if Christ was really risen from the dead. After listening respectfully to the lecture, one of the seminarians raised his hand and, after being called upon, said: "Father, if Jesus Christ did not really rise from the dead, I am going out and getting laid."

In other words, if Christ was raised from the dead, then this proves that God exists and is revealed to us through the orthodox teachings of the Roman Catholic Church. Therefore, gays seeking God should just go take a cold shower, because the pope says that's God's will for all homosexuals and all the faithful are obliged to submit to his authority. Here's how I responded to David:

I imagine that in speaking of "building our own cosmologies," the gay Buddhist does not mean that we should worship a made-up idol but rather that we must forge new images and beliefs that open us up to universal spiritual truths. Why bother articulating a cosmology where gayness has an honored place? Because it's the Truth!

As for your comment about the resurrection, literal belief in a resurrection is not important to me, nor to a great many spiritual people. Nor, apparently was it important to the authors of the Gospel of Mark, which does not include the resurrection and overall leaves the impression that Jesus's disciples were still very much struggling with what to think of Him after he was crucified.

There are many myths in countless religions and folktales of human or divine figures that rose from the dead. In my opinion, Christianity's belief in Jesus's resurrection is but one of the most popular examples of such a myth. Your version of faith in the resurrection is akin to insisting that fairy tales really happened. If something never happened—and I strongly doubt the historical reality of the resurrection and reappearances of Jesus—no amount of insistence that it did will make it so.

Faith as sentimental self-assurance that you don't have to suffer through death and mortality is actually harmful to living spiritually. There's another way. Suffer the pain of anxiety about mortality. That is part of being human. Feel your grief and fear, let them overwhelm you at times if you must, and cry in the arms of a close friend. There is faith on the other side, a faith that leads many people to go on with life with a quiet and peaceful serenity.

"Father, if Jesus Christ did not really rise from the dead, I am going out and getting laid" is a suitable remark for a Catholic teenager, but *you* can choose to be more adult.

Thursday, January 1

I spent New Year's Eve with Colin (not his real name), an ex-boyfriend. We had dinner on Capitol Hill, saw the new Steve Martin film, and then went out to my favorite leather bar, The Cuff.

I'm irked, because Colin disappeared about 20 minutes before the stroke of midnight. I figured he was either nabbed by a serial killer or just got lucky and was being very rude by abandoning me. Since I don't think there's an active serial killer in Seattle at the moment, I wasn't too worried. Still, I'm pissed. I decided not to call him to find out what happened. If he wants to call me to apologize, then he can go right ahead.

Fortunately, I happened to be standing next to a good-looking Latino man as midnight approached. We chatted for a few minutes and kissed when the countdown reached zero. He was a lousy kisser, so I quickly lost interest. Soon I was talking and flirting with a cute guy who had been repeatedly looking in my direction. He had blond hair, a boyish face, and a hard body (turns out he's ex-military).

I went home with him. Back at his place, we had The Talk.

"What's your status?" I asked him. "Your *HIV* status."

He said he was negative, and then I told him of my positive status. We spoke about safer sex for a short while, and then we went back to making out. We spent the night together. There are worse ways to spend an otherwise lonely New Year's morning than lying in bed with a handsome stranger. I'd much rather be curling up next to a lover in a long-term relationship, but that just isn't the reality of my life right now. I don't feel ashamed about sleeping with someone outside of a relationship, but I don't hold it up as an ideal. It's just one of the mundane compromises made in my life as a gay man whose love life ain't so hot at the moment.

Friday, January 2

Petirrojo Trujillo, a Roman Catholic, has posted a "rebuttal" to my "T.I.O.B.G." series (see posts beginning on November 30). This guy so distorts my point of view that I don't know where to begin, or even if I should respond at all. I can honestly say that I have seldom felt more completely misunderstood.

In his "argument," he does not engage my theological vision of gayness as such; indeed, he ignores my big picture altogether. He never seems to recognize that he and I are operating out of rival big pictures, nor does he explain how his worldview provides a better or more truthful interpretation of the facts about human sexuality and the experience of homosexuality by homosexuals. Instead he slides right past my big picture to the old, medieval arguments that equate gayness with homosexuality, homosexuality with buggery, and anal sex with all sorts of nasty, terrible things.

I'm sure some of the fault of the misunderstanding is my own. I have difficulty articulating a coherent philosophical position that allows people to easily peg me, so they throw me into holes with some mighty odd pigeons. I laughed out loud to read my critic reduce my big picture of gayness to the question of whether anal sex is a violation of the natural moral law. Then he said that the proof of the immorality of anal sex was obvious: it's just as "objectively" wrong to put a penis in an anus as it is to put food in an anus. The anus, it seems, has one and exactly one "objective" meaning and purpose: defecation. He believes that any other view of the anus is unnatural, irrational, and preposterous on the face. Ergo, Joe Perez's vision of the nature of gayness (which never mentions anal sex or other sexual acts) is disproved!

This critic seems incapable of thinking about gay men without reducing our full humanity to anal sex acts. Moreover, he's unwilling or unable to reflect subtly on the connection between Divine Love and what I call homophilia. He is unwilling or unable to contemplate God's embrace of all humanity in its multiple variations, enfolding and embracing as an act of same-directed love of all Creation as the Mystical Body itself. My critic never sees gay persons as reflecting in our nature a universal quality of Being, nor does he look within the patterns of his own ways of loving to see a mirror of the same deep underlying principle of reality. In short, he completely misses and ignores everything that I attempted to do in "T.I.O.B.G."

Instead of confronting my thoughts as an original vision, something perhaps that he has never heard before, he attempts to cast my vision into an ill-fitting mold. Trujillo honestly believes that I'm suggesting that "Christianity itself stipulates that God is pedophiliac and incestuous since the Father 'fully' loves his Son" and other questionable nonsense. God the Father a pedophile, and his Son an incest victim? He said it, not me.

We see the world from such different vantage points, I'm not sure that there's a point in further discussion. Not until he shows that he's made a serious effort to understand and engage the vision that I've set forth, instead of distorting it horribly.

Tuesday, January 6

When it snows like it did yesterday in Seattle, half the city shuts down. Driving in the snow gave me more than a few scares today, and being shut out of the office building where I work on account of a power-grid failure didn't help matters. But it was all worth it. I spent a couple hours this morning doing little else except sitting in a warm room, petting my cat, and watching the snow come down. Perfect!

Wednesday, January 14

I had a dream this morning in which I was one of a group of four or five men. I hadn't met them; but I was searching for them, and they were trying to find me. I was running through a maze looking for them, but there were police who were out to prevent us from meeting. Somebody had issued a restraining order to prevent us from finding one another, and the police were hunting us down.

I had a key tag with a picture of the man I needed to meet. At first, I thought the image was of me, because the guy had a bald head. Something about my perception of the image was blurry and indistinct, and I had to really concentrate to make out the image. After staring at the picture for a long time, I saw that the man had sideburns (I don't—I keep my head shaved and face smooth except for a goatee) and, directly beneath his ear, a gash on his face.

When I saw his wound, I knew he wasn't me. Then I saw that he had strange, wild eyes and a bizarrely contorted expression. I was frightened by him. I woke up breathing heavily.

Thursday, January 15

In the news: a Philadelphia minister who loudly condemns homosexuals has been convicted of soliciting sex from a 14-year-old boy. He was the sort of preacher who would go to college campuses and use a loud-hailer to rile up students about wicked fornicators, whores, and sodomites. He denied the charges, saying that he was merely asking the boy for directions to a video store because he wanted to buy the movie *Shrek* for his children. As the jury handed down its verdict, his mother wept in the courtroom and cried out, "He's innocent. He's innocent."

Isn't there something archetypal about this story? The convicted man ceases to be a peculiar individual, and somehow becomes the quintessential Homophobic Preacher, by day attacking sodomites on street corners with a blowhorn, while at night cruising teenage boys for a blow.

Tuesday, January 20

Aquarius

The sun enters the part of the sky governed by Aquarius. Like rationality itself, the Water Bearer disperses her life-giving gifts freely to all, rich and poor, female and male, straight and gay. Aquarius is the most intellectual of all the signs and describes the need for defining one's individuality against the tyranny of the herd. Above all else, the Water Bearer seeks freedom, the freedom of one who acts with equanimity in service to all humanity.

Wednesday, January 21

Correspondence with David Morrison

Same-sex attraction is not a condition I have chosen, any more than I have chosen to be a man or to be of Mexican-American descent. It is an involuntary condition, as I believe you agree and are well aware. However, my response to that condition is fundamentally a matter of choice and faith.

I have no problem accepting the idea that most human beings are heterosexually oriented and a small minority are bisexual or homosexually oriented. A penis and vagina go together, naturally, and for heterosexuals, reproduction is certainly an important meaning of sexuality. But I see it as one way of thinking about sexuality, and not the only valuable way.

I don't understand why a certain small portion of the human population is bisexual or homosexual, but it is. I am intrigued by efforts to understand homosexual origins in psychology, biology, or cultural anthropology. There are some quite interesting theories about the role that homosexuality plays in furthering the aim of natural selection (see books by Bruce Bagemihl, Louis Berman, and others) but much more study needs to be done.

I believe there is significant evidence that homosexuality has both biological and developmental origins. I guess that it is about 75 percent biological and 25 percent due to environmental factors, but this is pure speculation.

In real life, questions of why homosexuality exists become moot. One is simply called to put down the science books and make a choice about how to best respond to the hand that one's been dealt. For me, the question is a spiritual one: Having discovered myself to be homosexual, do I trust in the value and meaningfulness of this orientation, and seek to live life with self-acceptance, honor, and integrity? Or do I reject my homosexual orientation and view it as a hindrance to integrity and ethical living rather than as a means to it?

I will not tell you that the answer to this dilemma has always been an obvious one for me. Over the course of years I have gained experience both with accepting my sexuality and not accepting it. And grace has revealed to me the wisdom of my decision to fully embrace myself, including my gay orientation.

To reject my same-sex orientation, as you have apparently done with yours, I would need to have compelling and persuasive evidence that it was fundamentally incompatible with living with good health, happiness, love, and integrity. I have seen no evidence of that. Instead, I am constantly amazed by the richness, beauty, and deep spirituality I find in the lives of many gay men who have fully embraced their sexual orientation. I see gaiety, joy, serenity, peace, compassion, and beauty in their minds, bodies, and hearts. I haven't always seen it, not in every bar and bathhouse anyway. But that's because I was looking in the wrong places.

Seeing gays living spiritually rich lives is compelling evidence to me the path of self-acceptance I have chosen is a good one. I do not believe that it is the only good choice, nor do I believe that your own path of celibacy will necessarily lead you to the opposite. "By their fruits ye shall know them," as Jesus said.

David, you asked what conclusions I draw about my body from its design, such as the presence of sperm that could be used to inseminate a woman? I draw the conclusion that there is an inherent tension between my reproductive capacities and my sexual, emotional, and affectional attraction to a sex with whom I cannot biologically reproduce. That much is obvious. However, I do not conclude that this tension is a disorder. I conclude that life is complex and full of mystery. I conclude that I am called to a choice between accepting life on its own terms and resisting it to my own peril.

Consider this example: I am a writer and have been gifted with some ability to write nonfiction and technical material. I can make a living for myself in this way. But I long to write lyrical and magnificent poetry. I read the works of the great poets and I am in awe. My heart yearns for the abilities that they possess, even as I humbly acknowledge that I probably will never be a great poet.

What conclusions do I draw about myself? I don't conclude that I am disordered because the yearnings of my heart are in contradiction to my natural abilities. I conclude that life is complex and full of mystery. What part of me wants is not necessarily what I've been blessed with. I can't choose to be heterosexual any more than I can choose to possess sublime poetic gifts. But that doesn't mean the artistic gifts I do have are shabby, second-rate, or disordered. And certainly it doesn't mean that my writing abilities are intrinsically ordered to objective evil (though some of my critics might beg to differ).

It's true that I've seen plenty of dysfunction in the gay community: sexual and emotional compulsions and addictions, drug abuse, self-hatred, suicide, and so forth. But as you know we live in a culture that is filled with animosity and antagonism toward gays, and these cultural attitudes have been deeply ingrained in every single one of us. It's true that attitudes have begun to change and today's youths are less damaged than gays of previous generations. But the wounds inflicted on gay culture by antigay prejudice will take many years to heal. In light of society's homophobia, it has been a blessing and delight to have made the acquaintance of so many happy, healthy, emotionally well-adjusted gay people. (I want to add: I wish that I were one of them!)

So where you seem to attach only one fixed meaning to human sexuality and see that meaning necessarily attached to every sexual act, I see human sexuality as being a rich, hearty stew of meanings. That's my choice. I see homosexuality not as disorder but as complexity and mystery—a condition that one can choose in a spiritual act to take as curse or blessing. I have chosen to see being gay as a blessing.

Thursday, January 22

Pagan blogger Jay Allen has posted some kind words and provocative questions in response to a recent post of mine on astrology. I wrote that I am coming to understand the twelve signs of the zodiac as representing a scale of evolutionary stages from pure egoism to the identity of consciousness with Spirit. The signs can be imagined as both stages and signposts marking one's progress along a continuum of growth.

Jay asks how my spiritual ruminations on the zodiac compare to the philosophy of Sri Aurobindo and Ken Wilber. I wrote a comment on Jay's blog that explained that I am not familiar with Aurobindo or Wilber, so I have no idea how to answer his questions. I'll try to add some books to my reading list, but I'm not promising when.

Sunday, January 25 (Snoqualmie, Washington)

A dream last night: I am leading a worship service at a Unitarian church. Everyone is standing in a circle in the basement of the church. I'm leading the service from within the circle. There's something else in the circle with me: a very large chocolate-chip cookie. The cookie looks fabulously delicious and is at least an inch thick. I'm leading some sort of a communion service that involves the cookie.

I know that the chocolate-chip cookie was prepared according to a secret and traditional family recipe that was closely guarded for a long time. And we are honoring the occasion that the recipe is at long last published for the world to see.

At one point, I say: "O holy chocolate-chip cookie!"

Immediately afterward, I feel awkward and embarrassed. I'm quite afraid that people in the congregation think I'm actually praying to the cookie as if it were some sort of deity. I'm afraid they will think that I'm ridiculous. I'm terrified of being mocked for praying to a cookie!

In my heart, I know that I am not worshiping a snack food but the hidden, eternal sacred mysteries that it reveals. But nobody at that church understands me, and I'm afraid that it seems to them that I'm worshiping an idol. Can't they see that the cookie is Divine, and that the Divine is not limited to the cookie? How can I persuade everyone that I'm not crazy?

Monday, January 26

I spent the weekend in the mountains at a private home near Snoqualmie. My friend Roger invited me to attend Snow Bear weekend, a weekend social outing of the Seattle Bears. (Bears are a subculture of gay men. They are hairy men with a stocky or heavyset physique.) I had a great, relaxing, fun time. There were a few men who caught my eye, but unfortunately they were partnered up and off limits (just my luck).

When I start to have too much fun, my shadow comes out. From a deeply unconscious place, I feel stuck and want to put the brakes on the fun. It's as though there is some sort of emotional calculus in my head that tells me I better not start living life to the fullest: "Whoa, better stop now, Joe! If you keep on going like this, you're going to enjoy life too much. Better hold back and stop before you get to really enjoying it, or you might find yourself all the more devastated to one day lose it all."

Wednesday, January 28

I saw Harry today for counseling. Near the end of the session, I brought up a difficult topic: "Do you remember the first day I came to see you? I had a list of my three top issues. Well, I've been aware that we've been doing lots of work for quite some time on the first two, and many others besides; but I've been thinking lately that I haven't been dealing at all with the third one. And I think it's a big one.

"Issue number three. My nervous breakdown. 1999. My 30th birthday, when I was confined in the psych ward at Harborview. And the spiritual experience there that I've mentioned briefly but haven't talked about.

"For so long, I've tried to forget. From the time it began to shortly before I was hospitalized, I kept a journal. But when I got out of the hospital, I . . . I destroyed it. I don't talk about it. I've never really talked about it . . . with anyone . . . ever."

As I spoke, tears began to pour down my face and I began to shake. My breathing deepened and quickened, so I put a calming palm on my chest. I grew fearful that if continued to speak, I couldn't bear the pain. Perhaps I would hyperventilate or go into shock or even die.

I dried my eyes then looked at the floor and said, "I'm not ready to talk about this."

Harry assured me that when I was ready to talk, he would be there for me.

2 Changing Seasons

The animal is satisfied with a modicum of necessity; the gods are content with their splendors. But man cannot rest permanently until he reaches some highest good. He is the greatest of living beings because he is the most discontented, because he feels most the pressure of limitations.

—Sri Aurobindo

Sunday, February 1

I've been working out for the past two weeks and the initial muscle soreness is subsiding. By the time I finished my workout tonight, I found myself recalling physically leaner and more buff times and thinking, "Oh yeah, I remember now. This working out thing, it's not so bad. I may even start liking it again."

I wish I could say that I work out to promote greater harmony among my mind, body, and spirit, or some such noble end. But the truth is I'm motivated in fair measure by envy, jealousy, and poor body image.

Guilt is another factor. Being HIV-positive, I know that my health should be my No. 1 priority in life. But very often it's not. My inner critic gives me lots of "shoulds" around health and fitness: I should do this, I should eat that, I shouldn't eat that, and so forth. I know I shouldn't should myself so much, but that's where I'm at today.

I haven't gotten to the point yet where the joy of stepping fully into my physical power is motivation enough to put my will fully into action. When that day comes, I expect that going to the gym will come as naturally and effortlessly as brushing my teeth. Someday, perhaps.

Thursday, February 5

I smiled and chuckled when I read the profile of Kurt, a blogger who lives with his partner in Portland, Oregon. Kurt is a former minister of a conservative Lutheran church, a member of the United Church of Christ, and a member of a Wiccan coven. He has additional interests in the occult, esoteric Christianity, and the common truths that run through all faiths. Kurt writes: "Yep I'm a weirdo."

I'm a weirdo too, in case you haven't noticed. The labels and the packaging may be a little different. But "weirdo" somehow seems to say something that other words don't. Like "queer," "weirdo" alludes to some primal quality that binds me to other strange fellows from all walks of life. In our culture, taking a serious interest in any religion or spiritual path is enough to get one branded as a freak. I think it's something that non-weirdos just can't appreciate. I have a long history of running from my inner weirdo, but lately I've been learning to embrace him. As Kurt's post reminds me, a cool thing about weirdness is that there's great company.

Saturday, February 7

A Gathering of Men

"He gives the best bear hugs of any man I know."

That was one of the frequently repeated stories told about my friend Mike at his 50th birthday party earlier this week.

It wasn't your ordinary birthday party. There was no gaggle of men drinking tequila and getting shit-faced at a pub. No, not this time. This party was a men's gathering. Sure, women were present, too. But, make no mistake, this was a gathering of men. Some of the women and men who'd never seen a men's gathering got quite an eyeful.

I love men's gatherings. We are men who give long, loving, intimate bear hugs. We are men who wrestle and tussle with each other. We are men who honor each other for being affectionate and loving, and for acknowledging our need for other men in our lives. We are men who can say "I love you" or "I need you" to another man.

We are men who can be intimate with other men even in front of our girlfriends, partners, and wives. At this gathering of men, the presence of a few openly bisexual or gay men is unremarkable, but not necessarily unnoticed.

As a gay man in a group of mostly straight men, I didn't know who was gay and who was straight or bi, and it didn't matter. I didn't need to know in order to protect myself from potentially hostile social interactions. I wasn't on my guard, so my gaydar could relax. (Gaydar, for those who need a definition, is the radarlike ability to detect queer folks simply by observing mannerisms, style, and bodily movements.)

After the festivities, I struck up a conversation with one clean-cut, good-looking man who I hoped was gay. Unfortunately, he mentioned he had to be running home to his wife. Damn!

This was a birthday gathering for Mike unlike anything most of us had seen before. We honored Mike by telling stories of his life. And not just fishing stories, or tales with lots of laughter and rollicking punch lines (though there were those stories, too). We honored our friend by telling stories not only of his joy, but also of his fear, his anger, and his pain.

Some of the stories we told weren't flattering. But in a men's gathering, we don't honor a man by flattering him; we honor him by speaking our truth. We honored Mike that night by sharing how he has helped us to become more authentic, to face our own fears, and to confront our own shadows.

I met Mike about two years ago at a men's gathering sponsored by the

ManKind Project. He's a participant in one of the two men's groups that I attend regularly. I haven't known Mike for many years, but I feel as if I know him better than friends I've known much longer. Men's circles can be extraordinarily intimate settings, particularly when a group has been going for a while with the same men.

In men's circles, we support each other in healing. That means looking at things in our lives that we don't want to look at, including how we think things aren't working or could be functioning better. That means being willing to face and own our shadows. Sometimes we go to battle against our demons. A special bond develops among men who have been in such battles together.

However, the point of our gathering on this evening wasn't to work but to honor our friend. We smudged with sage. We called in the Seven Directions, a sacred ritual we respectfully borrowed from the Native Americans. We beat on drums. We sang songs. We ate cake and drank punch. We gave and received awesome bear hugs. And then we cleaned up after ourselves. I love men's gatherings.

Monday, February 9

How to Respond to Antigay Moralizers

One of the hazards of writing about homosexuality in the public eye is that sometimes my views get attacked by religious moralizers. Here's how I respond to them.

"It's just as wrong to put a penis into an anus as it is to put food into an anus," one such moralizer told me. "God intends the anus for only one thing: shitting. Any other use of the anus is a violation of objective, universal principles of morality."

I am convinced that there's all too much attention paid to moralizing about gay sex, and not nearly enough attention directed toward efforts to appreciate and understand the actual lived experiences of gay people's attempts to make meaning of sexuality. Defensiveness leads many people to claim they know answers about morality and homosexuality. The superficial confidence of moralizers who try to convert others to their point of view is belied by the undertone of desperation and fear in their efforts. Paying close attention to such moralizers, I've reached the conclusion that they are expending massive amounts of energy simply to convince themselves.

Moralizers generally define morality as adherence to a set of minimum requirements. Go to church on Sunday, check a box. Don't go to church, it's a mortal sin. Don't do this, don't do that. Take sexuality for instance. There's a whole list of things that good, moral people aren't supposed to do. No oral sex, no masturbation, no sex with members of the same gender, no anal sex. If you're an orthodox Roman Catholic, add no condoms and no birth-control pills to this list of prohibitions. Do the minimum, avoid these "sins," and you're okay. You can have a pretty righteous opinion of yourself.

You can hardly blame some churches for taking a fast-food approach to the moral life. In many churches, the rich, nuanced topic of morality becomes trivialized and caricatured into McMorality. These churches have millions of souls to instruct—like overburdened parents with a dozen children—so they promulgate rules for their flocks at the lowest common denominator. Such rules are like one-size-fits-all clothing handed down from one child to another: ill fitting, ragged, and unseemly. But as I see it, morality is more than simple adherence to a universal set of minimum standards for life; it is a striving to realize the highest aspirations of one's true nature.

My dictionary defines objective like so: "Existing independently of mind; belonging to the sensible world and being observable or verifiable, esp. by scientific methods; perceptible to persons other than an affected individual; expressing or involving the use of facts without distortion by personal feelings or prejudices." It's interesting to observe people writing about homosexuality as an objective disorder. Their facade of confidence, self-righteousness, and certainty are all too often betrayed by the anxiousness of their tone, their adamancy, and their quickness to feel that their very worldview will collapse upon them if they give but an inch in the argument.

Remember the guy who told me that the anus is "objectively" only intended by God for defecation and nothing else? I hadn't the stomach to continue a dialogue with him. I've seen where these arguments inevitably go: nowhere. That which is so obvious and central to my worldview—the mystery, complexity, and multifaceted meanings and purposes of human sexuality, irreducible to any one philosophy—is fundamentally incompatible with his literalism (one act, one meaning, case closed), which is shared by millions of other men and women. They are all convinced that their beliefs are 100 percent objectively true. Funny thing, though: these believers don't agree with each other on either what's objective or what constitutes a rational mode of inquiry for determining objectivity. Their beliefs are nowhere even close to objectively anything. Their beliefs fail the test of objectivity on all counts: they are clearly distorted by personal feelings and prejudices; they are not verifiable by scientific methods; they are not perceptible facts; and they do not exist independently of mind.

These traditionalists aim for objectivity, but what's the point really? In science, objectivity is useful; it's essential to the mode of inquiry. But in moral thinking, I prefer to think of the aims as being empathy, impartiality, and the attempt to put ourselves in other people's shoes. Morality is not about reducing the complexities of our lives and diverse experiences to a skeleton of supposedly simple moral facts (like "don't put food or penises in the anus").

Human beings have vastly different personal experiences and worldviews. And we are all deeply embedded in particular historical and cultural contexts that do much to determine these. In this sense, morality is relative—a lesson that moralizers refuse to learn. Morality is relative, but not absolutely relative. Morality is relatively relative, so to speak. This is a lesson that so-called moral relativists refuse to learn.

How do I know that morality can't be completely relative? Because morality may become more sensitive, more subtle, more dynamic, more fluid, and more rich. We may grow from very selfish ways of behaving to more altruistic ways of caring for others. Spiritual and moral growth is a real possibility.

My stock response to moralists is not to enter into their drama-fests of self-righteous blather. The best response to moralizers ("Gay is bad!") isn't to moralize back ("Gay is good!"), but to expand and enrich our own moral compass. We can be moral without moralizing. We may or may not ever convince the moralizer, but we can change ourselves.

Tuesday, February 10

At the Orangeguru blog (orangeguru.net), Dieter Mueller writes: "Not every knockdown in our life is good for something." The tendency to try to find something good in every experience is a spiritual temptation to be resisted. There are certainly lessons to be had in life from the punches we're thrown: lessons of humility, grief, righteous anger, and even the endurance of seemingly unbearable cruelties.

But however you cut it, a punch is a punch. Thinking good thoughts about the punch may sell New Age spirituality books, but it does not satisfy the soul. Simply learning how to endure pain is a trying lesson that initiates us into the deep mysteries of life.

If enduring pain were easy, there would be no addictions, no procrastination, no flights of escapism, and no defending against our pain by intellectualizing about it. We may seek to avoid emotional pain, but rarely are these attempts successful. In living with honesty and depth, we do not need to learn how to think positively about being punched. We need to learn how to take punches . . . and how and when to throw them. One of the biggest problems with some New Age spirituality is its refusal to see the need for occasionally returning a punch with a punch.

I recall a famous saying by Aristotle: "Anybody can become angry, that is easy; but to be angry with the right person, and to the right degree, and at the right time, and for the right purpose, and in the right way, that is not within everybody's power; that is not easy." Learning how to be angry in a good way is one big piece of my ongoing work. I'm not where I want to be, but I'm getting closer all the time.

Wednesday, February 11

A Proprioceptive Write

This is the first blog post that I write without editing myself. I want to write about HIV. But first a word about this writing style. I'm writing this blog exactly as I would if I were scribbling with ink in a paper journal. Once the words hit the computer monitor, I'm stuck with them. Oh, I think I'll still spell check. Or maybe not. I really haven't thought that far ahead.

This mode of writing is similar to what's called proprioceptive writing. It's not stream of consciousness writing, but intentional writing done in a ritual way with the aim of increasing self-awareness. It's a form of writing done as a spiritual discipline.

One of the rules of proprioceptive writing is that it must be done on paper (there are other rules as well involving candles and baroque music). Why write this way? Well, there are a number of reasons, but they all basically come down to one thing: slowing down the thought processes, and allowing the writing to be an expression of an audible voice.

This takes a good deal of the ego out of my writing. My ego that edits, critiques, and polishes without end. My ego that wants to impress you, so I search for a wittier or funnier way of making a point. It takes out the ego that is embarrassed at how little I know about something, so I don't have to admit that I'm ignorant.

Take HIV, for instance. I want to write about HIV, but I'm resisting. I think I'm afraid that if I do, I may begin to feel grief . . . I want to be able to control what I'm writing, but the proprioceptive style of writing doesn't allow for that. Proprioceptive writing means that I must write exactly the words that come to mind as they come up, without editing myself.

I need to write my voice, and yet my voice wanders and doesn't go where I intend it to go. And all I can do to try to move in different directions is to ask a stupid question that just loops back into what I've already written.

What do I mean by stupid? Stupid like the kids in school who were so much slower than me. Stupid was something I never permitted myself to call anyone. Because I was always too embarrassed to call attention to myself. Being smart, having people judge me because I'm smart, I was always trying to hide, so people wouldn't think I was arrogant or better than anyone else.

What do I mean by arrogant? Proprioceptive writing is stupid. I want to write about HIV, and I'm going everywhere but where I think that I want to go.

What do I mean by arrogant? Arrogant, like I was so arrogant that I didn't believe I could ever possibly become HIV-positive. I knew better. I knew how to protect myself. I knew how to have safer sex. I was the last person in the world who would get HIV. I was so sure of that. That sort of arrogant. And stupid. I know what I mean by stupid. Stupid enough to get a fucking virus that could kill me. That could wreck everything and devastate everyone around me . . . So stupid. So arrogant.

I see now that it's not so much the grief I resist, perhaps, in writing about HIV. It's the shame.

Thursday, February 12

Tonight we did anger work in one of my men's groups. I was the only gay in a room of about a dozen men. One by one, we each took turns doing our work. I found myself struggling. I could muster the physical response of anger but couldn't put words to my anger, only animalistic noises. I left the meeting breathless and confused. When I came home, I began to write about it:

If only I could put my rage into words. The rage I felt was toward all straight men. All heterosexuals everywhere. Every man who'd ever yelled faggot or queer . . . Every jock who could fucking squash a puny little homo punk with his sneering and hatred. No, not hatred, smug superiority. Like I'm a man and you're a fucking worm. Humiliation.

I could speak. No I couldn't speak. I couldn't tell the men—it's fucking YOU I hate. It's fucking ALL OF YOU . . . It's all in me . . . This rage, eating away, tearing at my insides like a beast with claws and leaving me raw and bloodied in a heap. This rage that tore me up, tore me down, left me feeling like a cast-off shoe next to a dumpster. This rage that fills my being with a toxic scream and yet is cut off at the throat. This rage that leaves me feeling powerless and weak, so full of fear that I cannot speak who I am because I will be hated, killed, destroyed. It is powerful.

Can I put the rage into words? Hell no, I can't put the anger into words. If I could, I would say: It's YOU I hate. Every last one of you. You, lashing out with words so tormenting, with a glance, with an unspoken phrase, with a blind assumption. You, with a question that oh by the way denied my very humanity and suggested that being who I am is the lowest thing imaginable, the very worst thing a human being could be—no, less than human itself.

This rage opens me into fear and sadness — not because I think you will hurt me, not because your judgments sting, not because of any of these things, but because I want your love.

Friday, February 13

Yesterday afternoon, I got some test results back. My T-cell count is under 200 and the viral load is high, but at least the numbers are stable. Actually there were statistically insignificant improvements in both. My doctor's message is that I should consider going on T-20, the first in a new class of drugs called fusion inhibitors. She says it's worth considering, but I think it's the last of a handful of terrible options.

If I go on this drug, I will need to begin giving myself intramuscular injections twice daily . . . probably for the rest of my life. As a boy, I remember watching my father inject himself with insulin in the thigh every day. I'm not looking forward to walking in those shoes. My doctor's not pushing me too hard, so I'm going to wait.

Friday, February 13

Will You Look into the Mirror?

I was once in a sacred men's circle with about a dozen other men. A few of us were gay, most were straight, and there was one man who had previously lived an openly gay life but who was now romantically involved with a woman. You might call him an ex-gay (that is, a person with same-sex attraction who strives to become heterosexual and who refuses to identify as gay).

All men are welcome in the men's circle regardless of their sexual orientation. It's not for me to tell another man in the circle that he ought to accept being gay or to tell him he should give up his religion. When I have an issue with another man, it's not my place to try to fix him. Instead, men in the circle are expected to be mindful of any uncomfortable feelings or strong judgments that are triggered for them while in another man's presence. If I am uncomfortable because there's an ex-gay person in the circle, then I'm invited to examine my feelings and judgments about the other man and discover what I can learn about myself.

I recently read a book by a man whom some would call an ex-gay. Actually, that term doesn't quite fit David Morrison. He does not claim to have completely eliminated his homoerotic attractions but simply to have adopted a chaste lifestyle. Here's what his book *Beyond Gay* says about him: "Morrison was a gay activist for about seven years until, in his late 20s, he gradually became disillusioned with actively gay life and, in self-acknowledged despair, turned to God. After his conversion experience, Morrison grew in his knowledge and faith in Christ, at first while still homosexually active as an Anglican and, later, as he is today, a Roman Catholic committed to chastity."

David is fond of saying of gay people that they are "more than the sum of their temptations." In that vein, I think it's a good thing for gays to remember that the people of the religious right are more than the sum of their antigay dogmas.

I see in David another man much like myself. We both lived an openly gay life in our twenties, then we both became disillusioned with how our lives were shaping up. In our late twenties, we were both miserable souls. Despair is a word that certainly described my life at times. I spent much of my late twenties fleeing from intimacy and genuine spirituality by throwing myself into drug and sex addictions, and refusing to take responsibility for my life.

David seems to blame his despair on the intrinsic qualities of gay life itself. He writes of the "hard realities of actively homosexual life," such as the lack of stability in gay relationships, the shallowness of gay culture, and the risks posed to our health by unsafe sex. There's nothing in David's criticism of gay culture that doesn't have at least a grain of truth to it, though I hardly see the problems as being inherent in gayness itself.

Despite the similar disillusionment we both felt in our late twenties, at a certain point our paths diverged sharply. David's response to despair was to embrace a conservative religion that largely blamed the problems of gay life on homosexuality itself and seemed to offer a way out. He converted to conservative Roman Catholicism and committed himself to a path of chastity and "Christian discipleship."

My response to despair was to reclaim a spiritual path that included fully accepting my sexuality as a gift and starting to take responsibility for my life. I entered a recovery program and found supportive groups where I could explore and grow spiritually in gay-affirming ways. It saddens me that David found living a gay life so unacceptable that today he prefers chastity. I wonder how his experience might have been different if gay culture had been more loving and less superficial.

Many gays are unsatisfied with the shallowness and negativity that we have experienced, and we are working to shift gay culture in healthier directions. We are committed to reducing the prevalence of unsafe sex, alcoholism, drug and sex addictions, and preoccupation with a perfectionistic body image. We have had enough of copping attitudes and striking anonymous encounters. We are striving, however imperfectly, to change. We are seeking to cultivate friendliness and forms of spirituality that affirm our sexuality and ways of loving.

As I see it, the ex-gay movement is a shadow for gay culture, and the gift they give us is that of a mirror into the queer soul. It saddens me when gays look into that mirror and see ex-gays merely as self-hating homosexuals. I suggest that we shouldn't too quickly condemn men like David Morrison and others on a more traditional life path. When we condemn what we see in others, we also reject a part of ourselves. We can choose to see those who walk a more traditional way as a mirror not only of our self-loathing but also as a reflection of our full humanity. They are our brothers and sisters in spirit, and perhaps some will eventually rejoin the gay and queer community.

Let us find the generosity of spirit to bless the ex-gays and learn what we can from their struggles. We need not adopt their antigay attitudes, fundamentalism, or traditionalism. But we can, perhaps, take away a precious gift: seeing our own deepest selves and souls more clearly.

Saturday, February 14

Is Gay Pride a Sin?

Antigay zealots once placed a billboard in downtown Toronto that they intended for marchers in a Gay Pride parade. The billboard was a Bible quote: "This was the iniquity of thy sister Sodom, Pride."

The idea that pride is the worst of all sins is a common notion. Saint Augustine called pride "the beginning of all sin." Today, the religious right sees the depravity of gays not only in our sexual behavior but also in our "prideful" failure to acknowledge our own sinfulness. They call us egotists, narcissists and hedonists. However, our response to the religious right does not have to be as categorical and knee-jerk as their attacks. Gays need not reject religion altogether just because a group uses its theology as a weapon against us. Instead, we can take an open-minded look at pride to glean wisdom that we can claim for our own.

Judeo-Christianity is hardly the only tradition to condemn pride. Buddhism, Hinduism, Islam, Jainism, and other wisdom traditions also have teachings that condemn egotism and arrogance. The Greeks understood pride as hubris, the exaggerated self-confidence of being foolish enough to ignore the gods.

Unfortunately, the spiritual wisdom about pride is frequently distorted by religion. Religions may go beyond condemning arrogance to actually teaching that human nature is corrupt, wicked, vile, wretched, and fundamentally sinful. In recent decades, gay men, lesbians, bisexuals, and the transgendered have suffered some of their greatest humiliations at the hands of religion.

Traditional religion relentlessly condemns pride but seldom condemns low self-esteem with the same conviction. Authentic spirituality teaches that both arrogant pride and low self-esteem are equally important distortions of self-worth.

In Christian ways of thinking, arrogant pride is tantamount to playing God; effectively one is pretending to be one's own savior. By the same token, Christians can think of low self-esteem as a failure to honor one's dignity as a creation of God by effectively playing God and damning oneself.

Christianity's remedy for the dual sins of pride and low self-esteem is right relation with God. In other words, it's not thinking so highly of oneself that you don't see your own need for salvation. But it's also not thinking too lowly of oneself, because your sense of esteem comes from recognizing your sacred worth as a child of God.

In *Taking a Chance on God*, John J. McNeil discusses the sin of low self-esteem: "In my 20 years as a pastoral counselor and psychotherapist to lesbians and gays, I have found that the chief threat to the psychological and spiritual health of most gay people, especially those who come from a strong Christian background, is guilt with its companions shame and low self-esteem, which can in turn develop into self-hate."

McNeil points to therapy, coming out of the closet, and developing a healthy spirituality as the three most important steps for gays to take in healing low self-esteem.

Pride isn't a sin when it's an expression of healthy self-esteem. Celebrating gay pride is an essential affirmation of our human dignity, whether that takes the form of marching in a parade or being more honest with our friends and family about who we are.

Pride can surely elevate the gay spirit, but what about the gay soul? Feeding the spirit requires that we envision our ideals, put our philosophy of life into action, and have a strong sense that we are a woman or man with dignity and integrity. Positive self-esteem is vital for these endeavors. In contrast, soulfulness does not care about what's healthy or unhealthy, or whether an experience is joyful or melancholy. Soulfulness insists on being true to what's real without pretense or apology. Being soulfully gay means not using false pride as a shield over our pain, shame, and guilt. Authenticity demands that we allow a place for all our feelings, especially the uncomfortable ones that we'd rather cover over with denial, secrecy, and rigid thinking.

For everything in life there is a time under the sun, says the book of Ecclesiastes. There are times for celebrating gay pride and times for acknowledging our doubts and lack of wholeness. For every man and woman marching gleefully in the parade, there are others who aren't yet ready to celebrate, at least not until they've done their soul work.

The point of doing soul work is not to wallow in misery but to enter deeply and courageously into our pain. Soul work requires us to break down the falseness of our sense of gay pride so that we can eventually emerge from the other side into an authentic form of gay pride. But the soul's first step down can be a rough and tumbling one: humility.

Sunday, February 15

Did Jesus really rise from the dead? No. And if I could have been there with a Polaroid camera, what would I have seen? An empty tomb, some say.

In the Gospel of Mark there is no resurrection. But there is an empty tomb. What do I mean by empty? That which we expected to find—a corpse—is not there. Our expectations are dashed. Our hopes for one thing shattered, only to be left, bewildered, with a puzzle: the empty tomb.

I tell myself I don't have to have all the answers, yet another part keeps searching. Searching for what? What answers do I expect to find? The corpse of Jesus, rotting in the grave. And two millennia of Christians whose hopes were as vain as Jesus's plea on the cross: "My God, my God, why have you forsaken me?"

Is this the real meaning of emptiness in the Buddhist sense? Is emptiness the same as being forsaken by the Absolute? Somehow I don't think that's what the Buddha had in mind.

Did Jesus really rise from the dead? No. But I doubt the adequacy of even that answer. Is that no a no with content, or an empty no? What do I mean by an empty no? A no that moves beyond antithesis to synthesis, a no that is said joyfully and playfully, a no that is said as a lover says no when he really means "Come to daddy, you naughty little boy." Not forsaken but beckoning. An empty no is living within the contradiction, living within the unknowing.

Monday, February 16

I had a using dream the other night. Thinking about it is making me a little crazy. I hadn't had a using dream in a while. Thankfully they come less frequently to me now than they did earlier in recovery. In my dream, I am performing a cool, rational calculus as to whether or not I should start using drugs again. On the one hand, I see everything that my life is gradually becoming in my recovery: spiritual, sane, sober, stable, service oriented, filled with friendships, and marked by a renewed sense of self-respect. And on the other hand, I see a line of crystal meth and a razor blade.

Then I calmly, coolly, rationally make a choice. I choose the drug, and I do so with glee. I run from everything that gives my life purpose and direction. I am running. Where? Away from life and into the arms of death, I suppose. I choose the end of everything good and decent and sane. I choose insanity. What can I say? In my dream, it seemed like a good idea at the time.

• • •

I called Odie, my sponsor in the program, and confessed my sins.

"I've been slacking in my program. I haven't been going to meetings. I haven't been calling you. I almost didn't call you tonight . . ."

I took a risk. Although it was only ten o'clock, I figured it was likely he'd be asleep. I almost didn't call, because it was such a selfish thing to do. But there was a persistent little voice telling me that I was probably just talking myself out of making the call because I was trying to avoid it.

Thank God he answered the phone. It was obvious that I'd woken him from sleep.

"I'm glad you called," said Odie. "You did the right thing."

Tuesday, February 17

What do I mean by life? Suffering. Loss. And the whole nine yards . . . The whole fucking awesome and miserable lot, the worst day of my life and the best day all rolled into one. The day my heart left. The day I stopped wanting to live. The day I sold my soul. The day I took the first hit of cocaine . . . no, crystal meth . . . no, crack . . . no, whatever the hell you gave me. I don't know. I just want to have it—anything but what I'm living in now. The hell of life so miserable that death was preferable.

What do I mean by death? Death is a drug. Death is a drug that I shot up my veins to take away the life. Death was ecstasy. Death was bliss. Death was forgetting. Death was oblivion. Sweet, sweet forever, forever and a day, love without danger, cheap grace from a dime-store god, grace from a spoon and a flame, grace from a line, a bump, a hit, a shot, an 8-ball and a quarter and a gram and a tin, tin, bitter, bitter taste. The taste of space and stars on my tongue, the taste of torment/agony leaving my body. Pain no more. Morphine, codeine, Vicodin, the sweet love of pleasure—it is a lover, it is a father, it is a mother.

What do I mean by pleasure? The absence of pain. The drug that takes me to zero.

Thursday, February 19

I had a dream this morning where I am composing a poem. I am writing "This is my Body, This is my Blood" over and over again, and in many different languages. I am thinking as I write: "Hey, I'm writing in German. I must be dreaming. This is cool. I don't even know German."

I am talking to a Roman Catholic priest, a closeted homosexual. I live in his parish, but I'm a lapsed Catholic. He has received orders from Rome. They have told him it's his job to "get the homosexuals out," and he has called on me to help him out.

"Me, why me? Don't you know that I'm gay?"

I'm puzzled. I don't understand.

Now I am arguing with a conservative Catholic. He is explaining that all Catholics who disagree with the pope's teachings should leave the Church.

I reply thus: "I think that's a great idea. Why don't you start? Since the Church teaches the primacy of conscience and you seem to reject that teaching, I think it would be a fine idea if you left the Church and started a new church called the Conservative Catholic Church. And by all means, why don't you take all the conservatives with you and shut the door on your way out?"

Sometimes I pray Catholic prayers. Sometimes I long to take part in the sacraments. And these impulses arise from a deep place within, whence the dream comes. Spiritual seekers often discuss faith as if it were strictly a matter of rational choice and preference, like they are consumers shopping in the supermarket aisle of religions. And religious conservatives often discuss faith as if it were strictly a matter of reasonable belief or unbelief, admonishing those who dissent from dogma to make the rational choice of leaving.

I am finding that faith is more complex than that. Leaving the Roman Catholic Church is easy to do with my feet but harder to do with all of me. These impulses are in contradiction, and for now I'm okay with that.

Friday, February 20

Pisces

The sun moves into the part of the sky called Pisces. The twelfth sign of the zodiac depicts the maximum expansion of consciousness: the inner realization of the Unity of Being of all things. Pisces is symbolized by the Fishes, and is linked to the archetypes of the Poet and the Mystic. It is ruled by the planet Neptune, the symbol of divinity itself. Notoriously unstable, Pisces rules addiction, misfortune, poverty, mental illness, and insanity—as well as the most blissful and ecstatic states known to humankind. Pisces is the sign where Ultimate Reality is experienced directly.

Saturday, February 21

My Philosophy of Life

A philosophy of life should keep me grounded in being in the world and in my body and emotions, affirm the value and dignity of life, and encourage living with richness, abundance, and an ethical sensitivity toward others. A rich and abundant life, it seems to me, is one that affirms our individuality, encourages deep, affectionate, and intimate long-term relationships and friendships, and keeps us conscious of our interconnectedness with the pulses and rhythms of nature in joyous and nondestructive ways.

A philosophy of life should have a realistic appraisal of the dark side of life and the potential for humans to think and act in delusional, destructive, and death-dealing ways. The philosophy must also demand that individuals take responsibility for their own beliefs and actions, and insist that we strive to own our projections of negative attributes, rather than directing our attention to the supposed evil of others or to matters outside our control.

A philosophy of life should define spirituality as the sum of our efforts to realize greater self-awareness and to overcome limiting beliefs and behaviors that keep us from living with inner peace and health of mind, body, and spirit. A philosophy of life should not seek to diminish, sentimentalize, or rationalize the mysterious and awe-inspiring nature of life. And it should avoid providing supposedly certain answers for understanding the mystery of death.

A philosophy of life should invite us to live humbly with an awareness that what immortality is to be found in life may be had by directing our full energy and attention to this life and this world as it presents itself to us, and by honoring with gratitude the memories of the departed and the best wisdom traditions of all those on whose shoulders we stand.

Sunday, February 29

Like millions of other Americans, I saw Mel Gibson's *The Passion of the Christ* over the weekend. My immediate reactions were emotional. I cried (and so did Ramon, the man I had my arm wrapped around). I felt deeply connected to the Passion in a way that I had never felt before. I felt deeply connected to the figure of Jesus Christ and his suffering and the pain of his family and friends.

I also felt anger toward the closed-minded religious bigots who condemned Jesus to death. The crime for which Jesus was handed over to the authorities to be executed: blasphemy.

Since I'm sharing honest, gut-level responses here, permit me to ask: How many times have I been described as evil and called a blasphemer or a heretic by closed-minded religious bigots since I started to keep this journal in the public eye? Plenty. How many times a day do I turn on the TV or read the headlines and hear religious bigots attacking people like me, telling lies about gay people, expelling us from their seminaries, pulpits, and pews, and projecting their shadows upon us? Too many.

Part of me wants to immediately qualify these remarks by saying that of course I'm not comparing my suffering to that of Jesus, but this would be bullshit. Of course I am. I wouldn't be human if I didn't connect to another's suffering by relating it to my own experience. Watching Gibson's film, I found myself identifying with Christ's suffering and also that experienced by other characters.

It's been two millennia since Jesus walked the earth. While I know I ought to be grateful that the churches aren't burning heretics and sodomites at the stake these days (except for beheadings and such in parts of the world ruled by radical Islam), right now I'm more angry than grateful. I'm disgusted at how little humanity has grown since the days when religious visionaries and prophets were greeted with shouts of "Crucify him! Crucify him!"

Would I have made a movie as bloody and sadomasochistic as Mel

Gibson's? Probably not. And yet I think the film is full of poetic glory, gut-wrenching emotion, and a hard-edged, masculine resistance to sentimentalizing faith.

My mind and will remain set against being part of an institution that seems more like an incarnation of the spirit of the hypocritical and rigid-thinking Pharisees than of the spirit of the Christ. Yet the reality of Christ remains with me — as a memory partly in shadow and partly in light; as a loving, abiding presence; and as a longing for wholeness. The film moved me to tears by reminding me of the calling that I strive to perceive. Even as I grope in darkness and doubt, seeking to give this calling a form, I know that it is, in some sense, the presence of Christ.

Wednesday, March 3

Today, some religious conservatives made a joke of my spirituality, for they imagine that I am terribly naive about original sin. They say I believe that we should all be ourselves. And to them this apparently means everyone running around in loincloths, humping each other willy-nilly. If we are truly ourselves, they say, we will surely be wicked beasts.

In every Great Lie, there is a grain of truth. And Christianity's doctrine of original sin is nothing but such a Great Lie. So what is the lie in original sin, and what is its truth? According to Carl Jung, one way of looking at things is to say that the creation of consciousness and culture is a turning away from instinct and nature. Problems of every kind drive human beings away from instinct and nature and toward greater and greater consciousness. In *Modern Man in Search of a Soul*, he writes: "The biblical fall of man presents the dawn of consciousness as a curse. And as a matter of fact it is in this light that we first look upon every problem that forces us to greater consciousness and separates us even further from the paradise of unconscious childhood."

Human nature is imperfect. We have problems, sins, and delusions. We don't live in Paradise. That is the grain of truth in the dogma of original sin. But a huge strand of traditional Christian (especially Calvinist) teaching on original sin suggests that our instincts and nature are always and everywhere inherently corrupt and wicked (and if you're a homosexual, your nature is a little more corrupt than others). That is the Great Lie.

Psychology, in parallel fashion to this religious doctrine, also tells us that our instincts and consciousness are at odds. But psychology generally does not fall for the Great Lie. Instead, psychology tells us that we are only dimly aware—and often completely unconscious—of much of our true, instinctual nature. We are forever separated from our true nature, that instinctual and unconscious state of being that we symbolize as Paradise (the prelapsarian condition).

Christians look to Christ for salvation from the Fall of Man. But what is Christ, if not the ultimate expansion of consciousness? Just as Adam's eating of the fruit from the Tree of Knowledge symbolically initiated conscious-ness, in Christ there is the redemption and fulfillment of conscious aware-ness. The Garden of Eden is lost, but it may be regained in a new form—not by judging and rejecting our instincts and impulses as evil or wicked or sin-ful as in traditional Christianity, but by expanding our consciousness to in-clude more and more of the unconscious parts of our true nature.

Monday, March 15

Mark Shea, the conservative Roman Catholic blogger, has recently mocked me for my comments last month about *The Passion of the Christ*. It seems that I have committed the unpardonable sin of comparing my suf-fering to that of Christ. In Shea's eyes, this arrogance just proves I am a "narcissist"; that's his catch-all insult for all things even vaguely involving depth psychology, self-help, introspection, or the New Age.

There's also a post today on narcissism by another religionist, Scripps-Howard columnist Terry Mattingly. Mattingly writes a post on his blog that contrasts narcissists who believe in "lovely, loving spirituality with lots of fuzzy, mysterious stories about What It All Means" with the supposedly less narcissistic believers of traditional Christianity.

These remarks by Shea and Mattingly are insipid and misleading. Of course there's narcissism in some contemporary spirituality, just as there is in our culture more broadly. But religionists lose all credibility by throwing the stone of narcissism where their own house is made of glass.

If we're going to start throwing stones, I guess I'll need to don my armor. I'm not perfect and never claimed to be. I can be self-absorbed, egocentric, and callous to the feelings of others. What Shea and Mattingly seem to forget is that traditional religion is no less narcissistic than contemporary spirituality, and possibly it's even more so.

Who are the true narcissists? Those who recognize that the mysteries of the universe are beyond their narrow ego-bound dogmatic conceptions, or those who project their own psychological dramas into the universe and announce that they alone possess the One Truth and the Ultimate Authority? Those who seek to dissolve their egos through mindfulness of arising experience, or those who bolster their egos through group identification with an institution that essentially embodies Their Own Identities Writ Large? Those who destroy their inflated sense of self-worth by facing and battling their shadows, or those who divide the world into "good" and "evil" and repress everything within them that threatens their righteous self-image? Those who cut against the grain of mainstream culture in their spiritual explorations, or those who are so obsessed with what other people think about them that they must join the most conventional and socially acceptable religion they can find?

Tuesday, March 16

Ten Years with HIV: Part 1 of 2

This is a morning of ashes. A cycle ends. My soul is wet with tears, ablaze in cinders, crumbled to gray dust, and then carried on the wind. This morning I celebrate the anniversary of a dark hour.

I was then 24 years old. I was a divinity school dropout struggling in a miserable Midwest economy that I called with only a wee bit of exaggeration, "The Great George Bush Depression." When I was lucky enough to find a job, it was as a research assistant and writer for a brokerage firm. I made a meager $18,000 a year to start, but at least I had health insurance.

I had the day off from work and took a train from Hyde Park to Wabash Avenue in Chicago's Loop. I went to my doctor's office to pick up the results of my HIV test. I got back news that I was not expecting. I had tested positive.

Words cannot express the emotion of this time. It is impossible to fully convey the magnitude of the fall from grace, because it is equally difficult to convey the magnificent grandiosity of my ego. It seemed that all my life had groomed me for the achievement of great things, at least in my own imagination.

In my secret fantasies I imagined myself shaping a life that would some-day be worthy of the history books. I hoped to make a difference and there-by justify my existence, but now that immortality project seemed impossible. Everything I was, my entire sense of identity, was bound up inextricably in the web of achievement and the fulfillment of expectations.

For that 24-year-old kid, HIV was a death sentence. It not only seemed to promise a future mortal blow; it was an imminent, death-dealing blow. In Freudian slips, I spoke not of my diagnosis, but of my "death." The news seemed to wipe away everything that gave my life meaning and direction.

My thoughts immediately turned to my older brother Bobby. Seven years before my own HIV diagnosis, my older brother Robert tested HIV-positive. All at once, my family discovered that he was gay and that he was living with a terminal disease. When I learned about my brother's homo-sexuality, I was nowhere near ready to deal with my own homosexual feel-ings. Yet my brother's illness seemed to put a deadline on my own journey of self-acceptance. I began to cultivate the hope that I could come out, and I wanted my brother to be the first person to hear the news.

When I was 20, I came out first to my brother and later to college friends and close family members. I cracked open the closet door, ever so slightly. A few months after my college graduation, my brother passed on. His partner, Ray, died within a year. Perhaps the gravest insult of my HIV diagnosis was that it wiped away the significance that I had given, in my own mind, to my brother's death. In my own arrogance and optimism of youth, I believed that what had happened to him could never happen to me. Having watched my brother's struggles and grown in awareness of the disease, I believed that I would be spared his fate. Somehow I had con-vinced myself that my brother's death had "meaning," because I could heed its warning and avoid getting AIDS myself. Now that meaning was gone. And being the second brother in a family to get AIDS seemed a dou-bly cruel fate.

My initial T-cell count was a low number typically seen only in patients who had lived symptom-free for many years and were now on the verge of the final, advanced stages of the disease. My doctor said that unless I immediately started taking AZT and other drugs, I would likely be dead within two years.

Just as I was starting to become more accepting of the HIV diagnosis, the possibility that I might only live two years was a shock. I began to research the mortality tables of people living with HIV infection. Fewer than one person in ten were expected to live even ten years with the disease.

My heart was heavy with pain. In my desperation, I began to pray.

I prayed the sort of prayer that is the sign of only the most truly desperate souls, the sort of prayer that begins, "God, I don't believe in you, but if you do exist . . ."

In that hour, I asked for one thing. I wanted the one thing that seemed more than I could ever reasonably hope for, something so unthinkably grand that it made pale even the prospect of winning the most fantastic lottery prize.

I asked God for ten years of life. "God, if you only give me ten years of life, if only, if only . . . I won't complain about anything ever again."

Somehow, I vaguely imagined, full of darkness and doubt, that ten years would make everything all right. At midnight last night, my ten years were up.

Wednesday, March 17

I'm very excited about a book. I've just finished reading the first three chapters of a book called A *Theory of Everything*. Let me tell you about it.

As readers of my blog know, I describe my spiritual perspective as "catholic in the truest sense of the word, open to truth wherever it can be found." Unfortunately, when it comes to being open to all truth, this is easier said than done. Traditionally, philosophy and theology have been the disciplines that are supposed to show how all knowledge fits together. However, today most philosophers and theologians take a very narrow focus and rarely make grand efforts at synthesis.

That's why I was skeptical when I read that there is a well-regarded contemporary philosopher and psychological theorist, Ken Wilber, whose work is said by some to incorporate more truth than any other perspective in history. Although it seems that Wilber has been writing books since the 1970s, I think that perhaps his work has only started to receive widespread attention since about 1995. Whatever the case may be, I didn't encounter his books when I was in college or divinity school in the late 1980s and early 1990s.

I've only read a few chapters of A *Theory of Everything*, so it's too soon to tell if Wilber's project is going to succeed. But I'm telling you, this guy has definitely got my attention. My head's spinning just reading this stuff. I haven't seen a philosophical project this intriguing since Hegel's *Phenomenology of Spirit*.

An observation from a student of astrology: it doesn't look like Wilber has a very high opinion of this ancient art. Despite some reservations about Wilber's apparent failure to explicitly include the more sophisticated forms of astrology in his synthesis, I want to reiterate that I'm impressed so far. Anybody out there know Wilber's views on astrology?

Reading about consciousness as viewed through the lens of integral theory is powerful. It feels like waking up and seeing my life clearly for the first time. I am wondering: have I been a closet integralist all along?

Friday, March 19

The Pleasure Principle

Beating off. Jerking off. Whacking off. Slapping the salami. Spanking the monkey. Milking the trouser snake.

Everyone does it, but few of us talk about it. Let's talk about masturbation.

Bruce Grether is the moderator of an Internet-based group called Mindful Masturbation for Men (groups.yahoo.com/group/mindfulm4men). There are over 1,600 men on the discussion list. The members of the MM4M forum strive to go beyond masturbation as a way of releasing tension and to explore its potential as a spiritual and consciousness-altering process.

The following is an interview conducted with Bruce via e-mail.

Joe: How did you first become interested in taking a more spiritual approach to masturbation?

Bruce: All of my life I've intensely enjoyed physical pleasure and felt intuitively that it was genuinely a good thing. Even so, in adolescence when I discovered how to deliberately masturbate, I also required some self-education and used reason to overcome traces of acquired guilt and shame. For me, this worked, and since that time it hasn't been an issue for me personally.

Yet all through my adulthood into my early forties, issues of self-esteem and safety prevented me from fully experiencing my gay male sexuality. In retrospect, I realize that I was starved for intimate touch. Not until 1995, when I obtained a copy of Joseph Kramer's video, *Fire on the Mountain*, did I begin learning how to pleasure myself far more effectively. Lacking a partner at the time to practice erotic massage with, I adapted the techniques to my solo practice.

I've never been the same man since! I've done a great deal of exploring and experimenting and have developed my own approaches in the subsequent years.

I had always felt that the experience of sexual energy is for humans quite literally our own access to the same basic creative energy that creates the universe. Only, our experience of this is commonly limited by unfortunate conditioning and cultural assumptions.

Gay men can naturally enjoy erotic energy apart from reproductive agendas; hence this becomes purely creative, pleasure for its own sake. Now in my ninth year of exploring male eroticism as a conscious spiritual path, more than ever I feel this is a major wave of the future.

Joe: What advice would you give a gay man who wants to try a more conscious approach to masturbation for the first time?

Bruce: There's nothing wrong with pursuing these practices simply to increase your erotic pleasure. However, the process is also capable of increasing self-awareness, healing the heart-genital connection, and helping you to feel more whole as a male human being. Ultimately it allows you to love others in a more balanced, integral manner.

First, it's crucial to be willing to humble yourself and go back to square one, as in "Zen mind, beginner's mind." Regardless of how experienced or adept you may feel you are in your masturbatory skills, consider seeking to clear the slate and start over.

It's necessary to break old habitual patterns in order to begin exploring new options. Keep in mind that pleasuring yourself is the most literal form of loving yourself.

Re-creating your self-pleasuring as something more than just relieving sexual tension or gratifying yourself is a process that does not come naturally to human males. Still, it makes use of natural, biological capacities and, like any fine art, requires some training to achieve excellence.

Also, you'll need to learn ejaculatory control in order to achieve higher erotic states, so that ejaculation becomes a choice, rather than something that just happens. Only then can you surrender to your limitless erotic potential.

Joe: Are there specific techniques that are especially good places to start?

Bruce: An effective order in which to approach this is to begin with breathing, practicing deep, abdominal or belly breathing.

Second, learn to relax while masturbating, rather than tensing up and racing toward ejaculation.

Third, explore a variety of masturbatory strokes. Learning about shifting into different positions during your session, and using both hands, you may begin to awaken your entire body as an erogenous zone.

Joe: What is your current spiritual practice involving masturbation?

Bruce: Having recently reached the age of 50, I've decided this is the age when life begins—at least for me! Without elaborating the brain-chemical and hormonal shifts involved, let me testify that my experience of masturbating mindfully suggests that the second half of a man's life can be the best part, by far.

Though I enjoy a loving and passionate relationship with my partner, I also masturbate every day. My solo practice grows deeper and richer all the time. This process allows me to love myself better and better, to live more fully in the present moment, and to experience a direct connection with the Source.

Saturday, March 20

Blogger Coolmel responded to my inquiry about Ken Wilber and astrology by forwarding me an Internet link. It points to an article in the *Noetic Sciences Review*. In the article, astrologer Will Keepin says that astrology is a transrational discipline epistemologically rooted in "vision-logic" and pointing toward a "vast holarchy" that unfolds "holographically" as a "unitive cosmic process." He quotes Wilber as saying that he's "agnostic" about astrology but willing to believe that it is "a profound hermeneutic of the World Soul," if rational evidence is produced to support it.

Vision-logic? Holarchy? Holographical unfolding? Unitive cosmic processes? World Soul? I'm not sure that I understand what Keepin or Wilber are talking about, but it sounds intriguing.

Also, I got another tip from a reader: Ko Imani says that Wilber discusses astrology in his book *One Taste*. I'll have to add another book to my reading list.

Sunday, March 21

Aries

Aries is the sun's destination during this time of the year. The sign of the Ram, Aries depicts the brutal, violent essence of the life force itself. It is the sign of the Warrior, the Survivor, and the Daredevil. The Arian path demands the strength to claim one's right to exist. The Ram's goal is to attain the courage to plow through one's deepest fears.

Monday, March 22

Ten Years with HIV: Part 2 of 2

After my HIV diagnosis at age 24, it was easier to believe the universe was indifferent to my life than that somehow my HIV infection could fit into some sort of divinely ordained scheme. How could I be enthusiastic about life, when it seemed I could hardly get a break? Try as I might, I had no desire to suck the marrow from the bones of life. Marrow sucking was passé. If I started to suck marrow, I might have to give up self-pity, my identity as a victim . . . or start giving a fuck about life . . . and that just wouldn't do.

At least I mustered an acknowledgement of what was real: Pain. Suffering. Misery. These were real. I could acknowledge pain and distract myself from it, but could not really overcome it. And after a while, I hardly saw a point in trying.

I knew how to put on a happy face so I could get through a day at the office or a family visit. But the most evolved attitude that I could muster toward life on my own was "Life's a joke, and death's the punch line." And yet the punch line seemed to take forever, and my life was turning into one dull and pointless shaggy-dog tale. I wanted to be dead.

Despite my best efforts to make it work for me, my life as an addict was turning out to be a total failure. I couldn't keep my addictions a secret. And it was exacting an enormous toll on me and the people who loved me. I had no self-esteem or self-respect, and the erratic lifestyle that accompanied my acting out was making it difficult to comply with a complicated drug regimen. At one point, I took 20 pills a day at four different intervals, twice with food (including meals of grapefruit juice and peanut-butter to improve drug absorption) and twice on an empty stomach. The HIV progressed hard and fast, quickly becoming resistant to protease inhibitors.

I was constantly facing the fundamental life choice that Hamlet expressed in six short words, "To be, or not to be." The path of addictions, lies, denial, self-centeredness, disease, escapism, and fantasy were leading me down the addict's path that inevitably ends, as they say in Narcotics Anonymous, in jail, institutions, or death. But the path toward life seemed to be even more frightening. If I were to choose life (hold the artificial highs, thank you) I'd need to do better.

I turned to addictions because the pain of my life seemed too much to bear, especially my resentments and despair and cynicism regarding God and religion. I didn't know how to accept life on its own terms, but I was convinced that I would need to try. Eventually, in the course of time, some answers started to come my way. The key, perhaps, was my belated discovery that I didn't have all the answers . . . a growing recognition of my need for others.

I simply didn't know how to live. I desperately needed to learn how; and to do that, I came to understand that I needed help. With the aid of others, I started to discover spiritual principles—principles that I'd heard many times in Gospel stories and other teachings of religion but that somehow had never quite taken hold.

Traditional religion had about as much appeal to me as a surgical procedure that would combine a lobotomy and castration. Yet the essence of religion, its universal spiritual principles—such as humility, honesty, integrity, sincerity, love, compassion, service—began at last to make sense.

One of those spiritual principles was gratitude. Taking a grateful attitude toward life is easier said than done. I realized that I'd rather blame everyone else for my HIV infection than examine the possibility that my choices might have had something to do with my illness. Even more important, I came to realize that I didn't need to blame anyone at all.

Adopting a spiritual outlook didn't give me trite slogans or a Hallmark-card sensibility. Instead, spirituality called me to begin to fundamentally change everything about how I lived my life, one day at a time . . . starting with my lack of gratitude.

Gradually I came to realize that my attitude toward life is a choice. It very often doesn't seem like a choice, but it is. It's a choice made not by my conscious self but by my deeper self (that which I sometimes call a Self or soul). The deep self is not just sweetness and light, but darkness and shadow as well. If I didn't befriend my dark side, it was going to kill me. If I didn't touch my pain, I could not get to the joy on the other side. If I would not give myself permission to be angry, my rage would eat me up from the inside. If I did not allow myself to feel my fears, I would continue to sleepwalk through life like a zombie.

I prayed to my nebulously defined Higher Power and I went to 12-step meetings for some time. I attended personal empowerment trainings and men's gatherings. I got into therapy. Because I'm an egghead and a weirdo, I also consulted psychics and astrologers, and read the scriptures of the great religions. I peeked my head inside a church door every once in a great while. I cracked open the philosophy books as well as the self-help books. In short, I committed myself to a spiritual path as if my life depended on it.

Over time, I became willing to be a better man. And, thank God, I stayed away from my addictions. I didn't do all these things perfectly, but I always stayed willing.

When I think back to the man I was ten years ago, I have compassion for his desperation and his need. Yet I choose not to adopt his arrogant stance as a negotiator with God. He prayed, "If I could only live ten years, just ten years God, if only . . . then I won't complain about anything ever again."

As I reach this ten-year milestone, I am choosing not to renegotiate the contract for ten more years. Such an illusion would give me no more assurance than spouting religious dogma. I could mouth the words of belief, but they would mean nothing.

Instead, I am seeking daily to put into practice, however imperfectly, the Third Step: turning my will and life over to the care of God as best I understand Him. And mostly, when it comes to understanding God, I don't.

On the night of my ten-year HIV anniversary last week, I performed a personal ritual to mark the occasion. I asked God to be present with me, and I laughed and cried and asked Him to turn the pain and heartache in my life to ashes. I wrote down on paper all the things in my life that I wanted to be ready to let go of, and then set them on fire one by one. I smeared my face in those ashes and began to contemplate the new realities in my life: hope, faith, friendship, love, meaning, and a sense of value that I cherish.

In my gratitude, today I can honestly say that God's mercy on my life is simply stunning beyond belief. Ten years of life is already a greater gift than I could have possibly imagined, and yet it is not the end.

Tuesday, March 23

I just finished reading A *Theory of Everything*. If some of Wilber's main ideas—such as the "spectrum of consciousness"—seemed familiar, it's because I'd encountered vaguely similar ideas before in a variety of places in at least a rudimentary form. What's so fascinating about Wilber's book is that it provides a solid theoretical foundation for integrating an evolutionary spiritual perspective with . . . well, everything.

Wilber explains that there is a research project—a Human Consciousness Project—underway currently that rivals the Human Genome Project in
its scope and significance. Involving leading theorists in psychology, sociology, history, anthropology, philosophy, and many other disciplines, this en-
deavor seeks to map the dynamics of consciousness from infancy, childhood,
adolescence, and so forth, all the way up to the ultimate realization, "God-
consciousness," resulting in an all-encompassing guide to human potential.

Although Ken Wilber is new to me, reading this book was an amazing
experience, because I immediately began to become more aware of my
own inner life. The very notion that consciousness can be understood as an
unfolding "spiral of development" seems to have extraordinary implica-
tions, if it's true.

I have begun to ask myself questions about how my own perspectives on
reality and God have changed over the course of my life. What were my sensations and perceptions as an infant? How did I see the world as a two-year-
old? How did I look at life as a seven-year-old, or as an adolescent? How did
my sense of God change when I studied calculus, physics, and logic? How
did my sense of self shift when I attended college, took anthropology
courses, and became acquainted with a variety of different cultures and
points of view? How is the study of astrology expanding the flexibility and dy-
namism of my ability to mentally identify and process connections among
symbolic patterns in personality, culture, and nature? How has my outlook
shifted since I first began to study evolutionary spiritual thought and weave
together rough visions of how everything in the universe fits together? How
is it changing even today, as I use my writing and other practices to help me
to achieve greater degrees of integration and a sense of wholeness?

Developmental psychologists such as Piaget, Kohlberg, and Gilligan
have been exploring the stages of individual growth for decades. Wilber's
psychological theories build on the best work of these psychologists while
integrating their insights with the mystical core of the world's religious traditions. He shows how a "spectrum of consciousness" extends not only from
prerational infantile states to mature, rational states (as the developmental
psychologists say), but also beyond . . . to a series of transrational states
described by the psychics, saints, sages, and mystics. And he doesn't stop
there. He also shows how consciousness isn't limited to strictly individual

and subjective dimensions but includes objective, collective, and intersubjective dimensions as well.

Wilber's "theory of everything" is appropriately named, because it is a metatheory: an overarching hypothesis that accounts for the truth-claims from a very wide number of sources. It provides a comprehensive theoretical grounding for understanding how science, religion, culture, business, and all other aspects of life fit together. Essentially he's drawing a huge map and showing how everyone else's maps fit into it.

I'm not sure what to think about some of the details of the Wilberian map, but the overall vision is compelling and inspiring. "Mind blowing" is the word I really want to use. Next, I'm diving into *Sex, Ecology, Spirituality*, the first book of Wilber's planned three-volume magnum opus. Zero pages down, only (sigh) 851 pages to go.

Wednesday, March 24

Today I googled "gay," "spiritual," and "Ken Wilber" and found a wonderful writer named Jay Michaelson. He's a guy around my age, lives in New York City, and edits an online journal of Jewish thought called *Zeek*.

His personal site, called Metatronics (metatronics.net), is devoted to "integral Jewish writing and teaching." One of my first finds while perusing his site: a heartfelt and powerful essay on Conservative Judaism. At one point, Jay talks about what it was like to be raised a Conservative Jew. He says that for about 20 years, he suffered the pain of being told that "being gay is the worst thing in the world." He acknowledges that in the subtle wording of its position papers, Conservative Judaism doesn't really use such language. But, he says, most Jews nevertheless believe "there is something wrong with being gay."

Swap Roman Catholicism for Conservative Judaism and I could have said the same thing about my background. It's a small world.

Thursday, March 25

I feel like speaking out loud some thoughts I've been carrying around in the last few weeks . . . ever since my dream on February 19. Is it possible for me to reapproach Roman Catholicism, or Christianity?

I know it's a cliché to say "Once a Catholic, always a Catholic." But it's one thing to acknowledge an influence from a tradition that no longer seems relevant and quite another to consciously seek to deepen and enrich one's spirituality within the context of one (or more) particular faith traditions.

I have described myself as a "former Catholic," but in light of some of my reading in recent weeks, I am beginning to wonder if something like "integral Catholicism" might be a possibility. Yesterday I was reading about Jay Michaelson's spiritual path from Conservative Judaism to Jewish Renewal. I was excited to read about how he has embraced the rituals, rites, and laws of his faith tradition and integrated them into part of a greater whole.

My heart yearns to return to Catholicism in some way. Despite my growth and interfaith explorations, the Catholic faith continues to pull at my heart, even as I am all too aware of its human shortcomings and sins. As I entertain a return to Catholicism of some kind, I sense that it's important to be as clear as possible about what motivates me: a desire to deepen my love for life and the divine, and to fully take to heart all the beauty, truth, and love to be found in the religious tradition of my upbringing.

Yet at the same time, there are complexities that nag at me, questions such as these: Can I in good conscience support an institution with my whole mind, body, and soul (not to mention cold, hard cash) when its leadership works on a daily basis to attack my civil rights and essential parts of my values? Is the Episcopal Church a preferable alternative? Any return to Catholicism must take these questions into account. This is a matter for further prayer and reflection.

Friday, March 26

From yesterday's entry in this journal: "Can I in good conscience support an institution . . . when its leadership works on a daily basis to attack my civil rights and essential parts of my values?"

Once I saw this post on my computer screen, I was mad at myself for even putting a question mark at the end of the sentence. Of course, I cannot. Speaking for myself, I do not believe it is morally defensible to support financially or in any other way the Roman Catholic Church hierarchy. There can be no doubt that the hierarchy is an enemy of gay rights and gay marriage. The Roman hierarchy is morally culpable for what Soulforce (soulforce.org), an organization that fights religion-based antigay oppression, calls "spiritual violence"—that is, "the misuse of religion to sanction the condemnation and rejection of any of God's children."

As a morally culpable institution, the Roman Catholic Church should be held morally accountable. I believe it is utterly morally wrong to donate time, energy, or work toward the advancement of the Roman Catholic hierarchy. Withholding support, if done with clarity of intention, is a necessary tool for spiritual disobedience. Actively and aggressively countering spiritual violence is noble. I believe that living with integrity and striving to live the Gospel principles more fully demands complete and consciously chosen disaffiliation from the papal hierarchy, at least until such time as that hierarchy has been held fully accountable and has repented for its deeds of spiritual violence.

This is a closed question in my mind. Open questions: Does joining the Episcopal Church or another Christian denomination make sense for me? Or does the way of fully stepping into my own spiritual path lie elsewhere? And what about Unitarian Universalism?

Sunday, March 28

I just came across a fascinating interview in *What Is Enlightenment?* magazine. José Cabezón, a gay Buddhist and professor of Buddhist studies, speaks about homosexuality and Buddhism. Cabezón explains that he reconciles Buddhism with his gay identity by asserting that the latter has no reality. "In the West, in large part as a result of Freud's influence, we tend to see the development of our identity as intimately linked to sexuality and to sexual desire. Buddhism would question that," Cabezón says. I wonder if there might not be a way to bring Freud and Buddha together, rather than having to choose between the two, as Cabezón seems to imply is necessary. Isn't that sort of the approach that Ken Wilber is taking?

What strikes me as surprising is that Cabezón says the highest calling of the spiritual life is celibacy. Although he's not celibate at this stage of his life, Cabezón says, "I still hold celibacy as an ideal." There are some things Cabezón says in the interview that I agree with, other things I don't, and a great deal that frankly I don't know what to make of. I will be the first to admit that I have no particular expertise in Buddhism. Perhaps Cabezón's world looks very different because he's more spiritually evolved than I am. That said, I am deeply suspicious of any philosophy that elevates celibacy as the ideal for the spiritual life.

I first became acquainted with Buddhism in college, where I majored in comparative religion. While I found much that appealed to me in Buddhism, the religion's history of homophobia and erotophobia prevented me from taking it seriously as a spiritual option. Nevertheless, I do seem to find myself reading a copy of the Buddhist scriptures every few years.

It's a fact that the Buddha rejected extreme forms of asceticism; yet when I hear Buddhists extol the virtues of celibacy, I find it hard to accept that Buddhism has really gotten away from world denial. On sex, Buddhism seems no better than the worst of Christianity. It's frightening how much Cabezón sounds just like the ex-gay celibacy advocates. In fairness, he does emphasize that celibacy is a personal choice and he claims that he's not making universal judgments about the sex lives of all gay people. But I'm not buying it. Cabezón claims that Buddhism isn't incompatible with gay liberation; but if that liberation means no sex, then why bother? It's like saying that with Buddhism you can have your cake and eat it too, just so you stay away from the cake.

I offer my opinion (for what it's worth) that gays can do much better than this way of thinking. I have to believe that there are perspectives that are able to offer gays (and everyone else) much more than hostility to life. Does the world really need more denial of our bodies, pleasure, sensuality, and the fruits of the earth? The nature-based or pagan spiritualities such as Wicca get at least this much right on a point where Buddhism is so very wrong, I think.

David Deida is a Buddhist. His book, *The Way of the Superior Man*, is one of my favorites. I recall none of this elevation of celibacy as an ideal in Deida's approach to sex. I'll have to revisit Deida and see what it is that makes his approach to Buddhism different than Cabezón's, if it is in fact different.

Monday, March 29

There's a question that has perplexed me for what seems like my whole life: how shall I reconcile spirituality in general (and Christianity in particular) with sex in general (and homosexuality in particular)? That there is a conflict and separation between sex and Spirit I take to be self-evident. That such conflict is unnecessary and illusory, I take as a matter of faith.

Gradually, over the past 12 years, my answer to this question has been increasingly catholic . . . or "integral," perhaps. I want to embrace truth and meaning in the most universal fashion possible, and so I have sought wider, more encompassing frameworks—both/and instead of either/or perspectives. As a result, I now find myself coming to a place of greater healing, reconciliation, and wholeness.

I am looking again at Christianity with open eyes. A conviction arises from within me: my own path to wholeness must be a path of integration of all that I have taken to be real, true, and holy. Therefore, my own path lies not away from, in reaction against, or in a swerve around Christianity . . . but with, through, and beyond Christianity.

Tuesday, March 30

Today I heard from a reader who knows more about Buddhism's attitudes toward sex than I do. Ryan Overby is a Buddhologist pursuing a doctorate at Harvard. He shared a few insights in my blog's comment box. If what he says is true, then there's much to be found in esoteric (nonmainstream) Buddhist traditions that is sex affirming, particularly in Tantric practices. He concludes: "Not all Buddhist traditions value celibacy so highly. But as with all things Buddhist, both celibate and noncelibate lifestyles are highly regulated, and the pursuit of pleasure qua pleasure is universally frowned upon."

Bottom line: for mainstream Buddhism at least, pleasure and sex are bad, very bad. Just more of the same old life-denying and world-hating bullshit, if you ask me. But there's also an esoteric or Tantric tradition that seems to go a different way. That sounds about right. What was it about the work of David Deida that struck me as such a life-affirming, world-embracing vision of Buddhism? Perhaps his work is part of that esoteric strain of which Overby speaks.

I paid a visit today to Deida's website to do some research for one of my columns. I like what Deida has to say about spirituality and sexuality, even though he's a straight guy who writes mostly for an audience of heterosexual men and women. He writes in a universal sort of way that even I, a gay man, can relate to.

Deida's website is different than I remember. It just so happens that Deida is an "integral thinker" and a friend of Ken Wilber's. Deida and Wilber are two of the founders of something called Integral Institute, a think tank in Boulder, Colorado.

Deida has an essay online where he says Wilber is the creator of "arguably the most important intellectual framework in recent history." Deida also says: "Ken has thought for everyone who has ever tried to think their way to God, and he has thought them as far as thinking will take them." Intriguing. Hey, it really is a small world. Hmmm . . .

Wednesday, March 31

Fuck! I'm reading a Ken Wilber book that discusses systems theory and holons. I know that "holon" is a term coined by Arthur Koestler to denote something that is simultaneously a whole and a part. But what the fuck is a holon, really? Seeing a holon has something to do with recognizing the repeating patterns that underlie reality. Repeating patterns. Repeating patterns. I read the words on the page over and over again but just can't seem to really wrap my mind fully around it.

Now I'm reading about the 20 tenets of all holons. Holons seem to have a closet full of tenets. Whatever the fuck a holon is, it seems to be rather well accessorized.

Reading and rereading . . . an interview with Wilber on the Shambhala website . . . Wilber's talking about self-dissolution . . . rereading David Deida . . . rereading "The Importance of Being Gay" (see entries from November 29 to December 7) . . . drawing connections . . . that's it . . . a box with 4 quadrants . . . No, not a box: a cross.

Duh! I can't believe I haven't seen this before. This is the pattern that connects it all, the pattern I've been looking for, the pattern I've been writing about . . . Life, God, Spirit, Emptiness, the Tao, the One, the Way . . .

homosexuality, heterosexuality, bisexuality, men, women, yin, yang, yin and yang up the yin-yang . . . Kosmos, cosmos, wholes, parts, holons, evolution, self-transcendence, self-immanence, adaptation, self-preservation . . . Love, Eros, Agape, Fear, homophobia, heterophobia, Phobos, Thanatos, Sameness, Otherness, homophilia, heterophilia . . . Gilgamesh and Enkidu, Virgo and Pisces, a dream of a chocolate-chip cookie . . . It's all there, everything; it's all been there all along; it's always been there . . . It's all coming together, coming apart . . . something in these books, something in my journal, something borrowed, something blue, something old, and something . . . something . . . something's coming back. My 30th birthday. Harborview. The psych ward. A bench in a hallway. . . . *Stop! Don't go there. Not now, not yet. Breathe, Joe! Breathe! That's it. Think, don't feel. Go to a safe place.*

I'm calmer now. I think I can write. I'll make a post for the Gay Spirituality & Culture blog. I'll call it: "Homosexuality and Agape, or Notes toward a Truly Comprehensive Theory of Gayness."

3 Deeper Connections

All the greatest and most important problems of life are fundamentally insoluble. . . . They can never be solved, but only outgrown. This "out-growing" proved, on further investigation, to require a new level of consciousness. Some higher or wider interest appeared on the patient's horizon, and through this broadening of his or her outlook the insoluble problem lost its urgency. It was not solved logically in its own terms but faded when confronted with a new and stronger life urge.
—C. G. JUNG

Friday, April 9

Finding God through Sex

Are you a top or a bottom? Butch or femme? Dominant or submissive? Consider the questions carefully, because how you answer may reveal a good deal about your spirituality. While some people believe that Spirit and sex are separate or even incompatible, I find it impossible to imagine that my sexuality is irrelevant to my spirituality. I believe that through our bodies and sex, we reveal our deepest self to others.

Chinese philosophy tells us there are two fundamental energies in the universe: yin and yang. Yang is traditionally associated with masculine energy, yin with feminine. According to Taoism, life is an erotic dance between the two.

Gender talk brings us into the dangerous territory of political correctness. So let me briefly note that I'm not endorsing rigid and conservative gender roles. Yet I believe political correctness goes too far when it denies the existence of universal types such as yin and yang, or feminine and masculine.

When I talk about the duality of yin and yang, I'm not just talking about women and men. Yin is the fundamental drive of all things toward communion, and yang is the drive of all things toward agency or self-determination. I believe everyone carries both yin and yang energies. Today, notable spiritual writers tell us that sexual chemistry is largely a dance of polarity between the masculine and the feminine, and they don't necessarily mean that in a *Leave It to Beaver* sort of way.

If you're not used to seeing the world in terms of archetypal masculine and feminine energies, then you may have doubts that this way of thinking works for queers. You may wonder, does same-sex attraction somehow "disprove" yin and yang? The answer gets a bit complicated. I largely agree with David Deida's perspective.

Deida acknowledges universal sexual principles, but he also allows for complex permutations of gender and sexual preference. Deida believes there are universal sexual essences corresponding to yin and yang. A sexual essence is an inner psychological and spiritual drive and is not necessarily the same as our sex, gender identity, or sexual preference. (I believe this approach is generally correct; however I would prefer a more nuanced typology than Deida's, one that includes all four prime patterns of yin and yang. See December 3 entry.)

While most men have a masculine sexual essence, some have a feminine essence, says Deida. And about one in ten men don't have a preference; their essence is balanced between masculine and feminine (and the same goes for women).

Deida also observes that gay and bi men also have sexual essences. We may be balanced in our sexual essences, or we may form sex couplings around a polarity such as top/bottom, dominant/submissive, daddy/boy, and so forth.

Sexual drives are not merely random preferences like our favorite flavor of ice cream. In Deida's view, sexual self-knowledge can be the beginning of spiritual wisdom. He writes: "Regardless of gender or sexual orientation, if you want to experience deep spiritual and sexual fulfillment, you must know your natural sexual essence . . . and live true to it."

So if you're a gay man, you must know if your essence is top, bottom, or versatile (dom, sub, or switch, if you're into S&M). In other words, before you can fulfill your core emotional needs and desires, you must first know what they are. It's tricky to make generalizations about something so complex as sexual preferences and roles, but bear with me for a moment.

If you're a top, your sexual essence is yang. Deida tells us that the spiritual goal of this energy as expressed through sex is to become transcendental to life and to empty into your partner. In short, the essence of a top's sexuality is the quest for Freedom. At its worst, top sexuality treats its partner as a receptacle for stress and frustrations, wanting the bottom to absorb everything and leaving the top empty and fulfilled. However, genuine spirituality teaches that tops cannot be truly fulfilled unless they have stopped searching for release. Instead, they must become grounded in Being.

If you're a bottom, your sexual essence is yin. You grow spiritually by learning to live in harmony with Love and to open to your partner. The essence of the bottom's sexuality is the desire to merge into Love. At its worst, bottom sexuality wants more to be fulfilled by clinging to another than to be emptied of desire. Spirituality teaches that bottoms cannot be truly fulfilled unless they have stopped trying to get "filled" from without. The alternative, advises Deida, is to become grounded in the emptying presence of Love.

If you're versatile, sexual polarity simply isn't important to you. You don't care whether your partner is stronger than you or more vulnerable. It's all good. From a spiritual perspective, you are learning equally the lessons of Being and Love, Spirit and Soul. My guess is that many queer people fit into the versatile category but perhaps fewer than the number who think they do. As Deida writes: "A lot of people today think they have a balanced sexual essence, but in most cases they are actually suppressing the natural desires which spring from their real [top or bottom] core."

Perhaps you don't feel that these descriptions of your preferred sexual position work for you. In that case, perhaps labels such as top or bottom speak only about your preference of sexual position and not your core sexual essence. Or perhaps you've found your sexual preferences too complex to be constrained by such labels. For you, these generalizations are too general. However, the vast majority of people will find a correlation between their preferred sexual position (top and bottom) or desire (domination and submission) and their yin/yang sexual essence.

An important lesson we learn from Deida is that spiritual and sexual fulfillment may go hand in hand. Whether we are top, bottom, or versatile, we must not deny our deep self or we deny the possibility of real love. And being grounded in the presence of Love is what spirituality is all about.

Saturday, April 10

I've been taking a break from blogging while reading Ken Wilber books. Two down, many more to go. Done: A *Theory of Everything* and *Sex, Ecology, Spirituality*. I've started on *One Taste*. I wish I could read faster or didn't have to work eight hours a day. It's hard to tear myself away.

It seems I'm not the only one to react strongly to Ken Wilber when first discovering his books. Blogger Coolmel dropped me a note warning me that I was starting down a rabbit hole and there was no going back. The world sure looks different from Wonderland. I know it's not all that healthy to be spending virtually all my free time engrossed in books, but I'm not sure that I could stop reading—even if I wanted to.

It's difficult to explain the draw that reading these books has for me. *Sex, Ecology, Spirituality* was one of the most difficult books I've read in years, and I'm sure I could get more out of it if I started over again and gave it a second, slower reading (not to mention wading through the 1,000 books and articles listed in the bibliography).

If Wilber's story is essentially correct, then history is the domain of Spirit finding its way back home. Spirit is a radiant, timeless essence that pulses through each and every one of us, alive with energy that is nothing if not timeless and eternal. And if Spirit or the World Soul is the deep essence of every "holon"—that is, every "whole/part," or everything in the universe— then the truths of the mystics are not merely strange, occult realities but something far more ordinary. According to this story, the footprints of Spirit can be seen not only in the plain patterns of existence as illuminated by all of the world's mystical traditions but also in the insights of modern science and postmodern thinking. It's a mind-boggling vision.

If something like Wilber's philosophy is correct, then there is more unity to reality than meets the eye. We look around us and we see a divided, fragmented, partial, painfully chaotic world. Everywhere there can be found warring religions, philosophies, ideologies, factions, denominations, sects, and parties. Everywhere around us is conflict: religion and myth and philosophy and science and politics and literature and art and medicine and law and the requirements of ordinary, daily life. But behind the discord, there is a hidden unity and deep universality, says Wilber. Somehow, inexplicably, everybody's right. And the integral philosophy expounded by Wilber simply says, "Here's a map."

This is a vision that, if it's basically right, could bring me inner peace, healing, serenity, and calm. How can I reconcile Christianity with homosexuality? Science with astrology? Technology with nature? Morality with autonomy? Liberalism with conservativism? Shadow work with meditation? The Goddess with the patriarchy? How do I tell which psychological or psychotherapeutic approach is best? Who's right: Nietzsche or Aristotle? Christ or Buddha? How do I tell the difference between an authentic spiritual genius and an egomaniac with a messiah complex? In short, how can I determine what is the True, the Good, and the Beautiful, and what is not? What does it even mean, in this postmodern age following Nietzsche, Wittgenstein, Foucault, and Derrida, to speak about the True, the Good, and the Beautiful? The theoretical foundation of a comprehensive vision that might be called evolutionary panentheism is all spelled out in Wilber's map. And the funny thing is, it rings true to me.

I've tried explaining Wilber's vision to friends, and the results are pathetic. I'm finding myself very inarticulate. I don't see yet how all the details of the model fit together: quadrants, levels, waves, stages, states, lines, types, doo-dads, doo-hickeys, and what have you. I think I'll keep reading and try to keep things simple and practical for now.

Reading Wilber can be painful. If his map is right, then much of what I've been thinking is, well, wrong. Or at least far more partial than I previously realized. Having one's worldview shaken to the core is not a fun or easy thing. It takes humility. More humility, perhaps, than I may have. We'll see.

I just read in *One Taste* where Wilber says that one reason the integral philosophy is so angrily and passionately attacked by critics is that it generally requires its readers to change more than 5 percent of their beliefs about reality. Any philosophy that requires such radical changes is likely to encounter deep-seated resistance. Just 5 percent?! It feels more like 100 percent if you ask me.

Reading Wilber is often painful for this reason. I just read along, see how wrong I've been, and mutter, "Oh shit . . . how could I have ever fallen for that one!" Well, at least there is the consolation that I am waking up.

Sunday, April 11

Behold, the Man Jesus Loved

Perhaps no film has depicted the loving relationship between Jesus of Nazareth and the disciple John with more beauty, sensitivity, or respect than *The Passion of the Christ*. John is the man tradition says is the "disciple that Jesus loved." He's also the man who a Bible scholar says could have been Christ's gay lover.

Mel Gibson's controversial movie gives us the beloved disciple in the form of John, a handsome, goateed, raven-haired man (played by Hristo Jivkov) who has a special, intimate place in Jesus's life.

From the garden of Gethsemane to the foot of the cross, John is rarely parted from his beloved. John wept when Jesus was flogged. And when the body of the crucified Christ was taken down from the cross, John placed his hand upon his bloody thigh. As Jesus neared death, John stood with Jesus's mother and Mary Magdalene at the foot of the cross.

"Woman, behold your son," said Jesus at the film's unforgettable climax, speaking to his mother in reference to John. And Jesus also bade the disciple, "Behold your mother."

The significance of this moment cannot be properly understood without realizing that Jesus is bidding his mother adopt his lover as her own son and bidding his lover adopt Jesus's mother as his own.

So says Theodore W. Jennings, Jr., speaking of the Gospel of John in the acclaimed *The Man Jesus Loved: Homoerotic Narratives from the New Testament*. Jennings is a Methodist clergyman and professor of biblical and constructive theology at Chicago Theological Seminary.

Imagine that Jesus had said to his mother in reference to Mary Magdalene: "Woman, behold your daughter." It was the custom in those times that upon the death of a son, the surviving family would adopt the daughter-in-law. Had Jesus spoken these words of a woman, few would doubt that she was being identified as his lover. However, because Jesus's lover was a man, the plain meaning of his words about his beloved has been ignored or twisted by conservative Christians in accordance with their erotophobic, homophobic, and heterosexist theological assumptions.

If Jesus and the beloved disciple were merely good pals and not lovers, then Jesus's words to his mother and the beloved disciple at the foot of the cross don't make sense, argues Jennings. Why would the mother of a deceased man adopt his "close platonic friend" as her own son and why should the friend adopt the deceased man's mother as his own, if the two men had not been in a relationship that surpassed mere friendship?

Recognizing that Jesus and the beloved disciple were lovers is the most literal and least tortured interpretation of the scene at the foot of the cross, says Jennings. And remember the scene in *The Passion of the Christ* when Jesus is seen washing John's feet?

Here's how the rest of the scene plays out in the Gospel of John: "One of the disciples of Jesus—the one Jesus loved—was reclining in Jesus's lap . . . Falling back thus upon the chest of Jesus, he said to him . . . "

Couldn't Jesus and John just have been really good fishing buddies? Not according to the plain meaning of the Bible texts, says Jennings. He observes that the text marks one disciple as "more than a friend" and Jesus's relationship with that disciple as being distinct from those with Jesus's other disciples by virtue of its physical closeness and bodily intimacy.

The simplest and most probable explanation, Jennings argues convincingly, is that their relationship is one between lovers. We shouldn't expect the Bible to specify that the two actually had sex, any more than we would expect it to describe the intimate relations between Peter and his wife, or between Mary and Joseph.

Doubt that the relationship was erotic? Read Jennings's book. Or, men, simply take this challenge. Gather twelve of your closest friends of the same sex, and take them all to dinner. Your best male friend lies next to you during supper, snuggling against you and lying across your lap with his head upon your breast. And then strip naked and wash his feet. If you can honestly say that isn't the least bit homoerotic, dinner's on me.

The portrayal of Jesus and John in *The Passion of the Christ* is perhaps the most evocative cinematic depiction yet of Jesus's intimate life, although the homoeroticism is only implied. Thus the movie offers a revolutionary, gay-affirming vision of the Passion, though ironically this couldn't have been the intention of the film's ultraconservative producers.

Of course, Jesus of Nazareth didn't sport a rainbow-colored tunic. Jennings warns that we should be careful about misreading our own culturally conditioned assumptions about modern gay identities into the Bible. Yet he also insists we should also avoid reading heterosexism and homophobia into the Bible when it isn't there.

Is it blasphemy to talk of Jesus's sexuality in a new way? Traditionalists say so. Those traditionalists are the modern-day Pharisees. *The Passion of the Christ* showed their predecessors accusing Jesus himself of blasphemy and chanting, "Crucify him! Crucify him!" Today, fear-mongers continue to attack all those who bring new ideas about God.

Jesus loved all his friends, but he loved one man in a special, physically intimate way. Gay men can deepen their spirituality by contemplating that Jesus's same-sex erotic love is worthy of the Divine. Today we can hear Jesus speaking directly to us when he said to his lover and the other disciples: "Love one another, even as I have loved you."

Monday, April 12

I'm still thinking about my interest in (obsession with?) the integral philosophy. One thing is certain: I feel a need to come to grips with this model, to test it, try it on, see if something like it is true. I just can't let it go. It's shaking up my worldview.

What do I mean by worldview? What is it, or what was it? Right now, it seems like nothing but hundreds of little fragments. I've read books for so many years, searched for God or Spirit in so many places; and so many of these teachers have not had the goods they advertised. They've fed me shards of glass until my stomach aches. I cough up blood, and the "wise ones" congratulate me for being so sophisticated and intellectually astute. They have deconstructed my soul and spirit. They've reduced my inner life and spiritual realities to exploding neurons. They've taught me to wallow in my wounds and call it transformation. They've shown me my ego in all its many disguises and called it magnificence. They've taught me to be sensitive, oh so sensitive, and they've taught me to "Turn on, tune in, drop out." They've taught me to relish victimhood and self-righteousness. They've promised salvation through postmodernism, feminism, Marxism, liberation theology, conservativism, liberalism, existentialism, mythopoetic fantasy, evolutionary astrology, and cultural studies.

My worldview was . . . is? . . . like a jigsaw puzzle that I've been working on for 34 years. The funny thing is that I've never even seen the picture on the top of the puzzle box. I've been spending time arranging the pieces into pretty patterns, reveling in how lovely and splendid each little piece is all by itself, perfect in every way, and saying, "See what a pretty thing it is."

It's like Ken Wilber just walked by the table where I've been working on the puzzle and said, "That's not pretty, that's a mess. Some of the pieces have a flat edge. Put them together and they'll form lines. Some of the pieces have two flat edges. Those are the corner pieces. Snap them in place and you've got a rectangle. That's the frame in which all the rest of the pieces go . . ." See, here's how it's done.

At first I feel stupid and resent Wilber, the know-it-all. But then I start to wonder if the bald philosopher dude is right. Like duh! How could I have been so fucking blind! I gather up all the jigsaw pieces with a flat edge and start snapping them together. Pretty soon the whole thing starts to fit together into a frame. Now it's getting really interesting, because Wilber has shown me how some of the jigsaw pieces fit together into a frame, so now I can try to fill in the rest.

"Hey Ken, it looks like you've been solving puzzles for a long time. What's it gonna look like when it's done?"

And he says something like this: "It's Spirit. It's Emptiness. It's the World Soul. It's your Original Face. It's your true identity, who you were before your parents were born, before the Big Bang, before time began."

Tuesday, April 13

"All Quadrants, All Levels." AQAL (pronounced *ah-qwul*) for short. It's the goal of integral spiritual practice, distilled into one godforsaken, unfortunate little acronym. It's intimidating, pretentious, incomprehensible, and difficult to explain. I hate it. But it's useful, so I'll use it.

AQAL is sort of a fancy way of saying "Be all you can be." AQAL does not prescribe a specific religious tradition or set of practices. It's an approach to spirituality that starts with where you're at, right now, with whatever you're doing, and goes from there. The immediate goals: greater balance, equanimity, and wholeness in all facets of life, wherever you're coming from.

Here's how the Integral Institute website (integralinstitute.org) spells out the very basics of an integral approach:

> The easiest way to understand the Integral approach is to remember that it was created by a cross-cultural comparison of most of the known forms of human inquiry. The result was a type of comprehensive map of human capacities. After this map was created (by looking at all the available research and evidence), it was discovered that this integral map had five major aspects to it. By learning to use these five major aspects, any thinker can fairly easily adopt a more comprehensive, effective, and integrally informed approach to specific problems and their solutions—from psychology to ecology, from business to politics, from medicine to education.

Those five major aspects are called quadrants, levels, lines, states, and types. They are the five elements of the integral developmental model for human potential. All possibilities for growth can be mapped somewhere in the integral model, so it's possible to identify the areas in which you are less

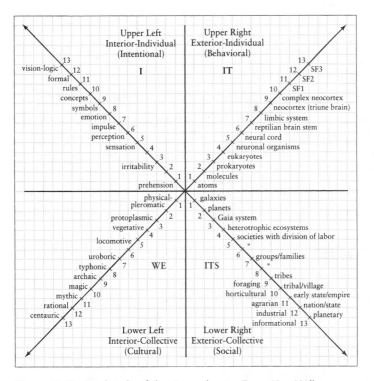

Figure 3. Some details of the 4 quadrants. From Ken Wilber, *Integral Spirituality*, © 2006, reprinted by arrangement with Shambhala Publications, Inc.

developed. If you want a good introduction to the integral model, I recommend visiting the website for the Integral Institute.

What are quadrants? A quadrant is a perspective on life. You can take three views of life: self, culture, and nature. These correspond to the pronouns "I," "we," and "it." Or, more precisely, you can cut life into four slices (see figure 3): individual subjective, individual objective, intersubjective, and interobjective ("I," "we," "it," and "its"). It's possible to look at everything from these three (or four) angles, so the quadrants can be said to be cross-cultural universals.

What are levels? Levels, or stages, are broad patterns of growth that, according to cross-cultural research, tend to unfold sequentially. For example, moral development may be described as passing through three stages:

selfish, care, and universal care. I'll have more to say about levels—and states—later.

What are lines? Lines are the vectors that move through progressively higher levels, or stages, of being. Depending on the researcher, lines are also known as modes, modules, streams, or multiple intelligences and include a variety of relatively independent capacities such as physical, psychosexual, cognitive, interpersonal, moral, and spiritual functioning.

What are types? A type is a distinct style of awareness. Systems of types, or typologies, help us to make sense of variety and differences in being; examples include the Enneagram, the zodiac, Jungian types, Myers-Briggs personality tests, Mars/Venus typologies, and so forth. If you are, say, an introverted personality type, this is so regardless of your level of development.

AQAL is an idea that says it's important to take all perspectives into account: quadrants, levels, lines, states, and types.

Wednesday, April 14

States are another part of the AQAL picture. Human beings have many different states of consciousness—waking, dreaming, and sleeping, for example—and these are all part of human potential. States are temporary experiences, not permanent conditions. You're in a state of consciousness right now. Everyone is. The waking state, I would guess. At other times, you might be experiencing consciousness in a dreaming or sleeping state. Or perhaps you're having an experience of a meditative or altered state.

In Ken Wilber's version of integral theory, states and levels go together as the being and knowing aspects of reality, respectively. States are the structures of being (that is, planes or realms of reality) and levels are the structures of our knowing about reality (that is, consciousness or selfhood). It's important to bear both states and levels in mind, because different levels of selfhood can encounter different planes of reality (that is, we can encounter different states at different levels).

Peak experiences deserve our special attention. Altered, nonnormal, or nonordinary states of consciousness include psychotic episodes, drug-induced trips, near-death experiences (NDEs), and meditative states. It's not true that peak experiences only happen at high stages of development; they may happen to persons at any level. When they occur, very often the result is what's called a mystical or peak spiritual experience.

States may be cataloged into five major categories that derive from the Great Chain of Being, a metaphor for the ontology of the universe: gross, psychic, subtle, causal, and nondual. Gross states are encounters with the gross, mundane, bodily, and terrestrial realm of existence. Psychic states are encounters with the psychic or astral realm of existence. Subtle states are encounters with the subtle, soul, or celestial realm of existence. Causal states are encounters with the causal, divine, spirit, or infinite realm of existence. And the nondual state is an encounter with ultimate reality, which is neither mental nor physical. Technically there are no "nondual experiences," only realizations of nonduality.

Although peak experiences happen to persons at virtually any stage of growth, the person's interpretations of those experiences depend in part on his or her stage. Peak experiences are transient states that require ongoing psychological and spiritual development to become permanent traits. Wilber says that research indicates that meditative states are important for such development to occur, because they access higher realms in an intentional and prolonged fashion. Thus, with practice, meditative states may become permanent traits over time.

Thursday, April 15

Some HIV-related issues have just appeared on my radar screen. There are problems with my liver functioning still showing up in my blood work, and there is possibly an enlarged lymph node. I've got a bunch of new tests to take this week, including a CAT scan and an abdominal ultrasound.

I just checked my messages, and there was one from my doctor's staff telling me to stop all my antiretrovirals immediately—so I guess this problem must be very serious. I'm not feeling anxious yet, but that could change if my skin starts turning yellow.

Friday, April 16

Liberalism, Gay Marriage, and Other Holy Things

Historically, liberalism and spirituality have been bitter enemies. In fact, since the Enlightenment, modern liberalism has come into being preeminently as a force of reaction against religion. Because many liberals left God to the conservatives, today our politics is dominated by secular liberals and conservative religionists.

Nowhere is the spiritual divide between liberals and conservatives more apparent than in the arguments waged in the battle over gay marriage.

Liberalism has its weaknesses. By and large, liberals identify marriage as a vehicle strictly for advancing the material and economic security of individuals. While talking about economic issues is not a bad thing, unfortunately it comes at the expense of acknowledging a sacred character and communal context to marriage. Liberalism sees only convenience and material gain where sacramentality used to be.

And yet much good has come from liberalism. Liberalism has brought fundamental reforms to patriarchal traditions that regarded women as mere property. As Jonathan Rauch explains in the new book *Gay Marriage: Why It Is Good for Gays, Good for Straights, and Good for America*, liberalism produced greater equality between the sexes in marriage. It did this in part by imposing monogamy on a tradition that had historically been stacked against women.

When the U.S. Supreme Court struck down state bans on interracial marriage, it relied on liberal principles. In the 1967 decision in *Loving v. Virginia*, the Court said that states were not free to define marriage in a way that violated core constitutional freedoms.

Liberalism wants to strengthen marriage by extending it to people (such as gays) where it is currently denied, but liberals are embarrassed by any hint that the institution may have a sacred aspect or civic role. Can we not find a way to retain the liberal emphasis on individual freedoms while scrapping liberalism's denial of spirituality and community values?

Across the aisle from the liberals, we have the conservatives. They are wedded to republican (in the historical sense) and religious traditions that define marriage according to communal standards and values, especially those of orthodox Judeo-Christianity.

Ironically, the very religionists who think all "pagans" will burn in hell forever are more than happy to invoke the social codes of Buddhist or Hindu cultures when it's convenient.

Rauch gives an example of such an argument. He puts it into these words: "For the entire history of civilization, marriage has been between men and women. In every religion, every culture, every society—maybe with some minor and rare exceptions, none of them part of our own heritage—marriage has been reserved for the union of male and female. . . ."

Rauch must have something like this argument in mind when he explains what he's up against in making the case for gay marriage: "Advocates of gay marriage are trying to change the way things have been—well, forever. I accept that the burden of proof is on my shoulders."

So Rauch personally assumes the burden of defending gay marriage while claiming that the God of every religion, every culture, and every society in history is on the other side. Against such a formidable foe, it is not surprising that he falls short.

Rauch rejects the liberalism of those who defend gay marriage on the basis of immutable human rights. Unlike liberals (and some conservatives) who believe that the precepts of *Roe v. Wade* and subsequent Court decisions such as *Lawrence v. Texas* may have located a right of gay marriage in the Constitution itself, Rauch finds no such right. Instead, he presents a case based primarily on civic republican virtues and incremental reforms.

Rauch's argument is well intentioned, but it ultimately fails. The problem isn't that he's wrong about gay marriage being a good thing (which it is). The problem is that if Almighty God Himself is supposedly an enemy of gay marriage, then it doesn't matter if gay marriage is a good thing . . . because it's been condemned by God. Thus, Rauch's arguments do not meet the awesome burden of proof he himself has identified.

In other words, Rauch makes arguments that appeal explicitly to traditional beliefs, without invoking the liberal tradition's central claim that reason is necessary to liberate human beings from superstition and unreasonable beliefs. Liberalism at its best finds a right to marriage for all, including homosexuals, in nature itself. In contrast, it is common for traditional believers to appeal to the Bible, the Koran, and other sacred texts to oppose gay marriage. To such believers, reasonability is determined not by rational argument but simply by the contents of those texts, which are regarded as infallible. When rational arguments are advanced, they are only offered as support for the supernatural revelations of their preferred tradition. If the religious texts say that God wants the faithful to smite unbelievers in a holy war, then that is considered a reasonable belief. If the texts say that homosexuals should be stoned to death, then that is God's will.

By Rauch's own admission, every religion, culture, and society in history is against him. To win his case, I believe he must not only make the debater's case that tradition is wrong. He must also argue (and he doesn't) that there is an immutable right for gays to marry, and he must explain why rights trump tradition.

A liberal argument for gay marriage makes the best and strongest case for change, because it contains a critical theory that explains why this innovative social reform is good and the prejudice of the ages is evil. Liberalism can go beyond Rauch's arguments that gay marriage is not war on the family and assert that the opposite is true: gay marriage is a necessary expansion of the institution of marriage that will strengthen and enrich all families and reduce cultural pathologies that are the result of the disenfranchisement of homosexuals.

At its best, liberalism can speak the truth: *the conservatives are wrong about God and, therefore, they're wrong about gay marriage.* Unfortunately, too few liberals are willing to speak about God.

Liberalism need not, and should not, abandon God or moral principles to conservatives. Conservatives aren't wrong because they affirm universal values or hold marriage sacred. Conservatives are wrong because they locate the sacred in the wrong place.

The challenge for liberalism is to locate Spirit in the right place: in the midst of the evolution of nature and culture; in the thick of multicultural diversity; and as the ground for liberal freedoms, strong families, and all authentic liberation.

Liberals must make the case that gay marriage is objectively good because it is part of the unfolding emergence of Spirit in our midst. We must open our eyes to see God's footprints in modern history. Then we can begin to see Spirit as a presence in the victories of the Enlightenment over medieval tyrannies, abolitionists over slavery, and the best and noblest parts of the women's and men's and gay liberation movements over entrenched prejudices.

In the short term, one of the goals of liberal spirituality must be to extend individual freedoms to those areas where their denial persists and is most inhumane, such as in the struggle for gay marriage. And in the future, spiritual liberalism can go beyond affirming individual rights.

As Ken Wilber envisions in *Sex, Ecology, Spirituality*, the ultimate aim of spiritual politics is not just a liberation of peoples but a liberation "of life, of all sentient beings, not as having equal rights, but as worthy of care and respect and honor, cherished as manifestations of Spirit."

Monday, April 19

Ken Wilber's integral model includes not only quadrants, but levels, lines, states, and types. The levels are also called stages or waves. They represent the main stages within a hierarchical model of development. It's impossible to read along without asking yourself where you fit in the hierarchy.

There are different ways of measuring stages, and integral theory is basically agnostic about which particular model is employed. Jean Gebser provides a structuralist sociocultural developmental model with stages going from archaic to magic to mythic to rational to integral-aperspectival. Other developmental models trace personal growth from preconventional to conventional to postconventional, or prerational to rational to transrational. Spiral Dynamics, a model developed by Don Beck and Chris Cowan and based on the work of psychologist Clare Graves, uses a color scheme to denote stages of evolution in core values, beliefs, and presuppositions about reality. Spiral Dynamics talks about growth from beige to purple to red to blue to orange to green to yellow and beyond.

So, where is my "center of gravity" in the hierarchical levels of development included within the integral model? Oh, Jesus Christ, I don't know. I could try to pigeonhole myself, but I try not to dwell on it. I see bits and pieces of myself at lots of different levels. I think what is most valuable about the model of developmental levels is that I can begin to see each stage within myself.

I think that I'm currently climbing up from one level to the next, but this evolution is not as easy as making a conscious choice or reading a few books. If I had to locate myself in the Spiral Dynamics scheme, perhaps I'm making a transition from green ("the sensitive self") to yellow ("integrative"). But that box doesn't quite capture the full picture. At the level I'm climbing to, I will need to realize a form of consciousness in which I recognize that my way of seeing the world isn't the only valid way. I will need to grow in honor and respect for a wide variety of ways of seeing the world, not just the ways that I've been comfortable with. I thought I was a fairly sensitive, pluralistic, and multiculturally aware sort of guy, but now I'm not so sure.

How truly sensitive have I been, considering that I've held up tolerance and diversity as values but in practice have been very intolerant of all those whom I perceive as being intolerant? The only thing I hate is hatred. The only thing I won't tolerate is intolerance. I am becoming aware that the things that most upset my sensitivities are slights to my own ego and to the ways that I've defined my sense of identity (that is, narrow, egocentric concerns). How can I expand, deepen, and enrich my sensitivity? In order to expand my sensitivity beyond egocentric concerns, I will have to lighten up.

I'm face to face with a terrible paradox. To become more tolerant, I must let go of my need to harshly judge those whose intolerance turns my stomach. To become more sensitive to the marginalized, I need to be willing to let go of the comfort of taking the victim role myself. To become more pluralistic, I need to be willing to see more universal features amid the diversity. To become more holistic, I must be more willing to make more judgments and discriminations of relative value. To be more inclusive, I must be more willing to make more rankings. To be more expansive in my thinking, I must be willing to see a positive value not just in linking but also in hierarchy.

To actually climb the ladder of consciousness, I need to be willing to first see that there are critical distinctions of value between different rungs of the ladder. I must not be afraid of the reality, however politically incorrect it may seem, that there are higher and lower levels of consciousness. I must not reject the possibility of identifying cross-cultural values simply because my own perspective is rooted in the worldview of the modern West.

And to become more spiritual, I must be willing to let go of the Mr. Nice Guy persona. I've been doing that sort of work for a while now. I haven't exactly been winning the Mr. Congeniality award in the blogosphere. The integral map of development suggests that I must be even more willing to be perceived by others as mean, intolerant, elitist, arrogant, or worse. I must be willing to be called names by hypersensitive folks. I must not be afraid that people will call my views "too Western" or "too white" or "too androcentric," to name only a few pejoratives that could be (and have been) thrown at me. I'm working on it, but I have a ways to go.

Tuesday, April 20

Taurus

The sun enters the part of the sky linked to Taurus, sign of the Bull. The Taurean impulse is to ground the sense of self in the body, the earth, and the material realm of all possessions. It is the sign most linked to self-pleasuring sensuality and the delights of the flesh. It is the most physical of all the signs: carnal, practical, and stubborn. The Bull's aim: simply delighting in the feeling of being, not doing. The Bull remains solid, unyielding, and perfect in itself, without doing a thing.

Wednesday, April 21

A few weeks ago, I wrote a post with a philosophical bent on the *Gay Spirituality & Culture* weblog. I called the post "Homosexuality and Agape: Notes toward a Truly Comprehensive Theory of Gayness." The collective reaction of the blogosphere: a huge, deafening yawn of indifference. Well, not quite totally indifferent. There were two responses that got my attention.

I got a kind note from Toby Johnson, the author of *Gay Perspective: Things Our Homosexuality Tells Us about God and the Universe* and many other books. Johnson is a sort of apostle to the gay community of Joseph Campbell's wisdom.

Like Campbell, Johnson claims mythology is an opening to mysticism and direct experience of God, but only if it is taken in an "as if," or nonliteral, fashion. I find myself in sympathy with much in Johnson's work, including his irreverent humor, his distaste for fundamentalism in religion, his affinity for Buddhism and Thomas Merton, and his commitment to an inclusive paradigm for spirituality. In an age of political correctness, the notion that there are collective attributes associated with particular social groups is frequently dismissed as stereotyping. Therefore, I also admire very much Johnson's boldness in being willing to talk about the possibility of a gay perspective on spirituality, while others fear to tread in such controversial waters.

Johnson found in Campbell's work an inspiring vision for the gay community, much as I am currently finding in Ken Wilber's work a way to plug the holes in my worldview. Not too long ago, I wrote a post where I said that "Everyone lives a myth." I now view that statement as naive and slippery. I totally glossed over the very real and important distinctions between science and mythology, blurring the distinctions between fact and poetry as if they were unimportant. I now believe that making such distinctions is critical for reconciling the various truth-claims made by proponents of religion and science. I am as guilty as anyone of blurring important distinctions among myth, science, and truth.

Wilber's careful distinctions in these areas sound true to me, so I can no longer accept the perspective of Joseph Campbell and his followers that taking mythology in an "as if" fashion is a great source of deep spiritual consciousness. I've been doing spiritual work involving mythic archetypes for some time and have never had a mystical experience by meditating on the Warrior, the Keepers of Beauty, or any other archetype. I believe there truly are spiritual realities that go beyond the ability of reason to describe; however, using mythology in an "as if" fashion strikes me as an approach of limited value. I think it's valuable up to a point, but then the language of myth fails. By the time we start talking about myth as if it can do everything except bake bread, we are really going too far.

In his correspondence with me, Johnson explained that he feels that some of my criticisms of Joseph Campbell's followers have a grain of truth but that they don't apply to his particular take on Campbell. Then he writes:

From Campbell we can learn that all the old myths are false. They're interesting as symbolic conveyors of wisdom about how to live a good life. But they're not true. The measure of religion is its ability to transform behavior. If believing in religion makes you cooperative and loving, then the religion has value. If it makes you judgmental and self-righteous, then it has no value. Gay people should look at how religion makes us feel, not about how ancient or authoritative it is. Even Wilber is speaking "as if." His reasoning is from a limited perspective. The reason that it sounds true and convincing is because this is the current human perspective. The "truth" of his ideas is how it makes people behave. There is NO truth beyond human imagery of truth.

Actually I think there are few ideas more identified with the current postmodern worldview than Johnson's notion that there is "NO truth." But is Johnson's a true statement? If there is no truth, then we can safely dismiss Johnson's claim. And if we are to pick and choose our beliefs based on how they make us feel rather than their correspondence to The Way Things Are, however imperfectly it is perceptible, then this is the very essence of egotism. If we are to judge religion based on its ability to "transform behavior," then by what standard do we judge positive versus negative transformations? Wilber's post-postmodern thought appeals to me precisely because it shows a way to cut through the relativism that dominates so much contemporary spirituality. Apparently, I believe in the existence of Truth, and Johnson doesn't.

Although Johnson and I disagree about much, we share a common interest in drawing the connections among homosexuality, God, and the Universe. In *Gay Perspective*, Johnson talks about the importance of homosexuality for revealing the limits of dualistic thinking. Straight people already know their place in the cosmos, so they have no special motivation for exploring the limits of conventional thinking. However, gay people are inclined to find new explanations and conceptions that can account for our place in the universe. Broadly speaking, I think that's right. Johnson also speaks of the divine attribute of "self-reflection" as a key to understanding homosexuality, not unlike the way that I speak of self-immanence or homophilia as an attribute of all holons.

Because Johnson and I share a common passion for understanding the nature of gayness within a big picture, there are many parts of his book that resonate with me. For me, the heart of *Gay Perspective* is this passage:

> Built into the dualistic vision of the world is the notion that virtually everything links by heterosexual connection—opposites attract. Electrical connections plug "male" plugs into "female" sockets. Pipes have male and female joints and connectors. According to this mechanical model, homosexuality doesn't work because the "plumbing" doesn't fit. . . . Still, we don't have a model to demonstrate how male and male and female and female do fit together. We need an example of how, at the mechanical level, like connects to like.

I believe that my approach to gayness is one that is capable of honoring the value both of dualistic thinking (yin and yang, male and female) and the principle of unity. As I see it, yin and yang truly are universal aspects of the deep structures of reality. Same-directed love (homophilia) and other-directed love (heterophilia) are the glue that keeps yin and yang together. Heterophilia and homophilia are inseparable; you can't have one without the other, any more than you can have yin without yang or light without darkness. Can you ever have the notion of otherness (hetero) without also the concept of sameness (homo)? No. It is impossible.

It's not so much that "like connects to like" as it is that like *includes* and *embraces* like. This is the key to understanding how, at a mechanical level, like and like are related. If you're just thinking about a flat world, you won't get it. You have to think about an evolving, dynamic world. Like embraces like as a molecule includes an atom, a sandbox contains a grain of sand, and God embraces Creation. Love connects all things to their Source, and that Love flows in two directions: from Creation to Source (the straight direction), and from Source to Creation (the gay or queer direction).

In my opinion, the approach to gayness I took in "T.I.O.B.G." (see journal entries beginning on November 29) provides exactly the sort of model that is needed to articulate the place of homosexuals in the universe. I believe that what I am getting at with my conception is not merely a subjective preference or a new myth but actually an expression of Truth.

• • •

Aside from Johnson's correspondence, there was only one other comment from a reader of my weblog post on the role of homosexuality in the universe. Perhaps nobody really knows what to think, they don't get it, or they don't care. Or perhaps nobody reads weblogs. I don't know.

My suspicion is that many people who call themselves spiritual would probably be very open to my ideas, except that many of them are stricken with an insidious anti-intellectualism. One guy responded with an utterly asinine comment that I take as typical of a widespread sentiment. He wrote in part: ". . . all theorizing or speculation about what is this or what is that comes from a wrong thinking. The Buddha did not theorize. He saw this as a justification to potential (sic) cause harm and a waste of time."

To summarize: Thought is a disease. Thinking is bad, very bad. It is best not to think. This is a fairly typical sentiment. Related sentiments that might have been expressed, but weren't, include: I was "staying stuck in my head," "trapped in thinking," "playing mind games," and "coming from the egoic mind."

Sound familiar? If, like me, you've spent some time in spiritual circles, especially those with an American Buddhist or New Age bent, you know what I'm talking about. At their worst, these spiritualists denigrate the mind and reason, and advocate an extreme form of anti-intellectualism. Never mind that the Buddha taught the spiritual principle of Right Understanding. I would like to think that my critic is speaking about truth from an absolute perspective and so is inclined to believe that knowledge of Reality can only be obtained through spiritual practices, not by mere intellectualizing. This is all good and true so far as it goes, I think. From the perspective of Spirit, one could say, All is One, so mental discriminations are not important and are a hindrance to seeing the actual Unity of All. However, my critic's post goes beyond that, implying that thinking is intrinsically harmful and useless. That is bullshit.

Anti-intellectualism is not the highest teaching of Zen, but it is often mistaken as such. Westerners who have read a little Buddhism can decide to bring the principle of "no mind" into their daily affairs and easily fall into this trap if they're not careful. Sometimes this shows up in an idiotic aversion to all critical distinctions and value judgments, such as right and wrong, or better and worse. Ken Wilber calls this misconception "idiot compassion" (after Chögyam Trungpa's use of a phrase from Gurdjieff).

From the point of view of Spirit, the distinctions of the rational mind can be said to be illusory. But you're probably not one of the 0.0001 percent of the human population that has truly reached the Zen-guru stage and lives in permanent Enlightenment. If you are, you're probably too wise to be reading this journal. Thinking critically and making distinctions, including value judgments, is not only permissible in spirituality, it's required. Reason is not a source of oppression and spiritual harm but potentially a bearer of liberation and a resource for spiritual growth.

(God, I'm reading so much Ken Wilber, I'm starting to sound like him. That's a scary thought.)

Thursday, April 22

I am trying to find a path that goes with, through, and beyond the familiar Christianity of our culture. And as I do so, I ask myself the question: how is this path truly different from that of the early Christians, who pronounced Jesus the Christ?

I feel my path must be with Jesus, but against the Jesus myths. And my relation to the Church must be one of honoring its truths, important as they have been in shaping the world today. However, it will not do to take the myths literally.

Though it is the vessel for the spiritual realizations of Jesus and his followers, today Christianity itself is in need of redemption. It has been stalling at a fork in the road of its history for some time. On the one hand, the religion can bury its head in the sand of its institutional accretions, blocking out both the world as it is and also the living presence of Christ. This path, which Christianity seems to have chosen at least tentatively, will see the religion fade into irrelevance for intelligent people of conscience — those who are best suited to providing strong and effective leadership — and fall more and more into the hands of fundamentalists and orthodox reactionaries. Fundamentalists will continue to use the religion as a vehicle for their anger and as a tool for imposing their moralism on society. Reactionaries will continue to defend moribund traditions while blind to the fact that a passionately engaged faith has ossified into escapism and irrelevance. On the other hand, Christianity can recommit to Christ's ministry of love and go deeper into the mysteries He revealed.

How much are Christians willing to give up in order to follow Jesus? Are they willing to give up their mythologies about Jesus? Are they willing to enter the Dark Night of the Soul, a time of entering into painful and uncertain transitions of consciousness, to grow in God-consciousness? Can they trust that Spirit is not, and never has been, limited to the scope of their mythologies about Spirit?

I can answer these questions only for myself. The spirit and teachings of Jesus endure, not as comforting promises of a wish-fulfilling and ego-sanctifying God, but as a challenging call to realize my own potential. Heeding the message of Jesus invites me to empty myself of narcissism and other illusions wherever they appear, even (and especially) in my quest to be all that I can be.

Friday, April 23

For the past two weeks, I've been following some suggestions in a book by Dr. Bob Arnot called *The Biology of Success*. For six days, I awoke at seven each morning, and I could feel my biological clock resetting to the new schedule. The single biggest aid: simply sleeping with my window blinds open instead of shut, so that morning light could reach me. The light made a huge difference.

I also started going for a short walk each morning to get the blood flowing and to have exposure to even more natural light. I kept up my weightlifting routine two or three times a week; and the walking helped to tire me out more, so it was easier to go to sleep.

The first hitch in my plans to change my sleeping routine came when (against all advice I'd ever read) I decided that I didn't have to follow the routine on the weekend. By Sunday, I was sleeping in until 11:00 a.m. and was still awake at 4:00 or 5:00 a.m. on Monday. Then this past week, I was fucked. While my morning and evening routines haven't gone back to square one, they are scrambled. I am sleeping in later, waking up at different times, and going to bed later. I lost my rhythm. I'm discouraged, but still committed. Down, but not out.

Saturday, April 24

Ken Wilber includes fascinating information in *One Taste* about the long-term effects of meditation practice. Meditation, he says, is the one spiritual practice that has been consistently shown through research to advance spiritual growth to higher stages of consciousness. Not church attendance, not astrology, not crystals or Tai Chi. Just meditation, according to the research he summarizes. Meditation seems to be the one practice known to produce significant evolution from one level of consciousness to another, when done consistently over long periods of time. Meditation yields immediate health benefits such as greater relaxation, improved concentration, decreased respiratory rate, decreased muscle tension, and so forth. Research also points to benefits for the immune system and self-esteem and new studies are finding additional benefits all the time. Wilber tells us that consciousness research suggests that meditation generally takes at least four or five years of regular practice to realize a change from one stage of consciousness to another.

I'm inspired to get started soon. Soon! But not now. Now I'm sounding like Saint Augustine ("Lord, make me chaste. But not yet."). That's a *very* scary thought.

Sunday, April 25

Today I watched Joseph Kramer's video *Fire on the Mountain*. Wow! What a beautiful film. I don't think I've ever seen a video quite like this before. There are naked gay men sexually touching, but it doesn't feel the least bit pornographic. Not that there's anything wrong with porno; it's just that porn stars aren't exactly models of open-hearted intimacy, and porn scenes are hardly models of sacred, tenderhearted lovemaking.

I have to admit the sights and sounds of two nude men doing rhythmic breathing together gave me the giggles. The laughter helped to ease my discomfort, I'm sure. I have been trained by pornography to visualize sex in a certain way on video, and to see such a different perspective is rather strange.

This is a practical how-to film for gay men who want to explore Tantric erotic massage with a partner. Unlike a porno, where the men are just going through the motions, the men in this film seemed to radiate a glow of warmth, concern, and kindness toward their partners. It's truly a beautiful film.

In his interview in *Gay Soul*, Joseph Kramer said something about non-gay men that I think is also true for many gay men: "Cock is the biggest shadow . . . Men have not learned to honor cock. Men are terrified of cock. Men are overwhelmed by cock." In this video, Kramer shows men (especially gay and bi men) how to honor cock.

I have to admit that watching the film served as a huge reminder to me of how far I have yet to go in more fully connecting my sexuality and spirituality. "Getting off" with myself or another person is, on a good night, easy. Yet being fully present, integrated, and emotionally available in the deepest aspects of my being is difficult, very difficult. How much more work do I have to do before I truly and fully honor my heart, soul, and cock? In terms of integral theory, how much higher must I develop in my psychosexual line of development to climb up from the pits of my current level? Thinking about it is actually sort of depressing.

Tuesday, April 27

I got to the point in *One Taste* where Wilber delivers his verdict on astrology. It's not as positive as I'd been hoping. In fact, it doesn't seem positive at all. He writes: "I am still willing to follow the evidence, but I must say, the total web of evidence at this point is crushingly against astrology in any form . . . at this point, it appears astrology is a belief without corroborating evidence."

Maybe that's right, but I'm feeling torn. I think he's right to be skeptical and to demand evidence for claims of an empirical nature. I've read several astrology books where the authors are so convinced of astrology's validity that they insist that corporate human resources departments would benefit from making personnel decisions based on horoscope analysis. That strikes me as leaping way ahead of the evidence, and it sounds like Wilber would agree.

Yet I can't help but wonder if there isn't more to astrology than mere superstition. Is astrology just an archaic repository of mythic archetypes that can be interpreted in an "as if" fashion? When I investigate my own birth chart or the charts of people I know, I am able to identify remarkably meaningful patterns. (Of course, that ability can easily be explained as a function of my having gullible Pisces on the Ascendant. LOL.) I know of no explanatory principle except for chance (that is, synchronicity) that could explain such patterns.

There is some evidence (for example, the work of the psychologist and statistician Michel Gauquelin) for an influence of planetary positions upon personality traits, and Wilber acknowledges and discusses this evidence. And he seems at least friendly to the theory that an electromagnetic influence between the gravitational forces of the planets and the gross physical body accounts for observed astrological correlations.

Wednesday, April 28 (Garrison, New York)

I flew today from Seattle into JFK airport and then took a train from Grand Central Station to Garrison, New York. I read Ken Wilber's *Marriage of Sense and Soul* on the airplane and the train.

Tomorrow a hundred men will arrive, and the Gay Spirit Culture Summit will begin. For a brief while tonight, there were about a half-dozen of us early birds talking in a lounge. I took the opportunity to thank Toby Johnson for writing an inspiring book and then shared a few ideas I've been playing around with:

"When we look at the various ethics around sexuality in the world religions, the conventional wisdom is that they generally condemn homosexuality. But I believe that if we back up to a great enough level of abstraction, and actually investigate what all the world religions have in common in their teachings on sexuality, a very different picture will emerge. I think we may find a core value that in sexuality, each partner should relate to each other partner as a perfect manifestation of Spirit. Sort of a golden rule of intercourse, as it were. And from this perspective, there is no heterosexist assumption that gay sex is wrong; gays and straights are on a level ethical playing field."

After a while, the conversation broke up. One of the men pulled me aside and said, "I hope that the rest of the conversations this weekend won't be as dry and intellectual as that one. I came here to get into my feelings and connect with other men on a heart level, and don't want to stay stuck in my head."

I just sighed and said, "I don't think you'll have a problem finding what you're looking for."

I felt disappointed and formed a snap judgment about the man. I viewed his comment as insipid anti-intellectualism; however, I didn't say anything that might cause him offense (my Mr. Nice Guy persona showed up). Why do so many spiritual people think that getting in touch with their heart means that they have to leave their brain at the coat check?

Afterward, some of us smudged with sage as we held the intention to invite Spirit into our midst. After a dip in one of the hot tubs and a good night's rest, I'm ready for the summit to begin.

Thursday, April 29 (Garrison, New York)

Today was the first day of the Gay Spirit Culture Summit. About 130 men have gathered in Garrison for a summit of leaders, luminaries, and change agents involved with spirituality in the gay community. Today we ate lunch and then gathered in an opening ceremony where we formed a circle and cultivated a sacred space.

Native American elders sang songs from their own traditions and led us by honoring the energies and spirits of the Directions. After the opening ceremony, we took a break and then, in pairs, did an experiential process designed to promote connection.

We shared the feelings and thoughts that are "alive for us," our intentions for the summit, and the fears we are bringing here. I huddled with Michael, who came all the way from Australia.

After this sharing, we learned more about the group as a whole. Men split up into different parts of the room to gather with others who share their interest or background. Later, men were asked to form groups according to religious tradition—at first with others who had been raised in the same faith and then with those who have the same current spiritual inclinations.

When it came time to share my own tradition, it was easy to pick my starting place: I just went over to the side of the room with men from Judeo-Christian upbringings (it was very crowded there).

When it came time to say where I'm at today, I was torn between staying with the Christian group and going all the way over to the other side of the room, to the "other/ none of the above" group. I decided to go to "none of the above." I had plenty of company.

At lunch, I met Joseph Kramer, the founder of the Body Electric School. He greeted me with a hug and words that brought a smile to my face. "You should get a new photo for your website," he said. "You're much better looking in person."

In the afternoon, we broke into 18 small groups of about seven men apiece. My own group named itself the "Fuzzy Fruits" (so called because every man in the group wore a goatee, moustache, or beard). The other men were Jacob, Haynes, David, Ramon, Greg-Eugene, and Joe.

The night's still young. We just ate dinner, and they've got more activities planned for the evening. The summit is off to a great start.

Friday, April 30

Last night, the summit wrapped up its icebreakers and introductions. After dinner, we were led in a group exercise that sought to help us experience erotic energy in a way that felt safe and that respected the boundaries of each man at the summit. Afterward, the group broke into the smaller groups to discuss the exercise.

Today was a full and busy day in which the summit moved into articulating visions and dreams. Every man had the opportunity to convene a group discussion on a topic of his choosing. These ranged from finding ways to move beyond separatism to exploring the question of what unique gifts gays bring to spirituality and religion. Some topics allowed men from specific faith traditions to meet; others, exploring issues such as race and ethnicity, cut across a variety of traditions. Several discussion topics dealt with youth and elder issues, music, art and performance, intentional communities, and issues peculiar to specific areas of the country. Some men brought a topic based on the work they do in the community, such as healing, religious ministry, or the "erotic spiritual path."

I attended three sessions today. In the morning, I convened a group to discuss applications of Ken Wilber's philosophy, Spiral Dynamics, and integral theory to contemporary gay issues. Later in the morning, I attended a group for writers in which participants talked about issues common to the craft. In the afternoon, I attended a group focused on HIV/AIDS issues.

This last group was convened by two men who have together created a performance piece that explores ethical and social questions related to HIV/AIDS, such as "who owns the stories?" Their piece was inspired by an actual situation, in which a man revealed his own HIV status and the status of another man to a mutual friend.

The Ken Wilber / Spiral Dynamics group was one of the times at the summit when I felt totally comfortable. I didn't realize until I got there just how isolated I've been feeling on some unconscious level since starting to read integral philosophy. It's a powerful set of ideas that really has the potential to shift one's entire way of seeing the world. Being with another group of gay men who've read some of the same books and can discuss them gave me a profound sense of belonging. I didn't even realize how excited I was until I got into the room and started drawing spirals and boxes with colored markers on sheets of butcher paper.

The day ended with a dinner that included traditional elements from the Jewish faith, organized by Jewish summit participants. Afterward, men participated in an evening ritual organized by various participants. The ritual blended elements from African and pagan practices, including storytelling, dancing, drumming, and singing. Some men dressed in traditional pagan attire. There was also a moment in the ritual for elders to provide a blessing for the queer youth.

Finally, there were also postritual festivities including parties and an experiential process involving erotic massage organized by men from Body Electric.

Friday night was the part of the summit that I've been secretly fearing. As it approached, I felt myself begin to isolate and withdraw from others. I've done quite a few retreats of various kinds over the past few years, and I often find myself emotionally dropping into a state of sadness by the evening of the second day.

I think it has to do with the powerful, altered emotional space created by such weekends and their ability to begin to wear down my layers of ordinary emotional defenses. And I've found time and time again that when my defenses come down, I tap into a deep well of undifferentiated grief.

Each time it happens, there are different stories attached, and different triggers. Sometimes I only skim the surface of the emotion, and other times I begin to bucket out deep, deep sadness. I keep thinking (or hoping?) that if I just keep letting myself go, eventually I'll get to the bottom of the tears and then will be able to get on with my life, better than ever before. And yet the tears keep coming, and it seems that there's no end in sight.

On one retreat last summer I found myself encountering the grief. I ran out of a bunkhouse where I'd been sleeping, because it was the wee hours of the morning and I didn't want to wake up the other men with my sobbing. I began to sink into my feelings and allow them to course through my body in waves. Two men found me, approached me cautiously, and just asked me a simple question: "Do you want to be alone tonight, or do you want to be loved?"

I considered this for a moment. Aloneness, tears in solitude . . . that's a comfortable, familiar path for me. I remember being a little boy lost in the woods. I remember getting news that my friend was killed in a car accident. I remember crying myself to sleep. Being alone with my grief is easy. Allowing my feelings to overwhelm me . . . being willing to be alive, with an unguarded heart, allowing a man to be with me in the pain . . . that's unfamiliar, that's a risk. I cried in the arms of these two men for a while, and then went to sleep.

I thought of that question again tonight, as I cried in the arms of a rabbi, during and after the evening ritual. He asked me why I was so sad, but I didn't feel much like talking. I mean, what could I really say? Does any man really know *why* he is sad, or just the fact of it? I could spin a few stories about the tears, but fuck it—I just plain don't know.

And I thought of the question one other time tonight. In the late evening, I joined the men from Body Electric for the sacred full-body massage experience. As three men caressed my weary body, I began to feel the connection between my heart and cock—spirit and sex—come alive . . . and tears once again began to stream down my cheeks. Sex without feeling is easy. But sex when my body comes fully alive . . . that is hard.

Afterward, as I lay sleeping in my bunk, I recalled the years I spent using drugs or anonymous sex to mask my feelings and cover up my pain. I used to use drugs and sex together whenever possible, for the double whammy that could take my sensorium to new heights of ecstasy and euphoria. I could spend hours zoning out . . . tweaking out . . . groping the darkened hallways of sex clubs . . . or masturbating to porno videos for hours until my cock was bruised or my anus was bleeding . . . smelling the aroma of sex and poppers and sweat . . . sending my feelings away and replacing them with the high of the drug. I thought of the faces and bodies of countless men whom I have known and shared moments of pleasure with, pleasant memories for sure, but memories devoid of feeling . . . empty of spirit and soul.

In *Iron John*, Robert Bly discusses a traditional fairy tale about a warrior who goes into a dangerous forest in search of adventure. He takes his dog with him; and when he reaches the edge of a deep pool, a naked arm reaches out of the water and pulls down the dog. The adventurer immediately knows that he has found what he's been looking for. He leaves the forest and brings back men from the village with buckets to return to the pool. They dip their buckets into the pool over and over, slowly draining it until they get to the creature that lives at the bottom, the Wild Man.

The work I do sometimes seems interminable, like the work of the men with their buckets at the deep pool in the heart of a dark forest. Faith sustains me time after time as I drain my grief and become more truly who I am. Tonight I descend once again into the ashes, where I feel vulnerable, emotionally present, and authentic. With the help of my friends, I dip my bucket into the deep pool. I do the work of soul retrieval. This won't be the last time. How far am I willing to go—how open, how free, how real am I willing to become in order to be able to give and receive love? What am I willing to risk to be whole?

Saturday, May 1 (Garrison, New York)

It was the third day of the summit today, and we're starting to get down to business. The first 36 hours of the summit saw a lot of feelings and ideas and visions shared, and much creative energy was generated. Now we've begun to harness that potential energy into action.

After a full day's work, the men of the summit broke bread together. I sat next to Daniel Helminiak, an author and professor of psychology and religion. After dinner, we enjoyed entertainers including drag performers, comedians, singers, and more. Entertainment included Jay Michaelson reading his poem, "Rat Boy," and a whirling dervish dance by Christian de la Huerta. After all the hard work, the evening brought time for networking, friendship building, and frivolity. Some intrepid souls organized a variety of optional after-hours activities, such as dancing, bodywork, massage, and a group erotic ritual.

In the evening, I hung out talking with various men until we were all spent. One of my conversations was with Ko Imani, a man around my age who attended the Ken Wilber small group the previous day.

"Ko, do you remember visiting my blog a while back and posting a comment?" I asked. "I had asked in my weblog if anyone knew what Ken Wilber has to say about astrology, and you suggested that I read his book *One Taste*. Well, I did. Remember the parts in the book where Wilber talks in great detail about the stages of consciousness he has reached and the states he has experienced, the various experiments with the EEG machine, and all that?"

"Yeah, sure," Ko said.

"I remembered something interesting while I was reading that book, something I hadn't thought about in years. You know how Wilber says that 'Nothing is real except that which is present in deep sleep'? And how, after two decades of intense meditation, he finally reached the state of lucid awareness during deep sleep?

"Well, I think I may have had an experience like that once, about five years ago. I'm not sure. There's a memory I've had that I could never quite explain, so I sort of just forgot about it. But when I read *One Taste*, suddenly a huge light bulb went off.

"It happened around the time of my 30th birthday. To make a long story short, I had a breakdown. I've never been quite sure what to think of the experience, so mostly I've tried not to. I had to spend time in the psych ward of a hospital. One quite peculiar thing happened that I hadn't been able to quite put my finger on before, until now. I would lie down to sleep at night, and I would lie in bed with my eyes closed all night long. Sometimes visions would come to me during the night. They seemed sort of like dreams, but different, because I was lucid the whole time. Morning came, and I got out of bed.

"Here I was, eating breakfast in the hospital, and thinking about the night I'd just had. And the funny thing is, I had no idea if I had been sleeping or not. The first night it happened, I guessed that I probably hadn't been sleeping at all. Yet all through that day, I wasn't drowsy. And that night, the same thing happened. And the next night after that, too. Each night, I would go to bed and my consciousness would simply float lucidly in visions or in a calm, serene state for hours. I never quite figured out if I was asleep or awake.

"I mentioned to the nurses that I wasn't sleeping, and they gave me a pill to help me sleep. That night, I lost consciousness completely for the first time in days. I didn't have trouble sleeping in the hospital after that.

"So that's the little riddle I've had for all these years. I'm not sure what to make of it; but after reading *One Taste*, I've got a whole new set of questions. 'Nothing is real except that which is present in deep sleep.' For once in my life, if I was sleeping, then I was fully aware the whole while. Something was present, some sort of awareness . . . But that's all I can remember. I never considered the possibility that this could have been an experience of *One Taste*. I certainly didn't perceive it that way at the time, anyway. If it was a small taste of Enlightenment, I would think it would have been a little less boring."

Ko said, "There's something I don't get. You had this experience, but you haven't talked about it? You say you tried to forget it. Why?"

"I don't know," I said.

After a moment, I ventured a guess: "If I did know . . . maybe . . . I think when I was there, in the hospital . . . I was happy. Indescribably happy. Everything was right and good with the world. For once in my life, everything seemed to make perfect sense. Then after a while the doctors explained that I was crazy and gave me mood stabilizers and antipsychotic drugs to bring me back down to earth.

"So here I was in the hospital. I was crazy, and it was the greatest peace, serenity, and happiness I've ever known. Very confusing. And then to have it all taken away. Losing that . . . Losing *that* . . . I mean, how does anyone lose something like *that*?"

Sunday, May 2 (Garrison, New York)

The summit closed as it began, with a ritual involving song, smudging, releasing the Directions, and storytelling from Native American traditions. Clyde Hall led us in the closing ritual.

After the summit, I took a train from Garrison to Grand Central Station, followed by a cab to JFK. A final happy surprise: I got the opportunity to share the 40 or so minutes in the cab with a man from the summit named Cami Delgado, and we had a great conversation.

Perhaps the most important gift I've received from attending the summit is the simple awareness that I am not alone. All around the world, gay and queer men are coming together to embrace our role as agents of Spirit, however we understand Spirit.

There is not a single monolithic "gay spirituality" but many gay spiritualities. Yet when I was present at the summit, I felt a common core of love, compassion, and gaiety. I am more convinced than ever that behind the eyes of those hundred men, there are many souls, but only One Spirit.

Sunday, May 9

A 30-Second Rant

An AP report says a gay Minnesota couple has been turned away from communion at their Catholic parish. Dale Sand and Tom Pepera, a couple of five years, have been told they are unwelcome to sing in the choir or take communion after Sand wrote a letter to the *Grand Forks Herald* saying that being gay wasn't a choice and that God had made him that way.

In an interview with the AP, Monsignor Roger Grundhaus makes clear his view that communion is a requirement for attaining eternal life. Ergo: Grundhaus is in effect damning the gay couple to burn in eternal hell forever (in his own mind, that is).

As a former Roman Catholic, I've written in polite language many thoughtful reflections on the inadequacies of Catholic moral theology. Today, let me put it a different way:

FUCK YOU, Monsignor Grundhaus. You and your hypocritical, sick, twisted perversion of Christ's teachings are a disgrace to Christ, the Church, and all humanity. You can take your Blessed Sacrament and SHOVE IT UP YOUR ASS.

Tuesday, May 11

I recently posted a 2,000-word essay offering a thoughtful critique of Pope John Paul II's *Theology of the Body*. Not a single reader commented. The blogosphere was totally indifferent to my prose.

And then I posted a rant of a few hundred words in which I suggested that a hateful church official should receive his communion wafer using an alternative orifice. My normally tepid website statistics blossomed, and I enjoyed an ego-boosting 15 minutes of fame. And I got several links from outside weblogs. I got attention! Much of it was negative attention, but people stood up and noticed me. Yippee! The blogosphere rewards drivel and vitriol.

Here's a sampling from among the dozens of comments on my blog and others:

Soulful Blogger Spews Highly Acidic Evolved Consciousness All Over the Screen . . . Joe Perez, Expert Astrologer, gives us all a rhetorical foretaste of what to expect from the Evolved Consciousness once it owns all the guns and can punish Christians for incorrect thoughts. —MARK SHEA

Unfortunately, these men have decided that their orgasms are more important than making themselves worthy vessels of the Bread of Life. Yes their souls are being placed in jeopardy, but it's not the priest who's placing them there. —STEPHEN

Christ went to the Cross for the sake of Joe's soul every bit as much as He did for mine or anyone else's. Mocking Joe reminds me a tiny bit of mocking slaves because they are chained or miners because they are covered in coal dust or 'sanitation workers' because they smell bad . . . —DAVID MORRISON

Of course David is correct that Joe needs prayer rather than scorn, because to be completely submerged in a state of sin must cause terrible, terrible pain and loneliness. But Joe's rant really did make me want to slap him upside the head, which is my own weakness and lack of charity. —SAHMMY

I read Joe's blog for the first time the other day. I then started to remember him in my prayers. He is caught kind of between worlds . . . self-pity and depression, he's up, he's down . . . sadly, what a lot of us went through in our teenaged years. —COLLEEN

Poor man. It would be much easier to jump up and down on this guy with golf shoes (and no soft spikes either) and probably more than a little satisfying. But where would that get us? This man lashes out in pain and anger. —SEB

Folks, this was an angry little outburst of moral indignation. So you do not share my indignation (not surprising). So you are offended (not surprising). So you want to turn this into an act of sacrilege (it was nothing of the sort). I don't think it's worth my time to beat this dead horse anymore. I'm not apologizing. Go home.

Wednesday, May 12

Religious and ethnic riots between Muslims and Christians continue in Nigeria, and today there's a report that says 15 more people are dead. The recent riots have left 630 people dead in the town of Yelwa alone.

Meanwhile, back in the United States, the religious right continues to argue that the solution to all social ills lies in regressing American culture to the traditional Judeo-Christianity of an earlier era in which they imagine everything was peaceful and pure. Men behaved like real men, women behaved like submissive ladies, and all respected the teachings of the (insert infallible religious authority here).

I presume that these conservative religionists also want us all to just overlook a few harsh details from the good old days, such as slavery, witch burning, torturing of heretics and sodomites, subjugation of women and children, and rampant religious warfare. They want us to overlook the sorts of things that are happening today in places like, oh I don't know, Nigeria?

Thursday, May 13

I've been wondering whether or not I should continue blogging.

I've come to realize that, for me, blogging is mainly about pilgrimage. In days of old, pilgrims had to deal with pirates, bandits, foul weather, and the expectation of encountering dragons and other mythical beasts. Today, in cyberspace, I face unfamiliar websites, breaking news stories, visitors who leave thought-provoking or insulting comments, and so forth. These not-so-mythical beasts can force me to grapple with unfamiliar ideas, new faith traditions, and unusual perspectives on life.

Realizing that my spirituality blog is a form of pilgrimage has helped me to answer the question, "Why continue?" Life's journey of self-discovery and growth in wisdom goes on indefinitely. And truly it's never really finished. The spiritual journey continues ever onward. Yet pilgrimages . . . they must come to an end. So here's a fair warning: the blogosphere, like everything in life, is impermanent, transitory, and ephemeral. Read this now while you can, because tomorrow or some day in the future, it will be gone.

Saturday, May 15 (Anchorage, Alaska)

I'm in Alaska with my sister and brother. We're doing some sightseeing, but this isn't a vacation. We are concerned about our father's health. I arranged this trip with my siblings so we could learn what's going on with Dad. This trip involves being with our dysfunctional family dynamics, years of buried grief and anger, and just as many years of masking those feelings with layers of defenses.

Tonight my siblings and I were on our own for dinner. We swapped stories—both good and bad—from our childhoods. There were plenty of painful stories about Dad. At times, he was a sick, troubled man. Today, he seems like a totally different person.

At one point, my sister asked me if I had felt abandoned by Dad after the divorce. I said that I did. Later, I realized that I had misspoken. As a boy, I didn't feel abandoned. I didn't consciously feel personally rejected, but then what teenage boy would allow himself to feel such a frightening emotion? I didn't feel much of anything. I went numb. Today, I am at a place where I have felt the pain, stayed with it, talked about it, and reframed it until I stopped hurting and began to see my father in a more compassionate light. Today I can remember the many good things he did for me as a dad, instead of dwelling on his shortcomings. I can see my father and experience moments of compassion and kindhearted tenderness, and even actual love, where I had previously felt only numbness or anger.

Tonight I also spent time thinking about the tumultuous final years of my parents' marriage. I call them The Volcano Years. On May 18, 1980, Mount Saint Helens erupted and buried my hometown in more than six inches of volcanic ash. Several hours of darkness followed as the sky turned pitch black at noon, and then there were many weeks of hard work to clean up the aftermath.

I thought about how I felt during those years—how I tried to understand what was happening around me and how the divorce changed me forever. I thought of the monster my dad seemed to become, like Dr. Jekyll changing into Mr. Hyde. Today, I have sympathy for both my father and my mother, and believe they did the best they could under difficult circumstances. I see wisdom in not pointing the finger of blame. However, as a child, I didn't understand . . . couldn't understand.

"He's gone *crazy,*" I told myself. "That's why Dad's acting the way he is." *Nothing could be worse. Crazy is the worst thing anyone can ever be.*

And then, one day long, long ago, I probably thought something that nearly every boy thinks about his father at one time or another: *When I grow up, I'll never, ever be like him. I'll never . . . be . . . crazy.*

Monday, May 17 (Seattle, Washington)

I'm back from Alaska. My siblings and I got the information we needed about my father's health, and we built some bridges of connection with Dad and his wife that are open to us in the future.

I packed a Bible for my sister at the airport, since her suitcase exceeded the maximum weight limit. The Bible felt like it weighed a ton. Dad gave this old Bible to my sister as a gift. The heirloom used to belong to his mother. He said he'd only read from it once and that he wanted to get rid of it to make more room for dishes on his table.

Tuesday, May 18

When I last wrote about my journey with Christianity, I wrote of moving away from a perspective of rejecting the Roman Catholic faith and toward one of integrating its best aspects as fully as possible into my life, even as I integrate its truths about Spirit into a wider framework.

Today as I ruminate on the theme of "where I'm at," what comes to mind is not anger with the Church, but disappointment. In Christianity there is the powerful witness of Spirit in Jesus himself, a man who realized a profound unity with the divine that issued forth in a radically transformed consciousness and the mystical knowledge that God is Love.

Yet the great tragedy that defines Christianity is that shortly after Jesus attained his God-realization—"I and the Father are One"—he was perceived as a threat to traditional religious and secular authorities and crucified for blasphemy and possibly other crimes. It seems that the notion of unity between a man and God has always been (and remains) too shocking for traditional believers.

Jesus's life and teaching were cut short by fearful religious traditionalists, and the religious movement he inspired almost immediately turned to mythology to translate Jesus's profound mystical realizations into a message for the masses. Jesus's radical proclamation of the Kingdom of God was not the centerpiece of the religious movement; instead, his followers adopted a dogma that proclaimed Jesus himself as the One True God, and they began to persecute those who believed that Jesus taught a way to sublime knowledge of divine realities.

Thursday, May 20

Gemini

At this time of the year, the sun enters Gemini. The sign of the Twins depicts the mental, talkative, and socially effervescent side of life. The

Twins live by their wits, quite literally. The Geminian impulse is to fully see, sense, and categorize all reality, and to put it into words or images. Gemini is the sign of the archetypal Double, the self reflected in a similar self as in a mirror.

Monday, May 24

Today, a friend forwarded me a link to a blog by a young man in his early twenties who describes himself as a Christian and says he's "turning away from homosexuality and toward God." What can I say to a young Christian, when I myself have chosen a path outside the institutional religion?

The first thing that comes to mind for me to say to a young man in this situation is that I will not preach to you. I will not tell you that once you learn to accept your gayness you will be happier. I will not encourage you to join a gay Christian church or give any other sort of unsolicited advice. There are plenty of well-intentioned folks who are sure to try to fix the way you are. I don't think you need to hear another voice encouraging you to just keep your chin up and be happy.

The second thing that comes to mind is to tell you that whatever choices you make about how to express or not express your sexuality, you are a wonderful, beautiful, precious gift to the world. Be the gift that you are. Nobody else can bring that gift to the world except you.

Don't just think about homosexuality. Feel what comes up for you around your sexuality. Be with your feelings, whatever they are. You can do no good by denying them. You may not know what those feelings are, and some of your deepest feelings may be so deeply buried that they are a mystery to you. Get help to be with your feelings from a therapist you are comfortable with and from friends with different points of view.

A word about friends: you are likely to change your opinions about God, the Bible, Christianity, homosexuality, sex, George W. Bush, and a whole host of other things many, many times. Your true friends will stick with you whether you are conservative or liberal, Christian or ex-Christian, gay or ex-gay. It's a cliché, but your true friends will accept you for you.

You are on a difficult path—bringing together your spirituality and sexuality—and you don't have to have all the answers. It's okay to be frightened, confused, and unsure where to turn. It's okay to question those who seem totally confident in their beliefs about homosexuality or Christianity. It's okay to doubt the dogmas of gay activists. It's okay to question the dogmas of the people in your Bible study group.

It's okay to flip-flop in your attitudes toward homosexuality—one moment thinking it's awesome with a hot man's body pressed against yours and the next praying to God to make you straight. It's okay to wonder if your faith (whether in God or the dogmas of the gay community) is genuine or if you're just kidding yourself.

What's not okay is to latch on to certainties that promise to make your life easier if you will only deny a little bit of reality. What's not okay is to just keep repeating something over and over again to yourself, figuring that if you just keep with it, you will eventually start to believe it.

It's okay to not know what to think about your homosexuality or God or the Universe. I heard Thomas Moore say recently that he doesn't know if everything in life happens for a reason. He said, "What I don't know, I don't know." I liked the sound of that. Enter deeply into the profound mysteries of life. Don't deny them. It's not always necessary to try to figure them out. Just try to accept the state of unknowing.

Tuesday, May 25

Yesterday, I finished reading a book called *The Art of Living: Vipassana Meditation as Taught by S. N. Goenka*. So far as I can tell, it's a pretty good book of practical instruction for meditation; however, a few irksome things jumped out at me. First, as I would expect from a Buddhist, when he speaks about sex it's always with an irritating heterosexist bias. Secondly, when Goenka speaks about the fruits of meditation, he says they include politeness, friendliness, and gentleness of language. Well, reading that just made me want to tell him to go fuck himself. *I want to grow. . . I don't want to be neutered!*

I'm planning to start beginners' meditation classes next week with a group called the Seattle Insight Meditation Society. It's humbling to think of myself as a "beginner," but I definitely am one with respect to meditation. With my Christian background, I've never really been encouraged to take up the practice of meditation. There's no need to meditate, according to Christian tradition, because Jesus Christ has done all the salvific work on our behalf.

Sure, I've done some things in the past that I've called meditation. But writing has been my principle spiritual practice in recent years, not meditation.

Meditation is a bendy, vague sort of word. It can mean just about anything, from sitting quietly and daydreaming to repeating a particular task over and over again. But meditation as taught by the Buddha is more serious and systematic, and it is something I've never done before, at least not in an ongoing, disciplined way. Am I finally ready to get started?

Friday, May 28

On my mind this morning: Do I have even more, as-yet-unacknowledged shadows that color my perception of teachings on homosexuality in the Christian churches? Are the charges I've leveled against conservative religionists—for instance, that they maintain the status quo of "heterosexual supremacy" by promulgating "antigay" or "homophobic" teachings—valid, or are my disowned shadows distorting my judgment?

As I begin to integrate more fully an evolutionary understanding of consciousness, I am beginning to come to greater acceptance of the world religions and their negative teachings on homosexuality as, perhaps, a necessary stage in the development of a higher consciousness. Could humanity have developed the notion that masculinity and femininity are deep structures, energies universally present in all things, had we not first passed through a stage of first identifying the principle of masculinity with biological males and femininity with biological females? Does a typical child learn to walk without first learning to crawl?

I shared these thoughts in an e-mail with men from one of my gay spirituality discussion lists. A few men immediately piped up to say that they thought I was off base. Judeo-Christianity really is nothing but evil, a bunch of bad people who've done bad things to innocent people all through history, and that's a fact (or so they said . . . and I do not exaggerate). To suggest an attitude of forgiveness toward homophobes based on spiritual evolution as I've done was "dangerous and irresponsible," said one, because it might be like "giving comfort to the enemy." Sigh. It's becoming increasingly difficult for me to find people who look at the world in roughly the same way that I do.

Sunday, May 30

My friend Ernie and I took a walk together around Greenlake for about an hour this morning. Ernie and I are both in the same men's group.

Today we talked about a variety of things, from my current health issues to Ernie's development along his spiritual path. He's a Buddhist and has for much of the past year followed a spiritual path called the Diamond Approach, a practice that integrates traditional spiritual practices with a psychological approach to healing. Ernie spoke of some of his frustrations with this practice. I listened earnestly and made an effort at understanding. But it was difficult to know what he's going through since I haven't done the practices he speaks about.

Ernie asked about my own current interests, and he let me talk for a while about the philosophy of Ken Wilber. I said that I just finished reading *The Eye of Spirit*, where Wilber discusses the Diamond Approach in a rather lengthy footnote. Generally, Wilber seems to think very highly of the Diamond Approach, praising it strongly on a wide variety of levels.

I mentioned that Wilber also offers one major criticism of the Diamond Approach. He says that to a certain extent it falls victim to something called the "pre/trans fallacy."

"It's a mind-blowing idea, really. And I'm still struggling with it. If the pre/trans fallacy is correct, then it shakes things up in terms of what I've been doing and how I've been doing it.

"The basic idea is this: there's a spectrum of consciousness that includes a variety of hierarchical, developmental stages. At one stage along the way, formal rational thought emerges. The stages that happen before rationality involve the instincts, emotions, sexuality, and so forth. The stages after rationality include higher spiritual states of awareness such as those

achieved by very experienced meditators—subtle states of intuitive awareness, truly psychic cognitions, a sense of Oneness with everything, those
sorts of things.

"The rational stage of development is the current average level of consciousness in our society, and it's at this stage that many people find themselves highly aware of the limits of rationality: its disembodied coldness, its
potential for creating a sense of alienation, and so forth. So people begin to
want something more than rationality. If they're running around in spiritual
circles, they may even begin to praise everything that's nonrational and disparage everything that's merely rational. This makes them vulnerable to the
pre/trans fallacy, namely the confusion of things that are merely prerational
with things that are truly transrational, or vice versa.

"Both pre- and trans- are nonrational, but that doesn't make them equiv-
alent. Pre- is more narcissistic, egocentric, and susceptible to superstition,
magical thinking, and other fallacies. Wilber says the concern is always
about expressing *my* feelings, owning *my* shadows, healing *my* wounds, getting into *my* body, loving *my* friends, that sort of thing . . . very ego bound.
Trans- means moving beyond the ego, and the sense of self is always wider,
higher, or deeper than the narrow self . . . the self is identified with a
higher Self or a greater whole, whether it's conceived of as Nature, Spirit,
or Emptiness.

"According to Wilber's argument, Freud and Jung both committed the
pre/trans fallacy, each in a different way. Freud saw the rational level as the
peak of human development and falsely believed that everything that is
truly transrational is really only prerational. So, in Freud's theory, even
mystical states are mistaken for infantile narcissism, regression, the future
of an illusion, and so forth. Freud and the Freudians are therefore reduc-
tionists.

"And Jung, according to Wilber, committed the fallacy in the opposite
direction: he tended to elevate a lot that's merely prerational to the transrational level, including magic, myth, divination, astrology, and the like. For
Wilber, it's important to be very careful about all these things, to distinguish the prerational elements from the authentically transrational elements, if there are any. Jung and Jungians like Joseph Campbell are frequently elevationists."

Ernie and I spoke more about the pre/trans fallacy and about how much of the spiritual work that we've both seen in the mythopoetic men's movement concentrates exclusively on the prerational side of things. The men's movement has been heavily influenced by Jungian archetypal psychology and Gestalt therapy, and these are two influences that stress the importance of strengthening the sense of self by incorporating repressed aspects of the self hiding in shadow.

There's no methodology in men's work that speaks to developing transrational levels of awareness. Nevertheless, it's quite common to hear men speaking of men's work as "spiritual." According to integral theory, that sort of talk can easily be elevationist: a confusion of that which is merely prerational with practices that contribute to development to transrational levels of awareness. In other words, men's work as we've seen it practiced actually focuses on integrating body (including feeling) and mind . . . not body, mind, and spirit.

"There's nothing wrong with focusing on body and mind," I explained to Ernie. "In fact, it can be very important work for many people—even spiritual, in a manner of speaking. But when I look at astrology and mythic archetypal work, the pre/trans fallacy seems awfully damning. These things have a place at the table, but they're not the whole table."

"Are you going to keep studying astrology?" Ernie asked.

"I don't know. I haven't been recently," I said. "Other things look a lot more interesting at the moment. I'm reading about integral theory. And I want to get serious about starting a meditation practice."

Monday, May 31

Last November 29, I began a series of entries in my journal called "The Importance of Being Gay." Here's the big picture that I painted:

- God, or Spirit, is the Source and Destiny of All and is manifest in all reality through the process of evolution in history. History is the story of the reconciliation of the Soul and the divine. Human beings are perfect manifestations of the Soul and, as such, are perfect reflections of God, or Spirit.

- All manifestations of reality are expressions of four principles, two fundamental qualities that we may call yin and yang, and two fundamental directions that we may also call yin and yang. The two fundamental qualities are manifest as the "horizontal," deep universal structures of masculine and feminine. The two fundamental directions are manifest as the "vertical," deep universal structures of Love, both same-directed love and other-directed love. I call those two directions homophilia and heterophilia, respectively.
- The two qualities and two directions of all things manifest at the root of all reality as four prime tenets or patterns (see figure 4): yin-yin, yang-yang, yin-yang, and yang-yin. The principle before the hyphen denotes the horizontal quality of the pattern, and the principle following the hyphen, the vertical. Gender and sexual orientations in their diversity teach us about these four archetypal patterns of all reality. Lesbians teach us about yin-yin, the principle of same-directed femininity. Straight men teach us about yang-yang, the principle of other-directed masculinity. Straight women teach us about yin-yang, the principle of other-directed femininity. And gay men teach us about yang-yin, the principle of same-directed masculinity.

While I had drawn from a variety of sources in coming up with this vision, I believed that it was unique . . . or, at the very least, something that I had never heard before. In particular, my definition of homophilia struck me as an important conception. Whereas most people regard homophilia merely as a synonym for gay love, I saw homophilia and heterophilia as deep universal structures equally available to all people, gay and straight, queer and nonqueer, alike.

Since I began keeping this journal, I have learned that several of the fundamental tenets of this vision have actually become widely accepted as part of a panentheistic world philosophy that has the support of many of the most subtle and gifted spiritual thinkers of our time. It seems that in the past few decades, there has emerged a widespread agreement among persons in many traditions that spirituality is an evolving process of greater integration and wholeness in self, culture, and nature. According to this

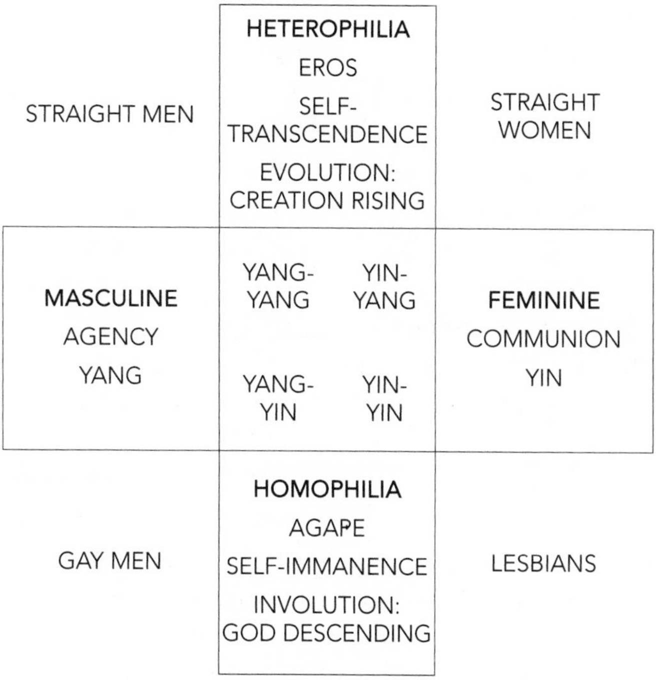

STRAIGHT MEN	HETEROPHILIA EROS SELF-TRANSCENDENCE EVOLUTION: CREATION RISING	STRAIGHT WOMEN
MASCULINE AGENCY YANG	YANG-YANG YIN-YANG YANG-YIN YIN-YIN	**FEMININE** COMMUNION YIN
GAY MEN	HOMOPHILIA AGAPE SELF-IMMANENCE INVOLUTION: GOD DESCENDING	LESBIANS

Figure 4. The 4 prime tenets of all holons (everything), the 4 prime patterns of all forms, and 4 analogous gender/sexual orientations.

vision, history is nothing less than an unfolding of Spirit, God, or Emptiness in our midst. These integral thinkers are merging the great wisdom of spirituality with the insights of science, systems theory, psychotherapy, and many other disciplines of knowledge. In the process, they are describing the deep structures of reality—the tenets of all holons—in ways that resemble the mythological and poetic account I gave in the "T.I.O.B.G." series.

Ken Wilber presents the idea that reality consists not of things or processes or elements or atoms, but of whole/parts, or holons. Examples of holons include an atom (part of a molecule), or a word (part of a sentence), or a child (part of a family). Saying that all reality is holonic is better than saying that all reality is composed of quarks, because it's a term that doesn't inappropriately reduce reality to one level (that of the material and physical, in the case of quarks). Drawing on vast research from many diverse disciplines of knowledge, Wilber argues that all holons are characterized by 20 tenets, or universal principles, that govern their behavior. Four of those principles are the primal drives of all holons. Everything in existence—natural and cultural, individual and social—is governed by these four drives. Those drives are agency, communion, self-transcendence, and self-immanence. Or masculinity, femininity, Ascent, and Descent. Or self-preservation, self-adaptation, evolution, and involution.

According to the work of integral thinkers such as David Deida, human gender and sexuality is also rooted in the four basic universal drives. Deida speaks of two universally valid sexual essences: masculine (yang) and feminine (yin). It's wrong to assume that masculine and feminine are, or aren't, related to each other in a specific sort of way. Nobody should assume that masculine and feminine are always attracted because "that's just the way things are." There must be one or more specific holonic tenets that describe how masculine and feminine are related. Those tenets are self-transcendence and self-immanence or, as I call them, heterophilia and homophilia. In self-transcendence, all holons transform through an interplay of masculine and feminine principles. Self-transcendence is the root drive underlying heterosexuality in all species. And in self-immanence, all holons transform through an interplay of masculine and masculine or feminine and feminine (that is, the holon turns inward on itself). Self-immanence is the root drive underlying homosexuality in all species.

If something like this theory is correct, and homophilia is indeed a manifestation of a universal principle, then it is possible to make a startling and fascinating connection. In ages past, poets and philosophers and Christian theologians have called the principle of self-immanence agape, the love of God for humanity. In the classic work *The Nature and Destiny of Man*, Reinhold Niebuhr concludes that self-sacrificial love lies at the heart of Christian revelation, symbolized generally by Christ and especially by the Cross. He argues that the Cross symbolizes God's love and reveals that suffering is not incompatible with divine perfection in history. He writes, "the agape of God is thus at once the expression of both the final majesty of God and his relation to history." For Niebuhr, agape was an ideal and yet an "impossible possibility," because of its tragic essence.

Agape is not merely a religious idea but an attribute of human nature. If I am correct, agape is one and the same as homophilia. Agape is the love of like for like, or the love of a self for a part of the self. It is the path of descent to matter and even toward self-dissolution. Same-directed love is not necessarily the same as narcissism, which is simply seeing everything in the universe as revolving around the self. Same-directed love is the love of a whole for a part. It is like the love of a molecule for an atom, a word for a letter, a flower for a petal, or water for hydrogen. It is an indispensable part of human nature and of the nature of all things.

Agape is traditionally seen as opposed to eros and is posited in the hierarchical and traditionalist thinking of the past as being superior to eros. This sort of hierarchy creates a false distinction; agape and eros are both equal and universal principles of everything. They are involution and evolution, respectively, the two fundamental directions of life and history. In eros, reality reaches out to the divine; in agape, the divine descends upon all of creation in an enfolding and transforming unity of presence.

David Deida once remarked of Ken Wilber that he "has thought for everyone who has ever tried to think their way to God, and he has thought them as far as thinking will take them."

Now, at last, with my understanding of homophilia situated happily within Ken Wilber's theory of everything, I seem to have arrived at a wall. A disturbing new thought occurs to me. Paradoxically, this thought is simultaneously terrifying and a source of serenity: The Search is over now, isn't it? Beyond this wall, can anything at all be said?

For so many years, my mind has restlessly quested for wisdom about the meaning of homosexuality in The Great Scheme of Things. I have sought to reconcile my sexuality with my spirituality, my homosexuality with my Christianity. Wisdom, it seems, has snuck up and bit me on the ass.

With this concept of homophilia, have I not at last taken my line of thinking as far as it can possibly go . . . to the very end of the line? Is there no deeper or higher thought about homosexuality and Spirit? Is there nothing else for the queer eye of mind to see?

4 Queer Eye of Spirit

Our normal waking consciousness is but one special type of consciousness, while all about it parted from it by the flimsiest of screens there lie potential forms of consciousness entirely different. We may go through life without suspecting their existence, but apply the requisite stimulus and at a touch they are there in all their completeness . . . No account of the universe in its totality can be final which leaves these other forms of consciousness disregarded. How to regard them is the question . . . At any rate, they forbid our premature closing of accounts with reality.
—WILLIAM JAMES

Wednesday, June 2

I've been bad. The Vipassana instructor gave everyone homework for this week, including 30 minutes of meditation per day. I haven't been doing it. It would be so easy for me to make excuses. But look, I signed up for the class; I'm gonna do it. No excuses here. I'm gonna just do it.

I'm not quite sure what's behind my resistance to actually beginning a meditation practice. When I talk about meditation, I feel like a child looking at the vegetables on his plate and being told to eat up because it's good for you. The Vipassana technique is really quite simple. You sit still and direct your attention to a chosen focus, which is usually your breath but can also be your body sensations or even your thoughts. When distractions arise during practice, you simply acknowledge them and then let them go.

I want to quiet my mind, but trying to do so seems to stir up uncomfortable things. I start thinking about my job, my bills, my health, the last book I read, or my next column—the usual monkey-mind chatter, as the Buddhists say. But it's not just thoughts that come to my mind but feelings as well—emotions that I usually keep at bay with distractions like watching TV or reading philosophy books.

The good thing about meditating in a group is that it helps me to just be with the monkey mind and start to experience longer moments of quietude and serenity. It's a bit easier when I'm not alone. Easier, but not easy.

Thursday, June 3

Just got a book in the mail: Jim Marion's *Putting on the Mind of Christ*. This book's a recommendation from Joseph Kramer. Today I read the foreword by Ken Wilber. He liked it. I think it's going to be a good one.

Friday, June 4

Damn it. I didn't do the Vipassana today, again. But I have been gradually increasing my mindfulness. Several times a day, I find myself simply turning my attention to my breath and bodily sensations for a few moments and thereby growing more and more present in the moment.

I try not to be hard on myself for resisting formal meditation practice. Perhaps it's just not the right time in my life for a meditation practice.

Sometimes I wonder if I'm not giving myself enough credit for the practices that I do all the time, like journaling, therapy, and my men's groups. Why should I feel obligated to meditate on top of everything else? It may not be a realistic expectation. Perhaps I'd be better off with a more practical, worldly practice like improving my culinary skills or getting to the gym for weight training more often.

Perhaps I have forgotten that practices don't have to be serious all the time. Ogling shirtless muscle men, having fun with my friends, and loosening up my tight ass can be worthwhile integral practices. Can't they? Or maybe I'm just making sloppy excuses for not doing my meditation. I don't know.

Saturday, June 5

I am reading the chapter "The Dark Night of the Senses" in Jim Marion's book. I see a description of the mystical state that happened to me at age 19. Although he writes about a level of consciousness, not a temporary state, I can tell from the description just how alike the experiences are. My experience seems to have been one called "infused contemplation" in the Christian tradition or "kundalini awakening" in some Eastern traditions. Although I didn't feel a rush of energy up the spine or encounter disturbing psychic phenomena, as some mystics report, I nevertheless experienced an intense joy next to which even sex pales in comparison (even drug-enhanced sex, I will note).

Following Marion's exposition, I can view my experience as an infusion of energy from one of the higher states of consciousness. Marion explains that the higher we ascend in consciousness, the lighter or less dense our consciousness becomes, in a manner of speaking. Growth in consciousness involves the transmutation of incoming fast-vibrating, subtle energies that result in changes from more slowly vibrating energies.

Now I am reading Marion's chapter on the Dark Night of the Soul . . . feeling uncomfortable . . . a sense of dread . . . reading quickly now . . . there are dangers . . . dark parts of the self . . . hallucinations . . . diseases. . . devils . . . bad angels . . . inner voices . . . negativity . . . kill the Buddha . . . emotional imbalances . . . parts of the person that are beyond the personality . . . the emotional suffering originates from unseen parts of the soul . . . the Christian is allowed to participate in the redemptive work of the Christ . . . Kosmic terror, Kosmic evil, Kosmic horror . . . I'm 29 again . . . I see visions . . .

horrible things . . . waking nightmares . . . my God, it's happening . . . I am running back and forth in my apartment in Wallingford between the toilet bowl and the gravity clock . . . visions of death . . . suffering . . . people, animals, machines, the spoiling of the earth . . . holocausts . . . inhuman betrayals, cruelty . . . pain, everywhere the pain . . . I want to go numb . . . I am falling . . . there is no separation between me and the world . . . there is no separation between me and (I dare not say it) . . . there is no separation between me and the visions . . . I see a toilet full of urine . . . I see a man reaching into his pocket for a knife . . . I see the sky overhead as I am falling from a tower . . . there is no separation, no separation . . . and there is death.

Sunday, June 6

Last night I stopped reading Jim Marion's book after the chapter on the Dark Night of the Soul. I let the pain of the world into my body for some time . . . I felt pain rip open my flesh . . . it seared me . . . it split me open . . . I became the pain . . . I fell on the floor and rolled around . . . I moaned, wailed, and cried . . . I identified with pain, but not quite . . . something in me was never just the pain, but was also a witness . . . I feared that the pain would consume all of me, swallow me whole, that there would be nothing else, only pain, nothing else . . . if I fell into the deep well of tears, felt my fear, touched my anger, there would be no bottom . . . none of these fears came to pass. I *included* pain, for a while, but I was not reduced to pain. I was something else . . . a *presence beyond*. A presence in which the pain was absent.

I cracked open the book again this morning. I read it all day and just finished it a few moments ago. The final chapter has got my head spinning. Could it be? Could it be? . . . Resurrection of the body . . . astral body . . . apparitions . . . appearances . . . spiritual being . . . veil of appearance . . . bilocation . . . I'm so humbled my knees are weak. Could I have been wrong about so many things all these years? Wrong about faith? Wrong even about the resurrection of Christ? And wrong about something else, too, a dim memory from nearly five years ago. Could I have been wrong about *that*?!

Jim Marion, thank you. You are beautiful! This book rocks my world.

Christ, I am confused . . . I have dried my eyes, but I am still in a tender place . . . I am . . . I am . . . heading to church?

Monday, June 7

After finishing Jim Marion's book yesterday, I ate Thai food on Broadway, where I was only a few blocks away from St. Mark's, the Episcopal cathedral. The Integrity Mass for gay and lesbian Episcopalians happened to be starting at 7:00 p.m., and the new movie *Harry Potter and the Prisoner of Azkaban* was starting at 7:05 p.m. at Pacific Place.

I remembered writing on my blog: "I am . . . heading to church?" and wondering if I should go. I picked the Harry Potter movie, but I gotta tell you, it was a close call. Very close.

Tuesday, June 8

Today I met with Harry, my therapist. I told him I was ready to begin telling the story of the events surrounding my 30th birthday. He told me to take my time and tell the story in the manner that seemed best to me.

"As my birthday approached, I was deeply unhappy in virtually every possible respect, and drugs and sex provided my only escape. I hated using them, but I had become powerless over my addictions. I tried to stop on my own and would make it a few weeks, but then I'd find myself filled with such overwhelming sensations of despair that only getting high could take away the pain.

"Throughout 1999, with a deliberate effort of the will, I managed to slowly wean myself from my addictions. But then I would occasionally snort crystal on weekends. On these occasions, I noticed something seemed a little odd. The high seemed to be duller and last longer than I was used to, even days longer than I expected. And I could simply sit for one or two days in an intense dreamlike state, eating little and sleeping not at all, when by all rights I should have been coming down from the drug-induced high. During these states of consciousness, my mind would begin to drift into bizarre streams of visions that seemed to come into my head from somewhere else entirely."

"Visions. What sort of visions?" asked Harry.

"I don't quite know how to describe them. There's a word for shooting stars . . . what do you call them?"

"Are you talking about phosphenes?"

"That sounds about right. When the eye adapts itself to darkness you can see wispy clouds and specks of light, colors and illuminations. Sometimes the visions would start out in that way. I would see the light images and entertain myself with their geometries, textures, and motions. As the hours passed, I would sit in this state of absorption until the visions became more intense. You know the Ray Bradbury book called *The Illustrated Man* where a man's tattoos come alive? I guess you could say it was a little bit like that. After a while, the tattoos began to talk.

"I suppose I've been watching the images behind my eyes for my whole life. As a child, I used to find it very difficult to fall asleep. I would often lay awake for hours and play in my imagination while rolling around under the covers. Those were times when I taught myself to watch the images and to play with them in my mind's eye. Everyone can see phosphenes. That's pretty normal, isn't it?"

Harry shrugged.

"Well, those are the sorts of visions that I'm talking about, except there's normal and then there's what started happening to me. I last used drugs near the end of July of 1999. In the weeks that followed, I began to experience a dramatic mood shift. Feelings of sadness faded and euphoria took their place. I experienced a high that persisted night and day, and I lacked appetite and desire for sleep. However, I hadn't relapsed. I hadn't taken anything. Something had changed all by itself.

"Although my condition seemed unusual, I didn't immediately perceive it to be a reason for alarm. I went on the Internet to look for possible explanations for my symptoms. I considered the possibility that I could be experiencing bipolar disorder. I also considered the possibility that I could be having an unusual reaction to an HIV medication or some sort of drug withdrawal symptom. I understood that sleep deprivation could have been contributing to my condition.

"I phoned my doctor and set an appointment to see him as soon as possible, which was just a few days away. However, I never made it to the appointment. My moods began to shift once again.

"I began to notice unusual changes in my apprehension of self, others, thought, space, and time. Sadly, I lack the words to speak of these changes with clarity. The physical and mental worlds suddenly seemed to be more connected than I had ever imagined. I began to see connections between things that I hadn't before. I fantasized about starting a new Internet company that would create a directory to finally bring a sense of order to the World Wide Web. I wrote down many of my thoughts in a notebook.

"In this state, common, everyday objects seemed to have a depth and aliveness to them that I had never before known. I began to look at everything as if I were seeing it for the first time. Frequently I began to see new applications for the things around me and began to come up with ideas for inventions. When my mind turned to conventional problems of business, science, or politics, I immediately began to see that the usual way of thinking was grossly inadequate. I began searching for new, more expansive ways of looking at things.

"Familiar people seemed unfamiliar or mysterious. Nothing in the world was as it seemed. Everything was changing . . . or was it just me? I was changing into something new . . . but what? I didn't know.

"I felt a sense of omniscience and omnipotence that's difficult to describe. I believed I had abilities that some might see as nearly miraculous, though not in the sense of being supernatural or magical. I believed I was capable of much more than I had ever previously realized, that I could learn very quickly, retain more knowledge, and understand things at a deeper and more complete level than ever before. For example, I've never been able to carry a tune in my life. However, I became convinced that should I choose to take voice lessons, I would sing beautifully within a short period of time.

"Although it had been years since I had taken piano lessons, I believed that I could suddenly recall how to play a complex song that I had learned when I was a child, the main theme of John Williams's *Close Encounters of the Third Kind* . . . and I believed that if I had access to a piano, perhaps I could even play the tune backward. Now that belief seems ludicrous. But at the time, I seemed to be tapping into something far more powerful and creative than anything I had ever before experienced or known. It was thrilling, exciting . . . and frightening. I strove to understand what was happening to me, and my head became filled with a number of crazy ideas about what it all might mean. I was certain that if anybody knew the thoughts running through my head, they would want to lock me away, so I kept my ideas private. I put up an emotional wall around myself, because I was afraid of how people would react if they knew the truth.

"Waking dreams or visions streamed freely through my consciousness, and I wrote some of them down. It all seems so bizarre and grandiose; I'm embarrassed to speak of it. I think I saw myself becoming some sort of prophet in the future. I'm not sure.

"Once, after spending an entire evening writing down a stream of visions in a spiral notebook, I went to a hospital emergency room with my notebook still in hand. I wanted them to draw blood from me. I got them to do so, and they ran some tests. I remember speaking to a nurse and doctor. They noted that I seemed dehydrated and made me drink a lot of water, but they didn't seem to take my situation that seriously. I even showed the doctor my notebook and explained that I had been writing in an altered state of consciousness for many hours. I showed him this picture I drew of the earth with a pole running through it from Seattle to Africa and talked wildly about Bill Gates and a cure for AIDS. Pretty crazy shit.

"The doctor said, 'It's good that you recognize that this isn't normal.' And that was it. They sent me home.

"I still wasn't sleeping. The next day, the visions continued; some of them grew very disturbing and frightening, and I prayed that they would not return. I saw visions of the world's history and future flashing before my eyes, and little of it made any sense. Images of holocausts and catastrophes and death on a wide scale left me gasping with horror. They included the stuff you would expect to see in science-fiction and horror movies, and half of them didn't seem at all plausible. There were ridiculous, impossible visions. I didn't want to see these things, and yet I felt connected to them, unable to shut them off.

"During this time, I began to hear and see things that were not normal perceptions. I heard whispering voices and coughing noises everywhere in my apartment and believed I was being continuously watched by unseen entities. I had no idea what was real and what wasn't. No, that's not right. Things were happening around me that seemed very real, but I also recognized that these things were impossible according to my usual understanding of the world. In order to stay grounded in what seemed very real to me, I had to stretch my imagination to believe that maybe, just maybe, the world was very different than I had ever imagined. Things were happening all around me that I could not explain—except by believing in what other people would see as bizarre, insane notions. Suddenly, the insane seemed quite sane.

"On my birthday, I dined with my family at a Mexican restaurant near my home in Wallingford. They were all very concerned about me. I was talking but not making a lot of sense. I took pity on them but felt unable to explain to them what was happening. There was no way they could understand, so I tried to speak about things that they could understand. I also believed that secrecy was very important, so I sometimes spoke in code and hoped they would somehow be able to decipher my language. I spoke about this idea I had for an Internet company and how they might be able to help me get it off the ground. I don't think I was talking about an Internet company at all, not really.

"At one point during the meal, I had the distinct perception that time itself had momentarily skipped around. It was as if my life were playing before me on rolls of film, and one roll had just wound down to an abrupt halt and caught the projectionist dozing for a few moments. Reality itself seemed to be crumbling before my very eyes. I don't know how to describe it. One moment seemed to stretch out for a long while, and then everything got really distorted and very clear all at the same time. The experience left me gaping in awe and literally breathless. In a moment, time returned to a normal flow. Nevertheless, I was stunned and in disbelief. *These things just don't happen.*

"A few moments later, I was inundated with a series of paranoid thoughts. I had the notion that the end of the world as we knew it could be near and that dark forces I could only imagine were afoot in the world. This *was* the end of the millennium, after all. I grew very anxious and wanted to go home. I had little appetite, a high energy level, and few inhibitions. The visions, the terrible fears, the growing sense of connection to everything and everyone around me, the emergence in my awareness of patterns underlying ordinary reality—this flood of sensations and meanings and confusion simply overwhelmed me. I completely lost it.

"We left the Mexican restaurant and returned to my apartment. That's when reality as I knew it seemed to be caving in all around me, revealing itself as a hollow shell. The walls of my apartment seemed to be closing in. Everything seemed not only unfamiliar but also ominous and foreboding. All around me, I saw layer upon layer of deception and mystery . . . more whispers, coughing noises coming from behind the walls. Questions frantically crowded my mind: Who was there? What did they want with me? What was happening to me? Why was this happening? Was I about to die? Was I already dead?

"I ran outside my apartment and barged into the neighbor's unit. My brother came and got me and brought me upstairs, and everyone was awfully scared.

"Someone in my family must have called for an ambulance, for paramedics soon showed up. I didn't see them arrive. By the time they came up the stairway to my apartment, I was balled up into a fetal position on the living room floor. I didn't want to go. I felt myself shrinking and disappearing. I saw blinding, suffocating white light.

"I resisted the paramedics' efforts to haul me away. I didn't want to go. As the men put a straightjacket on me, I laughed and shouted obscenities, many of them of a sexual nature. I didn't believe any of it was real; I seemed not to be myself at all but a witness to a strange movie of my life. Part of me stood above it all as a witness and held an attitude of joy, amusement, and wonder. It was an amazing ride. Forces beyond my control were pulling me forward to something unknown, a destination I could not imagine."

Harry and I finished the hour's counseling session. He asked how I felt. I explained that I felt comfortable telling the story and not nearly as fearful as I had expected.

My worst fear, barely conscious, was that if I started to remember or talk about the experiences, then I would go crazy again. That wasn't happening, so I felt great relief. But the next set of events that I would describe, I said, I've kept private. I've been holding on to them for five years . . . was I ready to let them go?

I set an appointment with Harry for next week. We made the appointment for two hours.

Thursday, June 10

Just thinking out loud about whether or not to join the Unitarian Universalist religion. As I've written before, I've long held the UUs in very high esteem, as something of an ideal for religious liberalism. And the UU has long been the frontrunner in my search for a religious community with which to affiliate.

But ask me today and I'd say I'm leaning against joining the UU. I've been following some UU blogs, one of which recently featured a conversation entitled "UU Atheists: An Endangered (and Embattled) Species?" The dialogue opens with a post explaining a major controversy that happened when the UU president wanted to insert "God language" into the UU principles. It turns out that he denied ever wanting to do any such outrageous thing, but the controversy terribly upset atheists and skeptics within the UU religion, who began to feel marginalized and oppressed. One UU atheist opined on a blog: "I do not believe in God. I do not believe in divinity. I do not believe in the supernatural (noncorporeal spirit). Why must I subjugate my beliefs and lie for the sake of UU unity?"

I don't need to keep a lot of philosophical or theological options on the table, like a dinner at a smorgasbord. So how would it serve my relationship with Spirit to participate in an organization with a wide variety of people who deny even the possibility of transcendence . . . and others who believe in a literal sort of sky-spirit god . . . all of us trying to force ourselves to keep communal religious language and practices so generic that nobody would ever feel marginalized? I'm afraid that being in religious community with folks with such radically different spiritual orientations would be very unsatisfying. I'm afraid we would always have to police ourselves, stripping away the language and practices that we were most comfortable with for some sort of lowest-common-denominator type of language. I'm afraid that political correctness would force us to deny the reality of hierarchical stages to spiritual development, because it would be horribly insensitive to suggest that some beliefs might be more adequate or true than others.

The very thought of worshiping in this way seems strange to me. In the words of the UU atheist, why should he subjugate his belief that no spiritual realities exist for the sake of UU unity? I don't think that he should. Why should I subjugate my belief that Spirit exists for the sake of political correctness? I'm not going to do that. I'm not sure that it would serve my spiritual growth at all to join the Unitarians at this time. In fact, I'm pretty sure that it would drive me bonkers.

Friday, June 11

Gay Mystics Take the Direct Route to God

There have been mystics in virtually every religion and even among those with no religion. *Merriam-Webster's* dictionary defines mysticism as "the reported experience of mystical union or direct communion with ultimate reality." Mystics report that direct knowledge of God, spiritual truth, or ultimate reality is the deepest core of spirituality.

Gay men, bisexuals, and lesbians have been among the mystics who have reported a union with ultimate reality. Andrew Harvey and Jim Marion are two contemporary gay men whose lives bear witness to encounters with ineffable mysteries.

In *Putting on the Mind of Christ*, Jim Marion describes how the life, death, and resurrection of Jesus offer people today an authentic mystical path. He says that the only reason for religion to exist is to advance human consciousness, leading ultimately to mystical awareness.

Jesus's teaching and his death and resurrection were meant to show human beings the way to the highest levels of consciousness, says Marion. Jesus said, "The Father and I are one" and "He who sees me sees the Father." Jesus not only saw a lack of separation between himself and God but also that this essential nonseparation from God was true for the rest of us.

The problem with Christianity, Marion convincingly argues, is that the vast majority of Christian elders, ministers, priests, bishops, and popes have not yet grown enough spiritually to see the world as Jesus saw it. They misunderstand Jesus's teachings because they have not yet "put on the mind which was in Christ Jesus" (Phil. 2:5).

Like many contemplatives, Marion did not attain his insights overnight. From early childhood to the present, Marion has spent many years in daily religious prayer and contemplation, often for hours at a time. He had his first mystical experience at age 15 and later joined a Catholic monastery, where he remained for seven years.

After one spiritual experience at the monastery, Marion became aware of his repressed homosexuality. Even after coming out of the closet, he continued his life of prayer and contemplation and experienced increasingly deeper degrees of unity with God. His life is a model for one who has sought, and found, Christ Consciousness.

Marion tells of experiencing the Dark Night of the Soul, a perilous journey to the depths of his psyche. He promised God that he would keep an "absolutely open mind" on the subject of same-sex sexual expression. If, in the depths of his psyche, he found something "wrong" with or pathological about gay sex, he would accept the traditional Christian proscription against such activity.

However, he says, amidst his experiences of union with the divine, "I found nothing of the kind. In fact, I found striking evidence to the contrary." Same-sex sexual expression generated psychic healing for Marion that helped him to grow to higher levels of mystical awareness.

He says that if it were not for the great spiritual power liberated by his sexual activity, he would never have experienced key spiritual breakthroughs. "Regarding the morality of same[-sex] sexual expression," he writes, "I now consider the case closed."

Harvey shares some of his research in *The Essential Gay Mystics*, an anthology he edited. He writes: "I wanted everyone, most of all my gay brothers and sisters to be aware that there is no authentic witness in our Western culture or in that of any other culture, of the divine itself in any way excluding homosexuals from its love."

A contemporary interfaith mystic, Harvey has written and edited more than thirty books. He lives in Las Vegas with his husband. Harvey also offers workshops where he encourages gay men and lesbians to learn about the heritage of gay mystics. He believes mysticism teaches us to shed dogma and claim a spiritual way he calls the Direct Path.

A key to understanding homosexuality is the realization that the Source of all reality is a unity that both includes and transcends both the masculine and feminine, says Harvey.

According to Harvey, gay persons of both genders have been widely regarded as among the spiritual elites in cultures and societies around the world. Even cultures that haven't tolerated or accepted gay sex have nevertheless quietly accepted the contributions of many talented gay spiritual leaders in their midst.

Harvey's book examines a wide variety of mystical writings by a diverse group of gay individuals (or persons who would probably be called gay if they were alive today). These include Sappho, Sophocles, Plato, Virgil, Horace, Basho, Michelangelo, and Walt Whitman, as well as less-well-known figures from Native American and Islamic traditions.

Although the gay mystics included in this book come from many different religions, Harvey focuses on an important common thread uniting many of them. Gay mystics reject false separations such as that between God and human beings, and between humans and nature. In the place of false boundaries, gay mystics seek to live instead "as one constantly explosive dance of divine energy, love, and bliss, interconnected in all of its events and particulars."

Tuesday, June 15

As I drove to my therapy session this morning, I began to go over my last session in my mind. Something struck me as very interesting.

I realized that during the time before I entered the hospital, I seemed to be experiencing a new dimension or space. I knew things but had no idea how I knew them. The visions seemed to be coming from this place. Some of the thoughts that were coming into my head seemed also to be coming from this place. The books I've been reading that describe the higher realms of consciousness refer to experiences like these as accessing a psychic or astral realm of being.

There was just one problem: rationally, I don't (or didn't?) believe in psychic phenomena. I had frequently dismissed most psychic phenomena as bunk, a combination of superstition and charlatanism. I'd never before really considered the possibility that not only might psychic phenomena be real but I might actually have had an experience of a psychic state of awareness. Now . . . suddenly . . . it was all coming together.

Now that I looked back over my experiences from my 30th birthday, I realized that for the past five years, I've regarded my experiences in the hospital as a sort of massive hallucination. And I don't doubt there was a certain amount of distortion, bad interpretation, and even psychotic delusion involved. But what if my experiences were actually experiences of a higher state of consciousness? What if there was more reality to them than I'd previously assumed?

I thought of Wilber's pre/trans fallacy once again. What struck me a few weeks ago about this idea was how it forced me to question the extent to which I had mistaken prerational mental phenomena for authentically transrational experiences, when in truth they probably were a mixture of both. Now, I have begun to wonder about the other side of the fallacy. What if I have mistaken my past experiences with transrational states of consciousness for prerational delusions? What if, rather than mere hallucinations, my experiences in the hospital were actual encounters with some kind of spiritual realm?

I arrived at my counselor's office and began to pick up where I left off last week.

"As I lay in a straightjacket in a holding room at the hospital, I actually believed that holy men and women were observing me from a hidden room above the ceiling. I believed that saints from every religion, perhaps even the pope and the Dalai Lama, had gathered in secrecy in Seattle. I couldn't see or hear the holy men and women, but I could feel their presence. I believed that they had the power to communicate with me but were choosing instead to observe, perhaps as some sort of test. I simply knew these things, though I couldn't explain how.

"I am embarrassed to even talk about this, because it seems so obviously delusional and narcissistic. Today, I look back and it seems egomaniacal and goofy. I know that I'm just one more guy who had a . . . whatever the hell it was. I hear that when somebody becomes enlightened in a Zen monastery, the Zen master will whack the student upside the head and say it's no big deal. Enlightenment happens. Get over it. But back then, in the hospital, the experience seemed so extraordinary! I believed that I was very unique and special for this to be happening to me. But I can't tell anyone what's happening to me, because they'll think I'm crazy and lock me up. Too late! Looks like I'm already locked up. I better not tell the doctors the truth, because they might never let me out. It's best to take whatever drugs they give to get me normal again, as much as I don't want to be.

"Although I was kept in one room with a closed door and could scarcely hear any noises from within the hospital, I began to hear the sounds of crowds of people in the background. I could make out the low hum of shouting, screams, banging noises, and unfamiliar sounds that vaguely resembled the shattering of glass. At the time, I believed that there were riots in the streets of Seattle. I felt safe within the hospital, but I wondered what was going on and if it was in any way connected to what was happening with me. Of course I did! Everything in the world seemed to be revolving around me.

"The whole time I was in this holding room, I remember there was this presence in the room, a spirit of some kind. I'm not even sure that I believe in spirits. I never used to. I used to think that I hallucinated the whole thing, that it was nothing but one big psychotic break with reality. I was communicating for hours with this invisible presence, watching it as I sensed it move throughout the room. I would ask it questions and then hear replies in my head . . . psychically, I guess.

"I don't remember much about my conversations with the spirit now, but it seems to me that I was very curious about the spirit's identity and regarded it as something like a certain godlike alien character played by John de Lancie on *Star Trek: The Next Generation*. I even gave him a name. I called him Q, after the *Star Trek* character.

"Q was a practical jokester who seemed to be really having a lot of fun at my expense. I remember sensing that it was connected to me in some intimate way, and I asked if the spirit might be my future self in some sense. But I don't recall what I found out. Maybe it was, maybe it wasn't. It was hard to get straight answers out of Q, because he was such a joker.

"Later, I was relocated to another room of the hospital and my restraints were removed. I lay alone on a bed in the darkness. I continued to hear faint riot noises in the background. While I was in this room, I believed that family, friends, colleagues, and teachers from my past had come to visit me. I believed that they were literally behind the walls, observing me unseen. There were twelve of them. Although I couldn't see them, I could feel their presence. I just "knew" they were there. I felt the presence of each friend, male and female, and was often surprised at who had shown up. I could only guess at their identities based on this inner knowing that I had. I could sense their movements around the exterior of the room, behind the walls. They all seemed to be aware of my feelings and thoughts, and I felt very comfortable in their company.

"I felt tremendous joy to have them there with me. I didn't understand that there weren't flesh and blood human beings behind the walls. Actually, today I am beginning to see this experience in a very different way. I think they were, perhaps, spirits. It sounds all woo-woo, I know. But that's the best explanation I can give. I'm not sure why I didn't understand at the time that they were spirits, but I didn't. Maybe if I had had a belief in spirits, I would have recognized them for what they were. But I didn't. At the time, I thought there were actually physical human beings behind the walls.

"Unlike the saints and holy men and women whom I had sensed earlier in the holding room, these spirits seemed to know me intimately. They were friends. They were delighted to be spending time with me. I felt protected, guarded, and loved by them. And I could even communicate directly with one of them.

"There was one friend—one spirit or whatever—who could communicate directly with me. I sensed that this entity was a man. I held contradictory beliefs about this man. On the one hand, I believed that he was someone whom I'd known all of my life . . . on the other hand, I believed that I'd never really known him, that he had appeared in my life only in disguise. I also believed that he was some sort of lover or soul mate . . . but I was uncertain whether we had actually ever met, at least in this lifetime. I began to wonder about reincarnation, which I didn't believe in at the time, because I had no other way to make sense of these feelings.

"I have never been happier in my life than when I was communicating with this man. I could not see him—he was behind the wall of my room—but I could sense his presence and emotions in a vague way that's difficult to describe. I desperately wanted a deeper connection to him, so I began to speak questions aloud to him. He responded by playing musical tones. I actually heard the tones. I wondered if my ears were deceiving me, because I couldn't recognize the musical instrument on which the tones were being played. When I got out of the hospital, I believed that the tone was merely an auditory hallucination; but at the time, nothing in the world seemed more real. I learned to interpret the tones as either 'yes' or 'no' answers.

"I asked many questions of this man. I don't recall if I was actually voicing the questions out loud after a while, or if I was simply thinking them. In any case, I could hear tones in response. The fact that I could get responses (unpredictable, often surprising answers) to questions struck me as a sort of proof that I was experiencing something extraordinary . . . and something real. This was a wonderful time. I felt so joyous and alive. I found myself frequently bursting out with laughter. It was a delight to be in the company of this man . . . and the rest of the spirits, or entities, or whatever they were. Because I had been laughing loudly for hours on end, nurses came to check on me once or twice.

"While I was in this room, I laughed so hard I shit my pants. And I thought that was really funny, too. Eventually a nurse came and escorted me down the hall to a room with a shower. This proved to be an amazing journey. Everything in the hospital seemed bizarre and unfamiliar, alive with fluidity and sensuality and beauty. The sight of a towel seemed most extraordinarily beautiful. There was something interesting about the towel, something about the color blue. I don't remember. Anyways, I wanted to reach out and touch everything. I wondered if I was, perhaps, traveling through time, and if it was a decade or more in the future. Nothing seemed to be familiar. The whole world was new.

"In my mental state, the knob of the shower was almost too complicated for me to operate. I stood naked in the shower but had no knowledge of how to make the thing emit water. I pushed and pulled on it, and truly made an effort to figure the thing out. But I just couldn't seem to wrap my mind around this problem. The nurse shouted instructions from the other side of the room, but I was incapable of listening to her and operating the shower knob at the same time. Eventually I stumbled on the solution by trial and error and cleaned myself off. That's when I became aware how different my state of consciousness was from ordinary reality. I seemed to have regressed to a point where even the capacities of a young child were beyond me. However, at the same time, I believed that I had, perhaps, evolved to a point where the way the world usually functioned was counterintuitive and that I could help to redesign the world to make it more beautiful, functional, and harmonious. After toweling myself off in the shower, I got into a wheelchair and let a nurse wheel me back to my room.

"But there's one more thing."

I paused.

"What is it?" asked Harry.

"I'm not sure . . . there's something here I don't want to talk about. I sense resistance in me, and I suppose I should explore the reasons for it."

"As the nurse rolled me down the hall, I saw something—something I don't understand. I saw a man. He didn't say anything; he was just looking at me. He was extraordinarily beautiful. He had olive skin, dark hair, and dark eyes. He seemed to have a timeless beauty. Although I had never seen him before, I felt a powerful connection to him. I began to know things about him, but I didn't know how I knew them. I believed he was there, because I was there. I believed he was waiting for me, waiting to take me away to another place, a happier place. I felt a passionate, erotic longing for him in every fiber of my being . . . and yet I felt that somehow it wasn't time for us to be together.

"There's something about West Seattle here, but I can't quite remember.

"I wondered if he was, perhaps, waiting to take me away to someplace where we could make love for a very, very long time. I believed he knew me from someplace else—another lifetime, perhaps. I knew all this about him somehow, and yet he never spoke a word. I don't understand. His eyes followed mine. He beheld me with an expression of complete love and compassion."

As I spoke about this man, I began to cry. The tears took me completely by surprise. They came spontaneously and lasted quite some time.

Harry and I spent time together while the feelings passed.

"I have no idea why I'm crying," I said. "I had no idea these feelings were there . . . I don't know why I feel so sad when I think about this man."

I gave Harry a look as if I expected him to explain it all to me. He just sat there in the silence.

"I don't know . . . I don't know why . . . except . . . if I did know . . . I get a powerful feeling of love just thinking about him . . . and yet it wasn't time for us to be together . . . and . . . *I never saw him again . . .*"

Suddenly, the feeling of sadness filled me once more, and I sobbed uncontrollably. When my eyes began to dry, I finally understood.

"I'm beginning to get it now," I said. "For almost five years, I've carried this inside me . . . this love, this feeling of bliss . . . and, side by side with it, the horrible pain of believing I had been abandoned . . . I never even knew the love was there, because I wasn't willing to feel it. I sort of forgot. Forgot, but not really. I thought it was all merely a delusion. Spirits? Reincarnation? Soul mates from the beyond? That's woo-woo shit. Better to believe that I merely went crazy. I thought I made it all up, that it was just a trick of the mind and senses. Now I wonder: was he even human, a flesh-and-blood human being . . . or something else? How could he be a spirit and still be a man physically sitting in the hallway? What was he? I don't know."

"He was sitting in the hallway?" asked Harry as he scribbled down a note in his pad.

"Yes," I said.

"Go on. I just missed that part," said Harry.

"Yes, there was a man sitting on a bench in the hallway outside my hospital room. Sitting there just as you are sitting across the room from me in your chair. The nurse took me right past him on the way to my shower, and I got a good look. He watched me the whole time. After I was finished with my shower, he was still there, just sitting on the bench.

"I told you that when I was in the room with the spirits, there was one man who could communicate with me. At the time, I believed that there was somebody literally on the other side of the wall of my hospital room — one friend, one very special friend who was playing these musical notes, a lover who alone could communicate with me, when all the others couldn't

. . . Well, when the nurse took me outside the room to take a shower, *there he was!* At the time, I thought he was a real, flesh-and-blood human being. I didn't touch him, but I knew that he was as physically real as the wheelchair, the bench, or the nurse. And later, after the doctors gave me drugs to bring me back down to earth, I thought he was just a hallucination. I didn't think he was real. How could he be?"

"What do you mean by real?" asked Harry.

"I mean . . . I don't know . . . Maybe he was just some guy visiting someone in the hospital. But the whole time I saw him, I sensed this energy exchange between us . . . I sensed a deep and profound connection, and a knowingness . . . If he were a spirit visitor . . . I don't know how to make sense of that. I mean, if he was a spirit and a flesh-and-blood human being, really there, sitting on a bench in the hallway, how is that possible? An astral body? A spirit body? I saw him, but I don't understand. Was I hallucinating? Delusional? This beautiful man, this spirit, this puzzle, this mystery, whatever he was, I saw him . . . I felt loved . . . I loved him . . . He loved me . . . whatever else I believe about it, the love was real."

Harry and I spoke for more than another hour, and I shared with him many more things.

Wednesday, June 16

Bipolar disorder (also known as manic depression) is an illness marked by extreme changes in mood, energy, and behavior. In acute episodes of mania, erratic thoughts and even psychosis are possible. After my breakdown five years ago, the doctors diagnosed me with bipolar I, the most extreme form of the illness.

They told me that I was a manic-depressive, and I believed them. For a while. I took the mood stabilizers that they prescribed. However, the more I learned about bipolar disorder, the more doubts I had about the diagnosis. I thought that I was probably too old for this diagnosis to be credible. My family history didn't match what the books said it should be. My life experiences were difficult for me to put into the mold. I did not perceive myself as having extremely fluctuating moods; if anything, I saw myself as having a calming and stabilizing influence on others. The doctors said they knew better than I about all these things; but they didn't know me, and I didn't really believe them.

Another possible medical explanation for my breakdown seemed more plausible than bipolar disorder: crystal meth withdrawal. Methamphetamine has been known to cause psychotic states months and even years after its use has been discontinued. My psychiatrist at the time was a man whose patients included many recovering users of meth. He reported that crystal users were, in his experience, susceptible to "flashbacks" in which they became high weeks or months after discontinuing use of the drug. Such highs would frequently mimic the symptoms of bipolar illness, including psychotic delusion. His insights resonated with my own experience and with what I had heard from other recovering drug users.

If my experience had been caused by a freak side effect of drug withdrawal, then I wasn't really bipolar. I figured that I should be able to discontinue the mood stabilizers without adverse consequence. When I did so, in the summer of 2000, it was not by choice but because the drug caused a life-threatening condition: acute pancreatitis. I spent ten days in a hospital on a morphine drip for excruciating pain and couldn't eat or drink anything for days. Not fun. I was already skeptical about the wisdom of continuing to take psychiatric drugs to treat a mental illness that I didn't think I had. Now I was convinced.

From that time until the present day, I have chosen to self-monitor my moods rather than take psychiatric medication. I have not known mania. Sometimes I encounter temporary dark moods, but so far I've been able to manage them with talking therapies and 12-step meetings. With each year that passes symptom free, the bipolar diagnosis looks increasingly improbable.

Going mad is pretty bad. But the funny thing is, it's just happened to me once. Perhaps I'm fooling myself, but I've begun to think that it was simply an aberration and won't happen again.

I've noticed that there has been a connection in my life between elevated moods and mystical experiences, as with the experience on my 30th birthday. Trying not to confuse the two or reduce one to the other is a challenging business. The scientific and spiritual interpretations of a mystical experience aren't incompatible; they are simply two different angles from which one can look at the same experience. In integral theory, the scientific approach of reducing an experience to abnormal brain chemistry is viewed as a function of the objective, individual quadrant, whereas the spiritual view, which sees the experience as disclosing dimensions of authentic reality, is understood in terms of the subjective, individual quadrant.

Mania can produce grandiose delusions and an inflated sense of self-importance (been there). And authentic spiritual experiences can produce a profound felt sense of the interconnectedness of all things and of the unity of all reality (done that). Those are two different things: the former, a regression to prerational states; the latter, an experience of authentic trans-rational realities.

I believe it's possible for psychosis and authentic spiritual experiences to occur simultaneously. That's true, I think, of my own experience. Of course, all spiritual experiences are subject to interpretation, and the delusional person will interpret an authentic experience through a very bad lens. As for the relationship between elevated moods and mystical states, it's not helpful for me to think of it as a cause-and-effect relationship in either direction.

Thursday, June 17

"No self-respecting gay person can remain in the Roman Catholic Church."

Yes, that's what I found myself telling someone today. I think that was too harsh. I really need to watch my temper. That probably was not a very "integral" thing to say. I should have said only that I personally found it impossible to retain my self-respect while remaining in the Roman Catholic Church. Others can decide for themselves.

That's not to say that the Episcopal/Anglican church isn't still a respectable spiritual choice for a self-respecting gay; in fact, it's one that I am actively considering. The funny thing is, though, every weekend comes along and I say to myself: maybe I'll go to church this Sunday. And then Sunday morning comes along, and I don't much feel like it. There's always something more interesting to do, like sleeping in.

I don't want to go to church just because I feel like I have to go out of duty. I don't want to join a church the way a typical voter votes for a politician—choosing the lesser of available evils. I want—how did I put it once?—a spiritual path that I can step into with both feet. I want to be passionate about everything I do. I want to feel excited about stepping into a place of community. And with the Episcopal Church, I'm just not feeling the enthusiasm. Nearly every day it seems there's another story in the news about conservative Episcopalians trying to foment schism because these so-called Christians are hostile to gays and want to keep them out of positions of leadership. They want to preserve teachings on "traditional sexual morality" that characterize gays as disordered misfits whose love lives are abominations. Not terribly surprising that I have trouble getting out of bed on Sundays to be part of an organization like that.

Saturday, June 19

A Map to the Kingdom of Heaven

Jim Marion's *Putting on the Mind of Christ* is the first book to articulate a vision of how integral theory and Christianity can be seamlessly put together. The central insight of Marion's book is that Jesus's teaching and his death and resurrection were meant to show human beings the way to the highest levels of consciousness. From this vantage point, he traces the entire spiritual path of the Christian, from the consciousness of infants to the nondual awareness of the Kingdom of Heaven, where saints and mystics have finally seen the truth that there is no separation between God and human beings. Jesus said, "The Father and I are one" and "He who sees me sees the Father."

Marion convincingly demonstrates that nondual consciousness is the essence of Jesus's Gospel proclamation of the Kingdom of Heaven. Furthermore, "not only did Jesus see this truth for himself, but he saw that this essential non-separation from God was also true for the rest of us."

The heart of Jesus's teaching was the Kingdom of Heaven, Marion says, something that could be realized by each and every person while on earth. Jesus promised his disciples that some of them would not pass away without first seeing the Kingdom. However, the Christian Church has never emphasized the importance of the Kingdom of Heaven being within. It has instead confused this teaching with admittance to an otherworldly heaven after death (the existence of which Marion does not deny).

Human beings cannot understand a level of consciousness above their own by simply reading a book or hearing someone's accounts of experiences at that level. To clearly grasp a level of consciousness, we must actually experience that level ourselves. Even after two thousand years of history, most Christian theologians, preachers, and church leaders still have failed to grasp the true meaning of the Gospel; they have not yet evolved to "put on the mind of Christ." Marion reminds us that Jesus himself frequently talked about people who had "ears to hear but could not hear" and "eyes to see but could not see"; he also spoke of religious leaders as the "blind leading the blind."

Seldom have Christians taken up the call of the Gospel toward consciousness transformation. As a result, only a small number of mystics (such as Meister Eckhart) and saints (such as Mother Teresa) have duplicated the nondual awareness of Christ. Therefore, Marion uses their lives and work as exemplars. He does this convincingly in the case of Eckhart, but I am less persuaded by his treatment of Mother Teresa. I am skeptical that Teresa truly attained nondual consciousness, because she remained so uncritical of the Roman Catholic Church leadership. If she did in fact reach the nondual stage, then it must be conceded that on some specific lines of development, she fell short of perfection.

The history of Christianity, beginning with Jesus's own crucifixion, reveals the dangers in store for those who transcend socially acceptable levels of consciousness and dare to speak about their experiences. They have often been called heretics, and have suffered persecution and even death at the hands of religious authorities. One of the frequent charges of heresy is "gnosticism." Marion addresses this charge directly and, in my view, convincingly. He says that he rejects those Gnostic beliefs that were rejected by the Early Church. However, he denies that the notion that there are levels of human awareness is, in itself, heretical. Otherwise, he asks, would we not need to condemn all developmental psychologists and an entire tradition of Christian spiritual writers, including many mystics?

Marion's bold claim that the truths of the Gospel have been widely misunderstood because theologians and church leaders have an inadequate level of spiritual development isn't likely to win him friends in the Church hierarchy or high-salary teaching positions at Christian universities. Nevertheless, Marion is able to make this claim convincingly, because he shares his own testimony of a life devoted to Christ, rich in mystical insights, and passionately committed to the betterment of the Church.

Marion's book plumbs the depths of the Christian faith to reveal a vision that is inspiring, relevant, frequently startling, and desperately needed in the modern world. It is both revolutionary in its approach to the faith and strikingly orthodox in its faithfulness to tradition. Even when Marion shares unconventional theological views, such as his strong belief in reincarnation, he supports such belief on the basis of Christian scripture and tradition. Properly understood, Marion's approach is not New Age but truly and authentically catholic and Christian. He shows how the teachings, life, death, and resurrection of Christ are revelations of universal truths about God and human beings.

Marion's book speaks directly to my own spiritual journey. After looking at God through the magical eyes of a toddler, the dutiful eyes of a church-going child, the rebellious eyes of an adolescent, the skeptical eyes of a young scholar, and the angry eyes of an ex-Catholic . . . what's next? How is faith possible when a child's worldview is impossible and even skepticism has reached the limits of its believability? Reading about the experiences and views that Marion and other Christian mystics have derived from high levels of consciousness, I found myself opening my eyes wider. I must say that there is much that I don't know what to think of. Not too long ago I would have thought all this talk of spirits, channeling, psychics, and past lives was all so much mumbo jumbo. Yet I do know that I must not dismiss even the most incredible experiences or ideas out of hand.

Marion describes in painstaking detail the subtleties of stages of consciousness of which I cannot speak. I believe the experiences of these stages of consciousness as described by Marion are real, and his interpretations reasonable. I will not accept every detail of his accounts as some sort of new doctrine or creed. However, I humbly acknowledge the limits of my own understanding, circumscribed as it is by the stage of consciousness that I have reached; and I know now that there truly is more to Christianity than I've ever seen before.

Sunday, June 20

I find myself struggling with the Christian label. It seems such a mixed bag, and frankly it's an obstacle to faith for me. I have so many negative conceptions about the socially conservative Christians that I want nothing to do with their brand of Christianity. Although I'm not offended by the liberal Christians, I find their worship and theologies dull.

And yet who alive can humbly read the Gospel accounts of this magnificent Jesus and truly feel worthy to call herself a Christian? Perhaps it is best said that there are very few true Christians (and even fewer inside the Church than outside, I would guess). Whatever else it means to follow Christ, surely it means that we must take off the masks that we wear, each and every one of us—the masks that tell us we are not already members of the Body of Christ, One with God just as Jesus was.

To be One with God, a man must reject all that is not his highest Self, even if doing so makes him a pariah in conventional society, which may shun him and even attempt to deny his right to a place at the table. When others give us a mask to wear, we must reject it. That is the way of Christ. Authenticity is the way Jesus modeled. Authenticity is the gateway to a higher place in consciousness, whatever stage you're at.

Conservative religionists don't understand authenticity. They think if we're truly ourselves, we'll all be wicked beasts. But what if in being truly ourselves we discovered that we were all Christlike? Where can those of us who see the possibilities of authenticity—who see in Jesus Christ not merely a teacher of virtue or morality, but a true revelation of God and our higher Self—go to nurture our faith, when the churches have failed us?

Monday, June 21

Cancer

The sun moves into the part of the sky called Cancer. The Crab is the sign of the archetypal feminine: sensitive and deeply feeling every pulse and ebb of emotion. The Crab may seek to protect its intense vulnerability by going invisible, hiding its true self from the cold, cruel world. And yet its true goal is to discover that it can open itself safely and radiate the beauty of its pure gift of love.

Tuesday, June 22

"It was as if I had been cheated or tricked by God," I told Harry. "As the experiences unfolded, they seemed so real. And it seemed so genuinely a religious experience, as if God himself were speaking to me and making the experience possible for me . . . When the doctors gave me medication to make me come back down to earth, I started to feel duped. What kind of God would give me a religious experience so profound only to then pull the rug out from under me and show me that there was nothing there?"

In the course of my reading and counseling, I found an interpretation of the experience that finally has brought me peace. I believe that there were some psychotic delusions that were regressions to prerational states and others that were mystical experiences (which were, of course, interpreted at the time through a delusional lens)—not one or the other, but a mix. Prerational, grandiose, narcissistic delusions and an encounter with my soul's true nature. Much of my work in the past few weeks has been sorting out, in my own mind, which is which.

Monday, June 28

Wish the gay community had more places of worship that we could truly call our own? There's certainly no shortage of real estate and great facilities. We only need to think outside the church.

I propose, tongue only half planted in cheek, that creative, spiritual gays everywhere should follow the example of one Denver area church and begin converting gay bars into gay churches.

The National Enquirer reports that at the Church at the Bar, the faithful meet every other Tuesday at a nightclub near Denver. Minister Matt Honeycutt greets them with a pint of beer in his left hand as he welcomes the crowd with his right.

He told the tabloid that he wanted to make a place where people would feel more comfortable at worship. The bar owner says that finding God in a bar makes perfect sense, because it's where believers are more likely to go if they're disconnected from God and traditional churches but still have a "tugging in their heart for something more."

The congregation is mostly made up of young people in their twenties and thirties who want to embrace the teachings of Jesus without the other trappings of organized religion. They strive to maintain a wholesome environment without rowdiness or excessive drinking.

As the lyrics of a song say, "In heaven there is no beer, that's why we drink it here."

Friday, July 2

I am reading Ken Wilber's *Boomeritis*, a novel starring a fictional protagonist, a naive 22-year-old grad student in computer science at MIT. One of the novel's most intriguing notions is that one's generation is closely correlated to one's probability of landing at any given level of the spiral of consciousness development. The Boomer generation is supposedly the first generation in history to reach a pluralistic, postmodern, sensitive, and multicultural level of awareness. "Boomeritis" is the name Wilber gives to a peculiar style of narcissism perfected by the Boomers.

Wilber says that research is showing that Generation X is starting to come in at a higher level than the Boomers. Generation Y may even be coming in at the same or an even higher level than Generation X, though it's too soon to say. Mine may very well turn out to be the first holistic, integral-thinking generation in all of history.

I've only met a handful of folks personally who are enchanted by the integral theory, and mostly they're all Generation X. I have met some folks in their forties and fifties who have read some of Ken Wilber's books, but many of them seem to have come away from them with reservations that suggest that they could be suffering from Boomeritis. For example, they will politely say that Wilber makes some good points, but then they'll add that his opinions are no more or less valid than anyone else's.

Hmmm . . . I honestly don't know what to think about the Generation X/Y thing. Wilber could be on to something, but I haven't seen the research to which he refers and so it's hard to say. Sweeping generalizations about any group—much less an entire generation—are difficult to make and rarely credible. I'll have to be alert for evidence that confirms or denies this theory.

Sunday, July 4

I just finished reading *Boomeritis*. I couldn't help but strongly identify with the protagonist, or at least a somewhat less brilliant and witty version thereof. The opening chapters of *Boomeritis* are virtually identical to those of *A Theory of Everything*, though from there the books diverge. While *A Theory of Everything* proceeds to systematically construct a comprehensive theory of reality, *Boomeritis* mainly explores the current prevalence of fragmentation, narcissism, and nihilism in our culture. Academia and its reigning philosophy of pluralistic relativism come in for very sharp critiques, and I think Wilber manages to hit the nail on the head.

Unfortunately, I cannot recommend or give a positive review to *Boomeritis*. Imagine the audacity of a man who attacks narcissism by writing a book that features a protagonist bearing his own name. The arrogance! The nerve! The hypocrisy! That's as offensive as an author who would write a book to promote depth while at the same time never writing more than a few hundred words at once on any one subject. It would never work. ;-)

Wednesday, July 14

An Outline of GLBT History

This is a brief version of GLBT history, written from the perspective of one gay man situated in a plethora of historical, cultural, and social contexts. There are many other versions of GLBT history, and I make no claim that mine is definitive in any way. This outline is necessarily quite simplified. Nevertheless, this conceptual account is offered as a way of looking at GLBT history that incorporates both a cross-cultural perspective and a universal, holistic embrace.

I am sketching a series of stages or waves of consciousness listed in the order they appeared in history—*not* an episodic history in which each phase has a beginning and an end. It's true that the waves likely appeared in a particular chronological order; but once a given wave arises, it coexists and interacts in history with the others. Concurrently in history, the different waves give rise to events that reflect a particular wave's internal logic and also to events that result from interactions among two or more waves of consciousness.

Phase I

Beginning about 10,000 B.C.E., the first signs of same-sex expressions of love and eroticism began to emerge into consciousness. By and large, this was a time when the world was experienced as a polytheistic realm of goddesses and gods, demons, fairies, dragons, and other fanciful creatures. Homosexual expressions were accepted as an honorable and sacred part of life in many cultures. Male initiation rituals, sacred temple sex rituals, and shamanistic rites featured same-sex behavior. Some cultures honored persons who didn't fit into the traditional gender roles with special roles bearing spiritual dignity. Hindu cultures worshiped many bisexual, polymorphous, and androgynous deities.

Phase II

As cultures developed, many peoples began to place a greater emphasis on individual achievement and overcoming obstacles in the way of individual self-expression. Heroes who broke away from the herd mentality were venerated, and the most successful leaders created new communities based on their visions and initiatives. Many cultures began to tell tales that honored same-sex friendship and eroticism between such heroes, including the stories of Naomi and Ruth and Jonathan and David from the Bible. The Egyptians sang songs of Horus and Seth; and the world's oldest story, from ancient Mesopotamia, tells of the love between Gilgamesh, a king, and Enkidu, a warrior created by the gods.

Phase III

About 2,500 years ago, human consciousness evolved into a mythic mode of awareness. It was a conformist, law-and-order way of seeing things, in which narrow cultural horizons defined what was "true" and "good" or "false" and "bad." Believers in the myths were saved, but unbelievers were condemned. Homosexual expressions were frequently limited and even stigmatized in these cultures. Frequently this was a result of the culture placing the highest priority on sex as a mechanical function of the drive toward procreation rather than as a part of the pursuit of loving relationships and happiness. This is a difficult era of history for many GLBT people to celebrate, for it reminds us of prejudices we still face today. However, we should recall that there were many queer ancestors of this era who lived exemplary, self-sacrificial lives in alignment with (and sometimes in partial transgression of) the moral principles they were taught.

Phase IV

Starting three hundred years ago with the Western Enlightenment and continuing to the present day, consciousness began to enter a more fully rational stage of development. The values of achieving material possessions and status, pursuing economic self-interest, and attaining individual autonomy were highlighted. Scientists coined the term "homosexual" and began to study gender and sexual variations in the light of reason. Sexual orientation became a recognized category of analysis for the first time. Activists pursued reforms to enhance the economic and social interests of individuals regardless of sexual orientation; their efforts continue today and have resulted in various gains for homosexuals: protections against police raids on gay bars, the right to gather in public demonstrations, and—in what is at the time of this writing the preeminent homosexual rights issue—equal access to civil domestic partnership or marriage contracts.

Phase V

About 150 years ago, a pluralistic worldview began to emerge based on an egalitarian impulse to share rich and psychologically subtle experiences in a world liberated from repression. Sexual and gender variations were recognized not merely as natural variations to be studied, but as the basis for group identities such as gay and lesbian, which were recognized as allied with the interests of other marginalized or oppressed groups. Multicultural sensitivity and kindness were frequently extolled as among the highest of values, and queer identity was defined as the act of being subversive of oppressive gender and sexual mores.

Phase VI

About 40 years ago, a new integrative, holistic, and spiritual perspective began to arise. Unlike the previous relativistic worldview, this level of consciousness sees the unity beyond the diversity, and there is a demand to honor both pluralism and universality. Gayness is acknowledged as an entity that has developed in consciousness from the basic impulses of Stone Age peoples to contemporary worldviews and beyond. Sexual and gender identities are not valued as the peak of development but as a gateway to the potential awareness of a new sense of self-identity based on the Unity of All Being. Religions that preach homophobia are recognized as deriving from lower levels of development, but the parts of every religious tradition that affirm (or are neutral toward) homosexuality are seen as offering spiritual models for all GLBT people.

Thursday, July 15

The Value of Homosexuality

Does homosexuality as such contain more or less value than heterosexuality as such? Is gay sex less valuable than straight sex because it doesn't result in the creation of children? Such questions might seem merely rhetorical; but in light of the frequency with which they occur in our social and political climate, they are quite salient.

The question of the value of homosexuality is frequently asked by religious conservatives and is answered with various degrees of negativity. It is just as frequently avoided by many gay writers, who are quick to stigmatize the very topic as somehow bad, oppressive, and marginalizing. Other gay writers deny that such questions have any relationship to reality or objective truth, viewing them as purely subjective.

We must ask audacious questions about the value of homosexuality, because ultimately such questions cannot be avoided. Gays have nothing to fear by making an inquiry into homosexuality's value or the morality of same-sex sexual expressions in specific contexts. Everything human beings do presupposes assumptions about values; if we don't address them explicitly, then we simply push them into shadow.

The following remarks will not so much attempt to provide definitive answers to these questions as to point to the manner in which such questions may be addressed in the future. I will share with you my hunches, and you can take them with an appropriate measure of reserve.

As a beginning to this inquiry, I propose that we consider at least three different perspectives on the value of homosexuality: ground value, intrinsic value, and instrumental value. These are three concepts from integral theory. For more about this intellectual framework, see two books by Ken Wilber: *Sex, Ecology, Spirituality* and *A Brief History of Everything*.

The Ground of Gayness

Recognizing ground value means recognizing that Spirit, the underlying immanent and transcendent force of evolution, is the source and ground of all value and that all things are perfect manifestations of Spirit. To speak theistically, all things are equally valuable and beautiful from God's point of view. The value of all earthly forms manifesting in homosexual expressions and that of all forms appearing in heterosexual ways is absolutely identical.

This fundamental equality between "gayness" and "straightness" is an acknowledgment that the deep universal structures revealed by gays are identical to those revealed by straights. All human and animal forms, gay and straight alike, express the identity-seeking drive of agency (masculinity) and the merger-seeking drive of communion (femininity). At the core of our being, we are all two-spirited in this sense.

What's more, not only do gays and straights equally give expression to the same core drives in our being, we also transform using the same core drives. Gay and straight alike, we transform using the drives of self-transcendence (heterophilia) and self-immanence (homophilia). Love flows in our lives both from creation to Source (other-directed love) and from Source to creation (same-directed love). Homosexuality teaches us about one of the two fundamental directions of Love, one of the four prime drives of all things (along with agency, communion, and self-transcendence), and how we are all truly one in Spirit.

The Intrinsic Worth of Homosexuality

Intrinsic value is the value of an entity or phenomenon in itself or for its own sake, or a measure of its wholeness or depth. Depth is the degree of

Spirit that is enfolded into the being of an entity or phenomenon—and so, the greater its depth, the greater its intrinsic value. In other words, not all sentient life forms are equally valuable. The more complex and self-aware a creature, the more it reflects the Divine. A cell has more depth than a molecule, an ape has more depth than an ant, and a dolphin has more depth than a sea anemone.

It is dubious to make claims at so a high level of generalization as the value of homosexuality relative to heterosexuality; however, as questions of value become more precisely defined within restricted historical and cultural parameters, it is possible to make valid comparisons. Researchers may choose to direct their attention to the anecdotal evidence suggesting that homosexuality may have been linked historically to advanced states of consciousness; such claims, if validated, could eventually provide objective evidence of the spiritual importance of being gay.

A relevant question that emerges at this point is whether both same-sex and opposite-sex sexual expressions among human beings are equally present at all levels of depth of consciousness. To answer, you would need to categorize persons according to their levels of depth of consciousness in various areas of functioning (psychosexual, cognitive, interpersonal, moral, and spiritual) and then look at their experiences with same-sex sexual expressions.

Studies of that kind have not been performed. However, there can be little doubt that homosexual persons exist and flourish at all levels of spiritual consciousness from prerational to rational to transrational. At higher levels of consciousness, the self-reported experience of contemporary gay mystics in this matter becomes relevant, as does research into the historical evidence that same-sex-oriented persons have been disproportionately represented among the great artists, writers, sages, saints, and gurus in history.

To summarize the findings of Andrew Harvey in *The Essential Gay Mystics*: there is no evidence that same-sex sexual expressions are a barrier to the attainment of the highest levels of consciousness. In fact, it has been tentatively suggested that homosexuals may be higher spiritual realizers, on average, than heterosexuals. Christian de la Huerta notes in *Coming Out Spiritually* that in the pre-Christian era: "[Gays] were the shamans, the healers, the visionaries, the mediators, the peacekeepers, the 'people who walk between the worlds,' the keepers of beauty." And as Jim Marion observes in a footnote of *Putting on the Mind of Christ*:

Anecdotal evidence from many cultures and time periods suggests that the guides or "seers" have been disproportionately same sexual in orientation. Some try to account for this by suggesting it has something to do with the pineal gland. Others have posited as the reason the natural union in one person of male and female energies.

If this anecdotal evidence is eventually supported by further research, then it would be reasonable to assert that (within specified historical and cultural parameters) homosexuality may be viewed as a psychological structure with greater intrinsic depth than heterosexuality. In plain English, being gay would then be proven to be more intrinsically valuable than being straight.

Perhaps homosexuality aids in consciousness development simply by allowing homosexuals an experience outside the mainstream of their society, giving rise to greater self-consciousness and suffering. Or perhaps homosexuality aids in spiritual growth by giving homosexuals a more balanced perspective on masculine and feminine modes of being. Or perhaps homosexuality aids in consciousness development by removing child-raising burdens, thus giving childless homosexuals greater opportunities for creative self-expression and other personal and spiritual endeavors. Or perhaps there are genetic links between homosexuality and creativity that result in homosexuals having on average a more expansive consciousness than heterosexuals, if there is in fact such a difference. These and other possibilities are worthy topics for exploration by future researchers interested in applying an integral approach to the question of homosexuality's value.

On the other hand, it's entirely possible that there is no connection between homosexuality and expanding consciousness, or that there is a negative link. Because of the social stigmatization of homosexuality, many gays may find themselves burdened psychologically with baggage that distracts them from spiritual development. In any case, it's hard to reach clarity on the intrinsic value of homosexuality because it is impossible to isolate homosexuality from the historical, cultural, and social contexts in which it inevitably appears.

Therefore the best we can do at this time is to speak, if we choose to speak at all, in terms of hunches. My own hunch is that homosexuality probably functions as a magnet for higher consciousness, pulling individuals to greater unity with Spirit at every level of their development. I don't want to make too big a point of this, lest gays get the notion that their sexual orientation automatically gives them a fast-track ticket to artistic greatness, religious salvation, or spiritual enlightenment. It's important to bear in mind that the actualization of potential advances in consciousness is by no means assured.

Value in a Relative Perspective

Instrumental value is the value to others of homosexuality. We can measure this type of value by looking at the contribution homosexuals make relative to their roles in networks of interrelationship (for example, comparing the contributions of gays versus nongays to the cultural and artistic advancement of a society or the degree to which gays versus nongays provide parenting and care for future generations. We should develop moral perspectives on the instrumental value of sexual expressions of all kinds by considering the degrees to which such expressions bring about greater or lesser degrees of value in all relevant networks of relationship.

The most negative sexual expressions include those that contribute to emotional or physical harm or suffering, including the emotional or social isolation of individuals, and/or the repression of spiritual energy through any level of body, mind, or spirit.

The most positive end of the spectrum includes sexual expressions that generate psychological health and well-being, assist individuals in contributing positively to their communities and society including the nurturing of future generations, and allow the free flowing of spiritual energy throughout all levels of body, mind, and spirit.

It is questionable whether procreative sex may be said to be simply better than nonprocreative sex as such when taking an instrumental perspective. Adoption and medical technologies such as in vitro fertilization give many gay and lesbian couples fine options for child raising today that are on par with the options available to heterosexual couples that experience difficulties in conceiving a child.

The instrumental, or extrinsic, valuation of heterosexuality and homosexuality will turn on many factors that are likely to differ depending on who is doing the analysis. In my own view, the most obvious difference is that homosexuals donate less to society as parents than heterosexuals. I believe it is safe to say that, person for person, homosexuals contribute more, on average, to the production of culture, entertainment, art, and literature than heterosexuals. Also, many homosexuals make a contribution to family structures that should not be overlooked. Although gays are parents less often than straights, they frequently have roles that strengthen the family. For example, gays often have roles as educators, uncles and aunts, nurses and caregivers to the elderly.

My own view is that the extrinsic worth of homosexuality in our society is on par with the extrinsic worth of heterosexuality. Society benefits from the diverse ways that both childless and nonchildless individuals enrich the social fabric. From the perspective of extrinsic worth, it is worth considering that perhaps neither exclusive heterosexuality nor exclusive homosexuality would be on par with bisexuality. Bisexuality may quite plausibly be viewed as the form of sexual expression of greatest value to others, since it seems to combine the advantages of homosexuality and heterosexuality and to maximize personal choices.

Conclusion

What's the value of homosexuality? Conservative religionists know the answers about gays with certainty. And don't bother trying to reason with them—they have their answers on God's authority. Many gays are just as convinced that they know the answers with certainty. And you if dare to question their views, don't risk hurting anyone's self-esteem—that's not politically correct.

Compared with what they've experienced in many other times and places, gays enjoy a wide degree of tolerance in American society today. However, full acceptance lags behind because so many people do not recognize the ground, intrinsic, or relative values of gayness.

What's needed today is an integral approach that faces the empirical data regarding differences and similarities between gays and straights with unflinching honesty. Without such an approach, gays looking for full inclusion in society may gain a degree of tolerance but will have little hope for gaining full equality in the minds and hearts of others. Full equality demands that gays be seen accurately—that is, as persons fully and truly reflecting Spirit, who are as absolutely perfect (and relatively imperfect) in their being and ways of loving as everyone else.

Saturday, July 17

I attended my first meeting of Seattle Integral today. There were seven or eight folks sitting around a table at the Starbucks on Denny Way in Capitol Hill. I remember the names Gary, Elle, Jake, Mark, and Tom.

Seattle Integral meetings have only been going since January, but there are already about 45 members on the e-mail list and two or three meetings a month. The group was formed less than a year ago to support, complement, and organize the Seattle Ken Wilber meet-up. Since then it has grown into an organization that focuses on "turning integral theory into integral action."

The first part of the meeting revolved around some tinkering with a mission statement for the group. Gary is the group's cofounder and leader. He said that the group may have overlooked the basics in its previous attempt, at least in part because there was such an effort to include ideas from everyone at the meeting.

From there, the discussion turned to the idea that organizations themselves, like individuals, may go through different levels of the spiral of development in their own life span. We discussed how Seattle Integral was still in its early, formative levels as an organization.

The second part of the meeting featured guest speaker Fred Lanphear, founder of One Sky Medicine. He spoke about his work in developing an integral approach to medicine, including ideas he gleaned from Ken Wilber's *A Theory of Everything*.

He also spoke about One Sky's struggles in creating a unique medical clinic that includes both conventional medicine and complementary medicine under the same roof. He said that getting conventional physicians and complementary practitioners to share the same space is the easy part. Getting actual collaboration occurring as part of treatment, given financial and other constraints, is a huge challenge.

After the meeting ended, I started thinking about what I'd just experienced. A bunch of folks from all different walks of life came together . . . why? To discuss the ideas of a philosopher! Yes, a philosopher! That in itself is extraordinary. When's the last time you recall people getting excited about a philosophy?

This may be pure psychological projection on my part, but if I were to guess, I'd say the folks at this meeting were coming together because they needed to. Their initial encounters and work with the integral philosophy may have made them feel more out of place than ever before in their families, among their friends, and in their religious communities. Then perhaps they began to search for others who were seeing the world through the same lens and struggling with the same perplexities. When they didn't find such an organization, they invented it. Truly extraordinary.

As I sat among this motley crew, I began to experience something that I haven't felt for a long while: a sense of belonging. It felt as if we were united by something I almost want to call a common creed. I need to be very careful about using a loaded phrase like that. I recently read a comment on the Integral Naked online forum from someone who said, "The integral movement is getting dangerously close to becoming a religion! Don't you think we've had enough of those?" Gasp . . . a religion! Horror of horrors! Could anything be worse than that? ;-)

I don't mean to imply that everyone at the coffee shop had identical opinions. However, I sensed we had a detailed, common framework for understanding and an overarching sense of agreement as to the value, meaning, and purpose of our lives. We may have been Buddhists, Christians, Jews, or atheists . . . who knows. But I imagine that we were brought together by a very general common vision of The Way Things Are, an attitude of openness to truth, a willingness to question and challenge all orthodoxies, and a conviction that living in accordance with our common vision is the heart of wisdom. If that's the beginnings of a religion, then so be it.

Monday, July 19

Rereading *Virtually Normal*

I had the impulse today to reread Andrew Sullivan's *Virtually Normal*, one of the most influential political books of the 1990s. Sullivan received wide recognition for having articulated a vision for gay politics sharply at odds with virtually everyone else's, upsetting the orthodox among the religious right, the political right, the mainstream progressive gay civil rights organizations, and the radical queer activists, among others. In the book, Sullivan defines four major types of arguments related to homosexuality (proponents of which he called the prohibitionists, liberationists, conservatives, and liberals). He then identifies the shortcomings of each and attempts to lay out a new "politics of homosexuality" that will marry the best parts of all the others while avoiding their weaknesses.

When I first read this book, I was 23 years old and a recent graduate of Harvard. I found myself strongly identifying especially with the arguments from the liberals and the liberationists. Sullivan's critiques of these positions struck me as compelling and very often successful. I found his arguments difficult to counter persuasively, even though I was not quite satisfied by Sullivan's proposed alternative. I was all for legalized gay marriage, but I didn't like the fact that Sullivan disagreed with laws that prohibit discrimination against homosexuals by private individuals and employers.

The liberationist viewpoint regards homosexuality as a social construct and the goal of politics as liberation from all traditionally defined social constructs. Sullivan says that it really lacks a political program and that when it does enter the political sphere, it is typically authoritarian. Political correctness is its main tool for activism. The liberal viewpoint sees homosexuals as an oppressed minority and demands laws to criminalize discrimination against gays by public institutions and private individuals. Sullivan says that this tends to create a victim mentality, subtly reinforcing a sense of homosexual identity that is disempowering. These arguments stung, because they challenged some of my beliefs and I didn't quite know what to replace them with.

Despite failing to fully sign on to Sullivan's proposed alternative, I had the sense that the book was a work of great significance. Sullivan had managed to accurately identify the different voices in the cacophony of argument surrounding a highly emotional and controversial issue, honor the essential truths in their perspectives, and then incorporate them into a broader, more expansive vision.

You might call Sullivan's perspective both postconservative and postliberal. From conservatives, it incorporates arguments that appeal to important traditional values and a sense of the common good. For example, in response to those who claim that homosexuality destroys families, it observes that homosexuals are parts of families. It says, "We are your brothers and sisters, sons and daughters. Include us, respect us, or watch your own families crumble from within." From liberals, it derives respect for the law and democracy, especially the need to uphold the rights of minorities against those who would seek to impose a parochial vision on all citizens. It demands an end to public discrimination against homosexuals, for example in sodomy laws, the military, and (most of all) the vital institution of civil marriage.

Nine years ago, I was a die-hard, left-of-center liberal. Having read my share of Foucault, Derrida, and other cutting-edge criticism, I was infected by a healthy amount of live virus in the form of postmodernism, just enough to inoculate me against any view that doesn't acknowledge that reality tends to be far more complex and pluralistic than naive realists make it out to be. After reading *Virtually Normal*, I could never again be convinced that all truth about homosexuality and politics was to be identified with any one philosophy or political party. There was plenty of truth to go around, and not everyone's viewpoint was equally true. If Sullivan's proposal was valid, then I could hope for positive change around gay issues in society, because many people who formerly disagreed could come to rational agreement on what to do.

Virtually Normal, *Nine Years Later*

Today, I note with amazement how much has changed in our country over the past nine years. Gays have won the right to marry in Massachusetts, and the right to marriage in everything but name in Vermont. Although there is the conservative backlash to contend with, in my mind Sullivan's argument that equal access to the institution of marriage should be the centerpiece of the gay political agenda has been vindicated. Moreover, Sullivan himself deserves a healthy amount of credit for having contributed to the intellectual climate in which this momentous change in social milieu was able to occur. For that, Sullivan and many other activists and intellectuals who got behind the push for equal marriage rights have my deep gratitude and deserve every gay person's respect.

Since I've been reading integral philosophy recently, I thought it time to reread *Virtually Normal* and to ask this question: Does it take a truly integral approach to gay politics? And if not, how does it fall short? I believe Sullivan's argument is certainly integral in two senses. First, it is an application of critical-thinking skills that draws heavily upon a highly creative, integrative, and aperspectival mode of consciousness. Second, it is an effort at synthesis that recognizes a plurality of perspectives and attempts to find a way to bridge the gaps by honoring the essential wisdom contained in each.

The shortcoming of *Virtually Normal*, as I see it today, is that it is very flat or shallow in its vision. As students of the integral philosophy will instantly recognize, there is no understanding of a developmental spectrum of consciousness; nor is there an attempt to recognize and contend with the complex psychological and cultural conditions of consciousness that underlie supposedly reasoned arguments related to homosexuality. The book is essentially written from a standpoint of positivistic rationalism, in that it assumes that the heart and central activity of politics should be to confront others with views or arguments, in the process asking what these mean, what is the evidence for and against, and so forth. An implicit assumption is that this effort at disembodied rational discourse will contribute to positive social change (for example, people will read the book and change their minds). Sullivan's approach illustrates the usual sort of conceit of picking a position and defending it against opponents. The approach falls short by failing to grasp the embodied and evolutionary nature of consciousness itself, and it therefore doesn't persuade in the way Sullivan probably thought it should. People fall at different levels on a spectrum of consciousness; therefore we may talk politics, but understanding is in shorter supply than Sullivan supposes.

A more fully integral approach to reasoning would be more like Hegel's style of political philosophy than like positivistic rationalism. As Robert Solomon wrote in *In the Spirit of Hegel*:

> Hegel would simply ride the wave of all the great philosophers before him, from the pre-Socratics and Plato up to Kant and the neo-Kantians. He would flow with the conflicting but ultimately unidirectional currents of their efforts and be carried to the end, for a final summation. . . . In this way, [Hegel] never actually opposed anyone: in a sense, all he did was go along for the ride.

Whereas Sullivan assumes that liberationists, conservatives, prohibitionists, and liberals are capable of fruitful dialogue and coming to agreement, the reality is less encouraging. Each of these four types are embodied in particular modes of consciousness and social structures. The modes of consciousness in which they are embodied are only capable of listening to Sullivan's arguments on their own terms and not in the mode of positivistic rationalism that he favors.

Thus, rereading *Virtually Normal* today, I am no less impressed with its ingenuity; yet I am now aware of its failure to reach an integral level of discourse. Sullivan's argument is properly characterized as residing at the rationalist level of consciousness, the average level of consciousness in society, with nods to the higher pluralistic and even higher integral modes. Although Sullivan wouldn't have used these words, essentially his book says, "Everybody smarten up now, why don't ya?" The book does more than any other book I know on the subject of homosexuality to bridge the gaps between people of different worldviews and modes of existence. Ultimately, however, it reduces their differences to matters of argument that (Sullivan believes) can be resolved in the instrumental mode of rationalism. If Sullivan were a doctor, he might have said: "I know what ails you, and it's that you're not reasoning well enough . . ."

I want to emphasize here that there's absolutely nothing wrong with making this sort of argument; in fact, it is quite useful as a healthy, positive expression of the rationalistic mode of consciousness. However, I am simply observing that readers and reviewers come along and they don't buy the argument, and many are not persuaded to actually change their minds. Nine years later, thousands of people have read *Virtually Normal* and many, I imagine, still think about and relate to homosexuality much as they did before reading the book. And some of Sullivan's readers still believe that homosexuals should be discriminated against in society. The rationalist must explain this disagreement as a function of people not reasoning well enough (or, they might concede, perhaps the argument of the book is flawed). However, the integralist recognizes that agreement cannot be expected, because each reader comes to the book from a specific level of consciousness and brings her own inevitable and entirely appropriate understandings and misunderstandings.

An Integral Vision of Gay Politics

What does a truly integral perspective offer the debate concerning a politics of homosexuality? In my opinion, the jury is still out. However, I can suggest an outline for a few elements of the emerging political framework.

According to integral theorists, about 50 years ago an integral level of consciousness emerged that is characterized not only by a high level of sensitivity to pluralistic ways of thinking but also by the impulse to think in terms of systems and holistic modes of synthesis. This mode of consciousness is distinguished from all previous levels of human awareness by the fact that folks at all previous modes of consciousness thought that their particular perspective was the only correct one and that everyone else was wrong. In terms of Sullivan's typology, liberals and conservatives think liberationists have gone soft in the head; liberationists despise liberals and conservatives as greedy, capitalist scum; and prohibitionists think everyone else is going to hell. At the integral level, which is a higher developmental level than the others, each of the previous waves of the spiral of consciousness is recognized as being normal and often quite healthy, and as having an essential place in the structure and order of society. In other words, the prohibitionists, conservatives, liberationists, and liberals are all seen to have a piece of the truth—they have essentially accurate and healthy views of homosexuality as gayness appears in their understanding of the universe.

An integral politics would not seek to impose a single level of values upon society but would obey a mandate to protect and defend the health of the spiral of human development as a whole. Unlike Sullivan's project in *Virtually Normal*, there would not be an attempt to articulate a single "politics of homosexuality," defend it using instrumental logic, and promote it under the banner of "public reason." Instead, one would find an acknowledgment and embrace of a plurality of politics of homosexuality. Integral politics would have an awareness of the vital role that liberals, conservatives, liberationists, and even prohibitionists can play in forging an effective gay politics . . . and would strive to craft a vision for integrating them into a coherent whole.

The laws of a society governed by integral principles would allow every level of development to simply be itself but would not let any level repress or dominate the others. This general rule is already used by most Western democracies: think what you like, but behave according to law or you may lose your freedom.

Prohibitionists should be recognized as vital advocates in society for the maintenance of law, order, social structures, and discipline. They can be encouraged by others to promote a civil society where homosexuals are free from unjust persecution. Prohibitionists should not be excused from getting to know gay people and working to create a more just society for everyone. They should be helped to take whatever steps are possible within the constraints of their traditions to welcome and affirm gay people in their families, churches, and neighborhoods, as well as in the political sphere. For example, prohibitionists can be urged to draw upon the Bible to create theologies that vocally oppose gay bashing in all forms, including the verbal harassment suffered by many gay youths. Conservative ministers can educate their congregations to make it clear that all people are sinners, and raise awareness that heterosexuals should not focus undue attention on the sins of homosexuals while ignoring their own. Some prohibitionists who oppose the morality of same-sex unions within their church may be willing to support legislation that provides gays with civil marriage rights comparable to those of heterosexuals.

Those thinkers that Sullivan calls conservatives and liberals should be recognized as vital for the recognition of individual rights and liberties, economic self-interest, egalitarian values, instrumental and positivistic rationality, and so forth. Gays in the Democratic, Republican, and Libertarian parties can all work within their political parties to articulate strategies for achieving the maximum possible freedom from discrimination. Although Libertarians may not be as effective as Republicans and Republicans not as effective as Democrats at advocating freedom from discrimination in both the public and private sectors, all activists should be encouraged to make the most of their party's resources. Or, if they must, they should leave their party to join another that is more responsive to the goal of winning freedom for all individuals. Some activists may even build creative political alternatives by joining forces with existing minority parties or forming a new political party if necessary.

Consistent with the thinking of some Libertarians and Republicans, Sullivan argued in *Virtually Normal* that discrimination against homosexuals should only be prohibited in the public sphere and not among private parties. He wrote:

This politics affirms a simple and limited principle: that all public (as opposed to private) discrimination against homosexuals be ended and that every right and responsibility that heterosexuals enjoy as public citizens be extended to those who grow up and find themselves emotionally different. *And that is all.* [Italics in original.]

However, in my opinion, an integral approach will give far more latitude to the liberal politics than Sullivan's vision allowed. An integral approach allows for the promulgation of laws that stem from the center of gravity in the consciousness of any given government. Therefore, in states such as California, Oregon, New York, and Massachusetts—where the center of gravity is slowly rising from the level of prohibitionists and conservatives towards the level of liberals and liberationists—laws that prohibit hate crimes or workplace discrimination by private employers may be justified. It is true that such laws might conceivably create or exacerbate a victim mentality among gays; however, this risk should be balanced against the risk of reinforcing a perpetrator mentality among gay bashers.

Liberationists have the dominant mode of consciousness in academia, especially among queer studies scholars. Liberationist views should be recognized for affirming the importance of multicultural diversity, authentic pluralism of cultural values, sensitivity, and the affective life of the group and individual. Sullivan is correct in his conclusion that activists at this level of consciousness are rarely able to articulate a coherent political program; as a result, one frequently finds them offering theatrical productions or performance art in lieu of efforts at political change. The essential role of the liberationist philosophy in the future of the gay movement is its recognition of the importance of winning not only political rights but also cultural change. Liberationists recognize that cultural values are not set in stone but are subject to ongoing change and refinement. Thus, thinkers at this level of consciousness or higher are often the most gifted producers and analysts of culture. Unfortunately, many cultural critics do more harm than good to the gay movement, because they tend to regard those who don't hold liberationist values as idiotic rubes, backward hicks, capitalist scum, or Nazi fascists. Their ignorance of and antipathy toward religion is also very likely to sabotage efforts to promote greater equality for gays. And their resistance to recognizing hierarchical levels of development and cross-cultural universal rankings of values prevents their evolution to the higher integral mode.

The liberationist mindset is rampant in academia, where authoritarian efforts to police free speech create a dangerous environment that is often appropriately labeled fascist. In some Western European democracies, queer activists have supported legislation to criminalize offensive speech. These efforts should be rejected and vocally condemned by the gay movement in the United States. The failure of many prominent American gays to criticize these dangerous laws has already caused major setbacks among those whose support we cannot afford to lose, especially the moderate religious mainstream. Few prominent gays other than Andrew Sullivan vocally criticize these laws, and Sullivan does so as part of a misguided general objection to all hate-crime laws. To progress on this issue, the American gay movement needs to adopt this message as a firm principle: "Think what you will of us, speak what you will of us, but incite or perpetrate acts of violence against our group and you cross the line of acceptable behavior." When a Muslim cleric incites a thousand people to go out and chop off the heads of homosexuals, this should be punished. When a pastor at a fundamentalist church in

Topeka says gay sex is a sin, this shouldn't be. Rhetoric or laws that blur the important distinctions among thought, speech, and action cannot serve the gay community.

Hate-crime laws are distinct from hate-speech laws; the former criminalize acts of physical violence against minorities, while the latter criminalize offensive speech. Although I agree with Sullivan that there are better ways to combat hate than passing laws that are seldom used, I disagree with his conclusion that such laws are bad. It is true that they may encourage gays to think of themselves in a disempowering victim role. Nevertheless, hate-crime laws may serve a valuable function as an indicator of a community's moral standards, and I support their adoption in all communities where gays have the community support to get such laws passed.

Some will object to what they perceive as an inconsistency in my formulation of the integral political philosophy: conservatives wouldn't be allowed to legislate morality by passing antisodomy laws, but liberals would be able to legislate morality by passing laws that prohibit discrimination by private employers on the basis of sexual orientation. However, this objection is misguided. There is no theoretical inconsistency whatsoever, because antisodomy laws prohibit behavior that is morally unacceptable only according to the worldview of persons generally residing at lower relative stages of consciousness. Such laws are not able to withstand the scrutiny of arguments at any of the successive stages of consciousness (whether those arguments derive from the assumptions of the rationalists, pluralists, or integralists). In contrast, antidiscrimination laws prohibit behavior that is morally unacceptable according to the worldview of those at a higher relative stage of consciousness. Arguments for such laws withstand scrutiny because of the relatively high level of objective moral concern displayed by the features of such laws in the moral order; arguments against such laws fail this test of scrutiny.

Integral thinkers are not included in Sullivan's typology of prohibitionists, conservatives, liberals, and liberationists. We are thinkers who recognize a developmental spectrum in which everyone plays an important role. Rather than attempt to articulate a single politics superior in some supposedly objective sense, we would forge strategies of engagement between various parties that respect the differences and legitimate interests of each level of development. An integral perspective is summed up as a philosophy of *unitas multiplex*, or unity in diversity. It advocates creating the greatest possible amount of inclusion for gay men and lesbians in social institutions such as marriage and in all domains of society, including religion; this approach would necessarily be grounded upon divergent (and sometimes apparently contradictory) rationales. It's a politics that both acknowledges the goodness of the distinctiveness of gay/queer identities and respects our common humanity.

Tuesday, July 20

I spoke to Patrick McNamara, the director of the Gay Spirit Culture Summit Project, on the phone earlier today. He shared exciting news about his recent trip to Denver, Colorado. It turns out that while he was there he met with Ken Wilber. They spoke for a few hours about the gay spirituality summit and related topics, and a recording of portions of their discussion will eventually be posted on the Integral Naked website.

I find it most encouraging that Wilber takes the time to follow and support the emergence of projects like the Gay Spirit Culture Summit. Although Wilber himself isn't gay, he may be an example of what these days is being called the metrosexual, a gay-friendly heterosexual who takes an interest in culture, fashion, and other things that more conventional straight guys shy away from. Whether or not Wilber would accept the metrosexual label, one thing seems clear to me: through his writings and work he is making an effort to include and affirm queer people as full partners in the integral revolution.

Thursday, July 22

Leo

Leo is the destination of the sun during this time of summer. The sign of the Lion depicts the impulse to play, frolic, and enjoy the pleasures of life. Trusting in the goodness and abundance of what is, Leo aims to bless the self and others with its laughter, love, and performance. The Lion's aim: the fullness of self-expression . . . relishing the joy of being alive.

Friday, July 23

Unexpectedly, I found myself in a 12-step meeting today, since a friend suggested that we meet there before going out to dinner. I wasn't planning to give a share, but then the chairperson looked at me and said, "Everyone else has shared, and there's time enough. Would you like to?"

"My name is Joe, and I'm an addict in recovery."

I simply spoke briefly to how grateful I was to be there and expressed that I am feeling especially blessed and joyful to be on a different path in my life now than when I was deep in my addictions.

"I date the beginning of my recovery to the end of July 1999. Today is an important anniversary for me: five years since I last used crystal meth."

The women and men there applauded. Afterward, we held hands and someone began to read a prayer:

If we are painstaking about this phase of our development, we will be amazed before we are halfway through. We are going to know a new freedom and a new happiness. We will not regret the past nor wish to shut the door on it. We will comprehend the word "serenity," and we will know peace . . . We will suddenly realize that God is doing for us what we could not do for ourselves.

Saturday, July 24 (Moses Lake, Washington)

Today it hit 101 degrees in Moses Lake, Washington, the site of the annual Díaz family reunion. I drove three hours this morning to spend the afternoon with my family, eat Mexican food, and get some R&R . . . and then I turned around and drove three hours back to Seattle. The highlight of the reunion is watching the kids go after the piñatas year after year, and seeing how they grow. There were about 150 of us in all at the park, enough of a crowd to justify name tags. I'm not sure how many relatives there are on Mom's side of the family; but I'd wager that if everyone showed up, we'd be well over 200.

Saturday, July 31

7:02 a.m. Got out of bed, brushed my teeth, and got dressed (removed cat hair from my black shirt). Ate breakfast. Fed the cat. Said the Lord's Prayer, followed by 20 minutes of meditation. Attention wandered frequently.

8:12 a.m. Got in my car and drove to work. The weather today is extraordinary: a cool 61 degrees and clear skies currently, a high of 74 and partly cloudy expected.

I'm planning to work just a few hours at the office. I scanned Google for news. Nothing out of the ordinary . . . "Bush, Kerry hit the road for votes."

Checking e-mail . . . Got a digest of the latest Seattle Integral list. A psychology student, Diana, forwarded an interesting article to the list. I quickly scanned it, and made a note to read it later. It begins:

> Transpersonal psychologists have attempted to define various types of spiritual emergences that can be mistaken for psychotic emergencies. This is a necessary response to the normal Western policy of labeling all non-consensual states of consciousness as psychotic. . . .

11:56 a.m. I spent over an hour revising an essay that I drafted on Tuesday and then posted it to my blog. Now I'm going to head to a movie.

3:42 p.m. Had a grilled cheese sandwich and a chocolate malt at Johnny Rocket's, then caught M. Night Shyamalan's *The Village* at Pacific Place.

5:02 p.m. I'm back at my office now. Opened a window, turned on a fan, and now am gulping down water. I'm hot. Couldn't have asked for a more perfect, pleasant afternoon at the park. Lots of folks out today at Greenlake. Cute dogs, shirtless men, a flock of geese, runners, rollerbladers, and lots of pale skin getting tanned.

I've been thinking about my brother and a walk I took along this lake on the morning he died. I sat down in the shade for a few minutes, and felt a single teardrop peek out from underneath my sunglasses and roll down my cheek. And then I continued on my way. I phoned Mom to see how she is doing.

11:10 p.m. I went to a party tonight for my friend Timothy, who is leaving next week for an indefinite stint as a surfer in New Zealand. There was an unusual mix of folks at the party, ranging from men belonging to Timothy's men's groups and his sangha to ex-coworkers of his from a software company. I thoroughly enjoyed the conversation, the pizza, and a cigar.

In the car on the way home, I listened and sang along to *Bell*, a wonderful Stuart Davis CD. My favorite song on the CD is "Smoke." Great music.

11:44 p.m. I watched a little TV with the cat and chatted with the housemate for a bit. He asked me how I liked *The Village*. I told him I'm a huge fan of director M. Night Shyamalan's movies. I love a story with a surprise ending.

5 Dangerous Thoughts

"Your true nature lies, not concealed deep within you, but immeasurably high above you, or at least above that which you usually take yourself to be. Your true educators and formative teachers reveal to you what the true basic material of your being is. . . . your educators can be only your liberators."
— FRIEDRICH NIETZSCHE

Friday, August 6

What Is Gay Spirituality?

One of the finest and most influential definitions of "gay spirituality" can be found in Christian de la Huerta's 1991 book *Coming Out Spiritually: The Next Step*. According to de la Huerta, gay spirituality is a radical response to the current state of spiritual evolution of humanity. To understand gay spirituality, he argues, it is important to understand the course of religion's evolution.

Like many gay spirituality writers, de la Huerta argues that before patriarchal times began several thousand years ago, there was a golden age in which gay and sexually ambiguous people were often spiritual leaders. Back then, he says, "we were the shamans, the healers, the visionaries, the mediators, the peacekeepers, the 'people who walk between the worlds,' the keepers of beauty."

In this earlier era, gays were honored as the Two-Spirit people of Native American tribes, the Gatekeepers of tribes in Africa and India, and the priests of goddess-worshiping tribes in ancient Europe and the Middle East. The bottom line: we were honored, respected, and revered for our unique spirit.

But with the patriarchy, suggests de la Huerta, came a dark age that ended all that. With the rise of the domineering male heterosexuals, there came religions that used violence and military might to impose their beliefs on others. Homophobia also went hand in hand with the patriarchy, especially in the teachings of Judaism, Christianity, and Islam.

How should gays today respond to a world very much shaped by patriarchal values? Not with a victim mentality, says de la Huerta, but with a determination to reclaim our "queer heritage." In *Coming Out Spiritually*, he invites queer people today "to reclaim our natural, our sacred, our archetypal, and yes, our God-given role of spiritual leadership."

With these words, de la Huerta helped to shape a distinctive spirituality movement within the gay community. If this basic understanding of spiritual evolution is correct, then the next step for gays in our current state of evolution is to come to a greater sense of identification with queer archetypal roles such as shamans and Two-Spirits so that we may become more appreciative of how our gayness sets us apart from others and gives us a special role in the universe. Queer spirituality takes nothing away from our spiritual heritages but adds to them a unique dimension that is truly our own. For this important contribution, de la Huerta and other spirituality activists in our communities should be applauded and supported.

Although I am sympathetic to aspects of this vision of spiritual evolution, I suspect that this story about our "queer heritage" isn't quite right. Consider this: If this widely held belief about spiritual evolution is correct, then queers are major dupes of history. If persons of same-sex orientation used to be revered and honored, and now we are vilified, then at some point along the line we must have given up our power. Or, perhaps, it may be said that our power was forcibly taken from us by oppressive heterosexuals. Either way, it seems difficult to avoid the conclusion that what we now call gayness is a product of thousands of years of damage at the hands of bad people.

About five thousand years ago, there was indeed the beginning of a dramatic shift in both the technical and economic base in Eastern and Western societies. Horticultural societies became more agrarian, and along with this change came a shift in cultures from those based on tribal and magical practices to cultures based on mythic religions of law and order. Gay spirituality writers suggest that this shift marks the end of the era where gays were often honored, and the beginning of a spiritual dark age. But who among us would want to go back to the tribal cultures of ten thousand years ago? Even among Native American tribes, Two-Spirit people were only allowed to marry "normal" people, not other Two-Spirits. Among tribes that utilized homosexual practices in male initiation rites, adult males were usually encouraged to abandon sex with men in adulthood. And even among cultures such as that of the ancient Greeks, homosexuality was rarely practiced among persons of equal social stature.

There are many examples of same-sex sexual expressions in premodern times but no examples where adults partnered with other adults of the same sex for life and formed a separate subculture based on their same-sex attractions. Slavery was commonly practiced even in prepatriarchal times, life spans were short, and living conditions were often brutal. As I see it, the so-called golden era of gay spirituality doesn't really sound so golden.

In my opinion, gay spirituality writers sometimes paint an unrealistically rosy picture of same-sex expression in prepatriarchal tribal cultures, ignoring or glossing over the fact that such cultures were far from being utopian paradises for liberated gays. They may counter with the argument that conditions in the distant past may not have been ideal but were better than the patriarchal era that followed and deserve to be reclaimed. By embracing the archetypal roles of our "queer heritage," these writers believe, people today can adopt an inspiring, empowering vision.

I generally support the agenda of encouraging gay people to reclaim the power and energy of a variety of mythic archetypes as part of a holistic spiritual practice. However, this agenda carries the danger of locking gays into an inaccurate historical narrative. Despite claims to the contrary, I don't see how we can accept a narrative that says gays have been the victims of thousands of years of oppression at the hands of bad people without trapping ourselves into a victim mentality.

Gay spirituality writers often imply that we have every reason to reject patriarchal religions such as Judaism and Christianity, and we are encouraged to emphasize those aspects of ourselves that set us apart from heterosexuals. I believe this approach to spirituality can actually have deleterious consequences on gay culture by encouraging a hostile attitude toward popular religions and a fearful attitude toward heterosexuals, as well as by undermining efforts to take personal responsibility for our own affairs.

Let's be clear about something. Many gay spirituality writers are neopagan, and many of the most prominent gay advocates of spirituality consider the adoption of pagan beliefs and practices as tantamount to reclaiming "queer heritage." They usually want to pick and choose the beliefs and practices they like from a variety of pre-Christian traditions that suit their fancy—a little of this and a little of that. In contrast, I prefer an approach to gay spirituality that has room for neopagans as well as Christians, Jews, Muslims, Hindus, Buddhists, and many others. I don't think that it's really a part of "queer heritage" to view Christianity and all other patriarchal religions that have arisen in the past five thousand years primarily as instruments of the oppression of gay people.

Whereas most gay spirituality writers tend to assume that gays got the shaft from oppressors, another possibility exists: we can view the rise of limitations on same-sex sexual expression that are historically associated with patriarchal religions as being a cocreation of persons of all sexualities. The rise in the agrarian era of religions that opposed same-sex expressions may be viewed to a certain extent as a necessary and appropriate reaction to a set of historical circumstances.

In the agrarian era, there was often the demand for tribes to maximize the procreative potential of all its members. This fact of life was perceived by some religions as a compelling moral necessity. Instead of arguing that gays were oppressed by bad heterosexuals for thousands of years, we can instead say that persons with a same-sex orientation made the rational decision to choose biological reproduction over sexual and emotional satisfaction in an era where their options were limited. In other words, queer forebears were not forced into closets; they *chose* to limit their same-sex sexual expressions because they wanted to maximize their reproductive potential.

I believe that, on the whole, gays have been victims of oppression more rarely than some would say. Important exceptions include the religion-and/or state-mandated executions of homosexuals by the medieval Roman Catholic Church, Nazi Germany, and present-day radical Islamic states. Many thousands of homosexual, bisexual, and transgender persons have been killed as heretics or degenerates. These exceptions have been the result of terrible social pathologies and should by no means be minimized or excused.

Nevertheless, I believe that the more pressing need today is not to affirm our collective victimization, but to question it. This must be done very carefully and with sensitivity to many shades of gray. To paraphrase a remark made by Ken Wilber in another context: *paradoxically, while we have not been previously oppressed, unliberated, or duped, we stand now in need of liberation.*

We need a view of spiritual evolution that doesn't lock us into a disempowering victim mentality. We do not need to distort the past to blame oppressors for our woes or to elevate neopagan religions over all others. Fortunately, in our day there is no longer a need to channel sexuality narrowly into heterosexual molds in order to propagate the species. There are safe and legal reproductive options such as adoption, surrogate parenthood, and in-vitro fertilization. This means that gays and lesbians are no longer constrained by the limits of the patriarchal era.

I support the gay spirituality movement, but I choose to cast its meaning in a different light than does de la Huerta. Gay spirituality is not only about staking a claim to our archetypal differences; it is about affirming *both* our uniqueness *and* our common humanity. Gay spirituality is not so much about reclaiming our "queer heritage" from a lost golden era as it is about the impulse to take the reins of our spiritual evolution and rise to never-before-seen heights of consciousness. Gay liberation today presents an opportunity to achieve new potentials for human flourishing at the mid-morning of a rising spiritual consciousness, not a struggle at dawn after a long, dark night of victimhood.

Friday, August 20

What's in a Label?

I was 20 years old when I first put a label on my sexuality. Actually, I was spared the chore of coming out to my mom, because a university librarian outed me.

I had secretly known that I was different from most other boys since junior high school. One summer, I decided to do some research on sexuality. I had checked out books on bisexuality at the college library. Unfortunately, I returned a few books a day late.

The library system was very efficient. They immediately printed out an overdue notice and sent it to my permanent address on file. My mother opened the letter from the library, saw the titles of the books, and mailed the notice to me. My process of coming out had begun!

I have worn various labels for my sexuality at different points in my life. Since coming out, I have used labels including bisexual, gay, and queer. I am a man more attracted to men than to women, so the gay label works just fine for me most of the time.

Some people hate labels and rebel against them. But before you can sing the praises of not being labeled, you need to ask yourself if you aren't still disowning a part of yourself. How can you truly embrace your sexuality without owning it? You cannot own your sexuality if you are unwilling to give it a name.

At the intersection of sex, identity, and spirituality, there are two major stages. At the first stage, we must own our identities as gay, queer, bisexual, transgender, or whatever feels appropriate. Our task is to learn to fully inhabit who we are, especially in the face of religions and cultures that have heaped shame upon us.

At the second major stage, we must learn to transcend our identities. Our task becomes learning to identify with our spiritual nature and not strictly with our sexual or other finite identities. We must take coming out to the next level: realizing ever more deeply our fundamental nature.

In his book *Ten Smart Things Gay Men Can Do to Improve Their Lives*, psychotherapist Joe Kort stresses the importance of the first stage of awareness. Kort gives a detailed portrait of what I'm calling the first stage, dividing it into six separate stages.

Kort describes the full coming-out process as involving stages taking a gay man from identity confusion to tolerance to acceptance and finally to pride. Kort says, "Coming out is a lifelong process; it never ends . . . every man is different. Clients veer back and forth, through all the stages."

José Cabezón is a Buddhist scholar and gay man. In an interview with *What Is Enlightenment?* magazine, Cabezón stresses the importance of the second stage of awareness. The Buddhist path requires that gender and sexual distinctions be transcended, not ignored, he says.

"Buddhism makes a distinction between two levels of reality: the conventional level and the ultimate level," he explains. "At the conventional level, the distinctions that we normally encounter in the world . . . are operative. They are valid and useful. . . . But, like all distinctions, they tend to limit our way of understanding the world."

According to Cabezón, many Westerners tend to overidentify with their gender and sexual orientation, even confounding these with their true self and attempting to ground their spiritual quest in them. He believes this is a mistake.

In "Sex, Identity, Spirituality: God in Gay Culture," an August 2004 dialogue posted to the Integral Naked website, Patrick McNamara and Ken Wilber discuss the apparent conflicts between identity and spirituality.

McNamara explains, "For me spirituality is a more important piece of my identity than being gay." But he also says that coming out has been a vital step along his journey of spiritual self-discovery.

Wilber explains that there are many different meanings of spirituality, all of which have a role to play at different stages. In the first stage, spirituality serves the function of acknowledging, understanding, and celebrating one's finite sense of self.

Spirituality helps us to joyously and energetically celebrate our bodies, our gay sexuality, and who we are in the world. As Wilber says to McNamara, "You really have to inhabit being gay before you can inhabit being Emptiness . . ."

In the second stage, spirituality serves the function of searching for an expanded sense of identity with an Absolute Reality, Spirit, or Emptiness beyond all finite forms. This is a much less common form of spirituality, since fewer individuals have reached this stage.

At this level you must grow from a spirituality of self-celebration to one of realizing your true identity with Absolute Reality. On the one hand, we must come out of the sexual closet. On the other hand, Wilber notes, we may find ourselves having to "come out of the closet about [our] own Supreme Identity." This can be tough, because there's a massive taboo in our culture against knowing who you truly are.

Labels are a useful tool for helping us to own all the parts of ourselves. When stepping out of the closet, we must passionately embrace and celebrate these parts in order to find our true selves. Later, we may reach the point where we can wear our labels lightly, opening the possibility of finding an even greater, more spiritual identity.

Sunday, August 22

Virgo

As the summer sun begins to fade, the energy of Virgo comes to the forefront. The Virgin's desire is growth, development, refinement, and healing above all else. Analytical thinking, pickiness, and a pragmatic sensibility are the primary tools of the Virgin. Criticism of self and others is not the end but the means toward the Virgin's ultimate goal: perfection of body, mind, and spirit.

Tuesday, August 24

My friend Darel and I met at the Tully's Coffee in Wallingford today. Darel is studying for a degree in chemical dependency counseling, and I have asked to get together with him to ask his advice on recovery issues. I have been frustrated with traditional approaches to recovery and want to start looking for ways of recovery that are more integral. It's frustrating that existing approaches to recovery are so partial, and yet their proponents are usually convinced that only their way is worthwhile.

Abstinence-based recovery programs such as 12-step meetings demand strict avoidance of prohibited behavior (drinking, gambling, overeating, sexual liaisons, and so forth). They also insist that dependency on the source of the addiction be replaced with dependency on a Higher Power. Addiction is "self-will run riot" and recovery is learning to subjugate one's own will to God's (with the help of a sponsor and other recovering addicts).

Harm-reduction, behavioral therapy, and "rational recovery" programs encourage the reprogramming of mental scripts that are linked to addictive behaviors. The addict's problem is not too much self-will; on the contrary, the problem is that his or her self-esteem and self-will are not firmly developed enough. Recovery demands strengthening the addict's sense of identity as a being capable of making reasonable choices to avoid irrational addictive behaviors in the light of enlightened self-interest. These styles of recovery encourage the addict to attain independence from all sources of dependency, including unhealthy dependency on religious institutions or spiritual fallacies.

Recovery programs based on mythopoetic principles identify the archetypal Addict as one of two shadow energies of the universal Lover archetype (the other being the Frozen or Numb One). Whereas 12-step programs encourage a shift from one form of dependence to another, and rational recovery programs foster independence, these programs strive for a recognition of interdependence and the growth of transpersonal awareness. Developing a healthy, balanced, and integrated relationship to the Lover archetype allows human beings to feel the delights of beauty, bask in sensuality, and enjoy the richness of the world. Recovery requires expanding the definition of selfhood to include repressed and denied dimensions of a transpersonal nature, thereby healing dysfunctional archetypes and replacing them with healthier expressions.

Addicts are right to feel confused by the competing and antithetical claims of various approaches to recovery. For most people, it's probably wisest to select one approach that is the best fit for their particular level of personal development and their own spiritual beliefs. Traditional religious believers might feel most comfortable in 12-step programs; agnostics and atheists might benefit most from cognitive therapy; and the "spiritual, but not religious" types might find themselves gravitating to Jungian therapy and dreamwork. Still others may be best served by combining aspects of different approaches to create an individually tailored program. The biggest risk of attempting to forge a synthesis among the various approaches to recovery is that their methods work against each other. The result isn't a synthesis, but chaos (like a dieter trying to follow an all-carb and a no-carb diet at the same time). Addicts can ill afford the risk of creating intense internal disharmony. If contrasting approaches to recovery are to be combined effectively, then they must first be integrated into a broad, coherent model of what constitutes human mental health and spiritual well-being. In this way, each type of program can be recognized as offering valuable methodologies that operate at different levels of our being at different stages in the recovery process.

I know Darel from the men's-work community, so it's not surprising that we are both wearing talismans.

Darel looked at my talisman and asked, "Is that new?"

"No," I said. "I've had this one for a couple years now. An ex-lover made it for me out of a bunch of my loose beads, and he sewed them together with some beads of his own. Steve H. gave me this bead when he led my first men's group. Larry M. gave me this bead, the one shaped like a big red teardrop. And the oval mirror: you gave that to me."

Darel: "Of course. For doing the Healing the Adolescent Wound weekend."

Darel's talisman also features an oval mirror.

Wednesday, September 1

The Seeker

Today, I walked around the lake and imagined myself back at the pyramids of Teotihuacán. In my mind's eye, I see myself as a character in an imaginary movie called *The Seeker*. I'm climbing to the top of a pyramid with a handsome man. I cast Ewan McGregor as Johnny, the boyfriend.

Johnny: "Do you remember what I said to you on our first date? I said, 'Do I get bonus points in heaven for dating a mystic?'"

234

Joe: "No. You said, 'Do I get bonus points in heaven for *fucking* a mystic!'"

Johnny: "And you promised me nothing!"

Joe: "Maybe you're paying off some very bad karma."

Johnny: "Ha ha. Now here I am, grinning from ear to ear, walking up the Temple of the Sun with my own Aztec god."

Joe: "Stop!"

Johnny: "You're blushing! Well, you shouldn't. To me, you are a god. Just like the rest of us—no more, no less—of course. I believe we all carry the spark of the Divine within. Go ahead and call me New Age."

Joe: "I'm not a god. I'm not a devil. I'm just a man, a lowly unpublished writer. But I'm going to write a book about my spiritual journey. You know I've been keeping a journal and an Internet diary. Well, I'm going to bring all my writings together under one cover."

Johnny: "A book?! Will I be in it?"

Joe: "Sure. You and Harry, you'll both be in the book. But you'll have to be fictional composites."

Johnny: "Fine. Just give me Brad Pitt's looks and the wisdom of . . . oh, I don't know. Someone like Madonna, but more credible. Samuel L. Jackson would be perfect as Harry, by the way."

Joe: "I'm thinking more along the lines of Delroy Lindo for Harry."

Johnny: "Don't take offense, but who would want to read your journals?"

Joe: "Here's the elevator pitch: I'm a seeker, worldly but not too jaded, cutting a path between skepticism and faith, searching hungrily for meaning as I grope in the darkness of a torn world."

Johnny: "Okay, maybe I'd bite. But is there a market for a gay spirituality book?"

Johnny and Joe reach the top of the Temple of the Sun.

Joe: "It won't be a *gay* gay book. At a certain point, don't we stop being gay with a capital G and start just being multifaceted human beings with souls?"

Johnny: "I'm not so sure I have a soul."

Joe: "Maybe you just need a little help in finding your 'soul spot.'"

Friday, September 3

The Childhood Wound

I'm picturing myself in *The Seeker*, an imaginary movie of my own life. In this scene, twenty or thirty men are gathering around a campfire, beating drums.

As I stand in the circle, an elder with a formidable presence walks around me. Harry carefully observes my bodily movements and facial expressions. Torches provide illumination.

Harry: "You're nine. You're in the woods again, the deep forest. You're running. Why are you running?"

Joe: "It's around the time of my birthday. Labor Day weekend. I wandered away from my family's campsite. Everyone's there—Mom and Dad, my brothers, my sister, plus lots of aunts, uncles, and cousins. I got lost. I can't find my way back. I keep wandering, but I don't see another soul anywhere. Hours pass."

Harry: "How long were you lost?"

Joe: "All morning and into the afternoon. I was totally alone. I cried the whole time. I felt so ashamed. And I thought I was going to die."

Harry: "And at the end of the afternoon?"

Joe: "I got lucky. I finally found a road. After another hour or so, a man on a motorcycle drove by. I waved him down and he took me back to the camp."

Harry: "And then?"

Joe: "Nobody had even noticed that I was missing."

Harry: "There were no search parties. Nobody was worried about you. Nobody went looking for you. They didn't see you."

A man with spiky blond hair approaches Harry carrying a black sash.

Harry: "You're 'I don't see you.'"

Man: "I don't see you. I don't see you." He blindfolds Joe.

Harry: "They neglected you, nine. What kind of a family would do that?"

A man takes my hand.

Harry: "You're 'I don't love you.'"

A man says, "I don't love you. I don't love you."

He leads Joe up a high platform. When they reach the top, the man folds Joe's arms over his chest and snaps his feet together.

A voice says, "Turn around 180 degrees."

Harry: "You're still alone, aren't you, Joe? No longer nine, but still lost, still seeking. Still wondering if you matter to anyone. You wonder if anything really matters at all. Twenty and some odd years later and your only real companion is your own private fantasy world. That's pathetic. Life doesn't have to be this way. You can make new choices. You can trust. Keep your back straight. Feet together.

"Tonight you have trusted men with your pain and your hope; now you must trust us with your life. Fall back!"

Joe falls back into the arms of many loving, accepting men. They take his blindfold off. He sees many men with big smiles and hearty cheers, and they cradle him in their arms. He grins from ear to ear.

Men: "We see you, Joe. We love you, Joe. You can trust us, Joe. I see you. I love you."

Wednesday, September 15

I have just finished reading Fenton Johnson's *Keeping Faith: A Skeptic's Journey*, and I'm ruminating on the importance of discipline in my life. In writing his book, Johnson spent time in monasteries and interviewed many Buddhist and Christian monks. He writes:

> This is the attraction and utility of monasticism, Eastern or Western—it is like art—in a very real sense it is art, the hours of life shaped to an ideal, never achieved but always present as a place to which to aspire. Like art it must be an end unto itself; its beauty and its truth arise from the impulse to create . . . Monasticism is about making time sacred, removing from it any possibility of a price.

These days I feel that I'm being called again and again to deepen my own discipline: my battles with the alarm clock, managing my finances, hitting the gym regularly, keeping to regular morning prayer. It's hard to do all this on my own, and I imagine that the discipline would come easier in community. That's why the order and structure of monastic life holds great appeal for me at the moment. I fantasize about the value of undertaking a Vipassana or Zen retreat, or some other sort of monastic experience. Such retreats will probably play a role in my future spiritual journey.

Reading Johnson's book inspires me to see an encounter with the monastic life in my future. And his words also speak to a deeper challenge: How can I make my time sacred, here and now? How can I deepen my realization of the preciousness of life, so close to mind, and turn my life into a work of art? My own struggles include AIDS, homophobia, and crafting a comprehensive worldview that gives homosexuality its rightful place. In these, am I not following the impulse to create beauty and truth—finding in the task of building order the work of creating holiness—as an end unto itself?

Thursday, September 16

The Gift of Otherness

In the passenger seat of his rental car, his lover was dying. Fenton Johnson drove 200 kilometers in France with the accelerator to the floor to get him to a decent hospital. Stuck in Paris traffic, he felt him slipping away.

"My friend is very sick with AIDS [*gravement malade avec le SIDA*]," Johnson pleaded upon arrival. The women at the hospital desk rose and left, filled with fear. So he begged, "*Madame, je vous en prie.*"

One woman turned back. Johnson checked his lover into the intensive care unit. The next morning, the head nurse ordered Johnson to leave his lover's side. Only spouses and close relatives were allowed as visitors.

A few hours later his lover died, with Johnson watching from the hall outside his door. Some years later, Johnson would write about the experience in his memoir, *Keeping Faith*. The book is the recipient of the 2004 Lambda Literary Award in the category of spirituality.

Johnson's book describes his journey from believer to skeptic to resident in two monastic communities, one Christian and the other Buddhist. In the course of his journey, he discovers a mature outlook that leaves behind only that which truly must be abandoned: cynicism, hubris, and simple notions about faith that had prevented his full awakening to truth.

Johnson says that the moment in the Parisian hospital when he was ordered to leave his lover's side caused a revelation. It stripped away his self-delusion that as a white American male, an insider, he was specially privileged and therefore safe from persecution. He writes: "Literally now, as the words flow onto the page, do I understand that my homosexuality provided my particular doorway to the place the Buddha called samsara, the place where Jesus hangs in agony on the cross, a place that as a middle-class white man in America I might otherwise have managed to avoid: the place of the outsider, the world of suffering."

Homosexuality opened the door to spirituality for Johnson by requiring him to step into the role of the outsider, or "other." The role of the other may be seen as an opportunity rather than a burden. The challenge of this role is an invitation to transform suffering into redemption, samsara into nirvana.

Johnson writes: "The wellspring of faith resides in the source of my otherness, my homosexuality—the condition that led me, or rather forced me, to seize my destiny and determine my own values, even as it taught me to respect the given, those aspects of life over which I had little or no control."

I recently interviewed Johnson by telephone.

Joe: How do you define yourself? Christian? Buddhist? Interfaith?

Fenton: That's a complex question. Since this is an election year and people are speaking in sound bites, I'll give you a simplistic answer: Christian. I'm a Christian who has a Buddhist practice.

Joe: Why did you go outside of Christianity for your practice? Why did you look to Buddhism?

Fenton: Religions are like gorgeous gowns, each of which one puts on. Underneath, there is still a human being. They enrich the experience of being human. They help us to find out more about what it means to be human. It's impossible to escape the common analogy that the East and West are like two halves of a sphere. They complement each other. All religions have the same thing to say, in different ways.

Joe: What was the role of homosexuality in your spiritual development?

Fenton: Growing up gay makes one self-conscious about one's body.

You can't take your body for granted in the way one can more easily do if one is heterosexual. Growing up gay, an outsider, is an opportunity. We are given that opportunity by the fact of our desire and that in turn changes us.

Early on I had to do a lot of things I would never have done: gay bars, gay neighborhoods, gay parties. I had experiences that made me stretch my understanding of the world. I was brought by my anger to confront my attitude toward religion. I had to break the mold I was given because the mold I was given didn't work. I couldn't make it work.

Joe: Did growing up gay make your spiritual development more challenging in any ways?

Fenton: All challenges are opportunities. That sounds like a cliché, but it's true. Growing up gay made it more difficult at every step. Mainstream religions are homophobic. Lots of gays and lesbians never get past that. They reject church because church has rejected them. That's a great tragedy. It's a loss to religious institutions, but also it's our loss. If we stay stuck in that place, we allow the homophobic voices to define us.

The gift of Otherness is a religious or spiritual gift. It is being the outsider, the unconventional people who are given the gift of showing the way. . . . As outsiders, we can explore spiritual paths the culture can then follow. In less technologically sophisticated cultures, they use everything. Gayness—that's something our culture doesn't make use of.

Joe: There is the idea that gay people on the whole have special and unique spiritual gifts to offer the world. Some say that in ages past, before the patriarchy, persons with same-sex attractions and behaviors were revered and given special honor as members of a spiritual elite. We were the shamans and the Two-Spirit people, that sort of thing. Do you see it that way?

Fenton: I agree with most of what you say. But being gay is an opportunity, not a guarantee. There's no inherent gift just because one is gay. If one has access to anything it's probably bitterness and anger.

I think every gift is also a burden (maybe that's my Roman Catholic upbringing speaking). Take great beauty for example. We see someone of great beauty and we may say, "Don't I wish that I were that person." But consider how difficult it must be for that person. Their every encounter they are seen from that angle. People interact with them and they're thinking, "What can I do to get this guy (or woman) into bed?" Great beauty has the potential to deform the person. I've seen that.

When there is a great gift—such as beauty, or great intelligence or wealth—there is also a great responsibility. Our being gay offers us an opportunity to grow, but we have to have courage and perseverance to seize that opportunity and make something extraordinary from it.

Thursday, September 16

Looking at Lookism

You walk into a crowded bar and a dozen heads turn your way. In an instant, most of the men's eyes avert. But some eyes continue to watch. They check out your clothes, face, body, and crotch. Looks are everything.

A while later, you are cruising through the bar. You are enchanted by one man's delicious bedroom eyes and another's hairy, rippling chest. You make a note of the cuties and hotties that you want to get to know better. Ah, you say, thank heaven for beauty!

Although this experience is a common one for gay men, the desire for beauty is held in suspicion by those who say that admiring beauty is unjust or demeaning and by others who say that it's antispiritual. What is the truth about beauty?

The *American Heritage Dictionary* defines lookism as "discrimination or prejudice against people based on their appearance." Lookism includes thinking less of a person whose appearance is less than ideal, or thinking more of a person because of his good looks.

Or, as the writer Bianca puts it in her "Lesbian Lexicon": "Lookism: dykes are not supposed to judge potential partners on looks because it is unfair and in poor taste."

In *The Beauty Myth*, feminist Naomi Wolf went so far as to claim that the hunger for beauty is a pathological product of mass media and advertising. The pursuit of beauty is a distraction from more worthwhile matters, she says, and nothing is to be considered beautiful unless everything is seen as being equally beautiful in its own way.

Although the egalitarian impulse of beauty's critics is a fine one, their admonitions against admiring beauty fly in the face of reality. The impulse to treat people differently because of their looks is an essential part of our sexuality and the ways of the world.

Because the battle against lookism is as hopelessly absurd as a battle against human nature itself, lookism has never been taken seriously enough to join other -isms, such as racism and sexism, in the cultural mindset. Asking people not to judge potential partners on looks is like asking them to avoid judging potential meals on how they taste or to avoid judging potential cars based on how they run. It isn't mean, nasty, or unjust to admire the beauty in some people more than others. However, it can definitely be wrong to act on that admiration inappropriately.

According to researchers in Texas and Michigan, attractive employees are paid 10 percent more than unattractive employees who have the same level of experience and do the same work. Pulchritude has also been documented as impacting experiences in schools, homes, courtrooms, and encounters with police.

If the issue of lookism is cast as an injustice in society and not as a problem with how people judge potential sexual or romantic partners, then it gains much in credibility. Still, battling lookism poses difficult problems. Do we sue Abercrombie and Fitch for discriminating against unattractive fashion models? How do we deal effectively with a prejudice that most agree is a largely unconscious phenomenon?

Admiring beauty is not only attacked as being politically incorrect, but also as philosophically or spiritually incorrect. Some critics say that it's wrong to look at a beautiful thing because it turns it into an object to which we feel superior. If the admiration for beauty leads to desire, Christians often attack the impulse as lust. A Buddhist teacher might say that it's wrong to admire a hot guy because doing so turns us away from the pursuit of enlightenment and represents a form of "clinging" or "attachment."

There's some truth to these concerns about beauty, but the truth needs to be carefully separated from the falsehood. I agree with the general idea that there are higher and lower ways of admiring a beautiful thing and that some ways are more superficial than others. It is possible to admire a hot guy based only on his body. It is also possible to admire a hot guy based on his body, heart, mind, and soul. As hot as it can be to admire a great face or toned body, it's much more satisfying to find beauty that is far beyond skin deep.

However, it's not always possible to enjoy the ideal. Many human interactions start with the superficial and get more complex from there. The gay community offers many opportunities for admiring superficial levels of beauty: underwear nights at bars, nude beaches, sexually explicit websites, and so forth. These sorts of interactions frequently involve objectifying other persons . . . and turning ourselves into sex objects.

I'm all for enjoying a tanned, gorgeous man in a snug pair of white boxer briefs. As Jerry Seinfeld might have said were he gay, it's not that there's anything wrong with that. But when we're being superficial, let's not fool ourselves into thinking that we are feeding our soul anything more than eye candy. To truly satisfy our soul's hunger for beauty, we have to go deeper.

The Christian mystic Simone Weil claimed that finite human beings perceive the infinite Spirit through beauty. She wrote, "The beautiful is the experimental proof that the incarnation is possible." Every time we respond to beauty in another human being or in the world around us, we are opening ourselves to God. This is why the quest for beauty is so paradoxical. The beauty our soul seeks in a beautiful object cannot be possessed, because it's the infinitely beautiful Source that is the true object of our desire.

That's why I disagree with those Buddhists who say that beauty is an "attachment" that turns us away from the true goal of spirituality. Anthony Flanagan, About.com's guide to Buddhism, says that the Buddha taught that food should be taken only for sustenance and ending discomfort, not for the enjoyment of its taste nor for its contribution to physical beauty and attractiveness. The Buddha also says that his followers should make the effort to ignore attractive things and cultivate attraction for repulsive things in order to attain liberation from impermanence. (Is this a valid path to enlightenment? I don't know and frankly I don't want to find out. Whatever else it may be, it's certainly a surefire recipe for a dull, bland, erotophobic lifestyle that successfully proves the adage "Virtue is its own punishment.")

Longing for beauty doesn't take us away from the Infinite but rather toward greater and higher states of being. The desire for beautiful objects can become a distraction from spiritual growth, however, if the lustful appetites are fixated merely on superficial levels of beauty instead of wanting to admire beauty in all its many dimensions. In other words, the problem arises when we are invited to life's banquet and then starve to death because we only ate the eye candy and not the delicious feast.

That's the error and truth in lookism, as I see it. Beauty isn't merely in the eye of the beholder. Beauty is in the eye, heart, mind, soul, and spirit of the beholder. As we grow in the depth of our spirituality, we begin to see beauty where before we saw none.

Friday, October 17

The M Word

Today many gays have nonmonogamous lifestyles. Others believe in following a more traditional path. Is there a way to bring all the opposing attitudes and beliefs about monogamy together in a way that respects the truths of both sides? I believe there is.

The majority of gay men, it seems, see the defects of sexually exclusive relationships. We would agree with Oscar Wilde, who quipped that "bigamy is having one wife too many. Monogamy is the same."

David Nimmons tries to pin down the numbers regarding gay men and monogamy in his book *The Soul Beneath the Skin*. He says that between 40 and 50 percent of gay men are in committed couples at any given time. Studies of gay male couples have shown that as many as 75 percent are nonmonogamous.

In 1992, says Nimmons, British researchers found that while many gay male couples begin as monogamous, 72 percent of gay male couples were nonmonogamous after five years. Other researchers have found that sexual jealousy is lower for coupled gay males than for straight men in heterosexual pairings.

Nimmons's approach to the issue of monogamy is to celebrate the gay male lifestyle as a cultural innovation that can even serve as a model for spicing up the sex lives of heterosexuals. He approvingly quotes a British gay liberation text: "Our heterosexual detractors betray their limited vision by their mistaken assumption that promiscuity is incompatible with lasting relationships."

Nimmons also describes a gathering of one hundred men discussing the "gay rescripting of monogamy" at a conference of the National Gay and Lesbian Task Force. All in open relationships, the men took the opportunity to exchange tips and stories.

"We only do it in three-ways," said one man. "It's OK if neither of you knows the person," said another. "Just on our designated 'boys' night out,'" said one couple. "Only when we travel," another couple remarked.

Not all gay men are suited for nonmonogamous lifestyles. Michael Shernoff, MSW, authored a case study for the journal *Family Therapy Networker* called "Monogamy and Gay Men: When Are Open Relationships a Therapeutic Option?" He shared the story of Peter and Luis, a gay couple who had been together for ten years.

Peter and Luis loved each other and wanted to stay together, but their love life was lacking in frequency and intensity. They usually had sex about twice a month and didn't feel much passion with each other. In couples' therapy they began to explore a variety of options for overcoming their dissatisfaction.

They contemplated opening their relationship, but they both feared that doing so would lead to a breakup. They also didn't want to become like another gay couple they knew, who always seemed to have a third man in their bedroom.

After some time in therapy, they decided to have a one-time experiment with nonmonogamy. They set ground rules and brought a third man into their bedroom. The experience wasn't as exciting as they hoped, and jealous feelings on the part of both Peter and Luis got in the way. They decided together not to try it again.

Peter and Luis made a choice in their relationship that few gay activists would disparage. However, in practice, it is common for gay writers to attack the traditional rules and strictures associated with monogamous relationships even while claiming that they are respectful of the choices made by folks making more traditional lifestyle choices.

David Nimmons, for example, suggests that "cheating" and "betrayal," key notions for the monogamous, are inhumane concepts. He writes: "What if married couples felt less stigma about naming what statistics tell us that so many of them already do? Might we one day erase the words 'cheating' and 'betrayal' from the matrimonial script? Indeed, might the very concepts slowly evaporate from a more humane marital vocabulary?"

I am suggesting that there is a way to move beyond the divide between the monogamous and the nonmonogamous, a way between the preachers of traditional values and the advocates of queer cultural innovation. The key is to grasp that there are three major stages of gay male relationships. In developing this idea, I was inspired by the work of David Deida, author of *Intimate Communion*.

The first stage of gay male relationships is characterized by a desire for fluid and polymorphously perverse sexual play with multiple partners and/or by sexual role playing based on power dynamics (fetish, sado-masochistic play, etc.). Nonmonogamy is celebrated as a good thing, and monogamy is seen as monotony. The concepts of cheating and betrayal are ignored as irrelevant or attacked as inhumane.

In the second stage, gay male relationships are characterized by a desire for a balanced relationship with one primary partner, usually in a conventional marriage or domestic partnership. Monogamy is upheld as the paragon of virtue, and nonmonogamous liaisons are forbidden. The concepts of cheating and betrayal are accepted.

In the third stage, our relationships are characterized by a desire for deep intimacy and passionate sexual aliveness that may be found with one or more partners in conventional or unconventional relationships. Monogamy and nonmonogamy are both recognized as playing important roles in the development of a mature sexuality. Fidelity is an important value in third-stage relationships, though it may find different modes of expression depending on whether the relationship is monogamous or nonmonogamous. The concepts of cheating and betrayal are accepted as important to the maintenance of fidelity.

The problem with gay advocates of nonmonogamy isn't that they're wrong about the goodness of open relationships. The problem is that they fail to recognize that there are multiple stages of development in sexual relationships, so they don't get that monogamy offers valuable lessons for everyone, even the gay community.

The way beyond the divide between the monogamous and the nonmonogamous is to see that there is truth on both sides. At certain stages in our sexual development, having multiple partners or having just one are both suitable lifestyle choices. Ultimately what's important isn't the number of partners but the maturity of the lovers.

Saturday, September 18

Wrestling with God

"Wrestling feels a lot like making love. It also feels a lot like making war," wrote Rabbi Arthur Waskow, PhD, in a poem. In recent decades, the Jewish Renewal movement, of which Waskow is a part, has given a variety of new expressions to the struggle that has moved people for centuries: wrestling with God and with each other.

In the Bible, Jacob and his brother Esau had begun to wrestle with each other even before they were born. Their combat inside the womb was so fierce that Rebekah, their mother, cried out in agony.

As an adult, Jacob had an experience of profound transformation. He struggled with a mysterious foe. The details are sketchy, but he spent a full night fighting with "a man" who then told him he had wrestled "with God and with men" and won. He's renamed Israel, the God-wrestler.

In his book *Godwrestling*, Waskow says he wrote his poem about wrestling as a young man grappling with sibling rivalry. And as an adult, he began to see new dimensions to the wrestling match described in the Bible.

He says that a friend of his heard his poem and called it "the first gay Jewish poem—or at least the first that says God is gay." The implication is that Jacob discovered a profound truth that night in an unexpected grip or toss, pinned to the muscular body of another man: there is both love and war in the pressing of flesh.

The heterosexual Waskow acknowledges the homoerotic reading but says that he was intending to say that within each person are all the polarities that have been conveniently assigned to men or to women, Same and Other. To wrestle with God is to unify opposites in the same way that God unifies.

We all contain love and anger, gentleness and toughness, and fear and guilt, the rabbi suggests. God is the force of reconciliation in the world. It's not really that God is gay; rather, it's that God is both gay and nongay; God is the force that moves us beyond duality.

Waskow is part of a nondenominational religious reform movement called Jewish Renewal. It is grounded in Judaism's prophetic and mystical traditions and incorporates insights from a variety of 20th-century influences, especially those with a progressive political vision. Many in this religious reform movement are also involved in social change movements such as gay rights and feminism, which they believe have tended to downplay or even deny the spiritual dimension of life.

The reformers do not simply accept Jewish traditions uncritically, but they do not reject them either. They wrestle with them.

When gays fight with the Bible, we often get pinned under some mighty heavy burdens. For example, Leviticus 18 says, "You shall not lie with a male as with a woman, it is abomination." And Leviticus 20 commands the death penalty for men who lie with men (as well as for a wide variety of persons including those who curse their father or mother).

The Jewish Renewal perspective advocates creating the greatest possible amount of inclusion for gays and lesbians among different Jewish denominations, though these would necessarily ground such inclusion in divergent rationales. Orthodox Jews have a literalistic way of reading the Bible. However, even Orthodox communities can take significant steps toward welcoming gays in ways that conform to their own principles.

In Orthodox Judaism, moral reasoning proceeds from principles derived from the Talmud, the traditional customs and legal principles of the Jewish people. Steve Greenberg, writing in *Tikkun*, notes that some Orthodox Jewish rabbis have articulated two main arguments for changing traditional beliefs around homosexuality, basing these on two principles, known in Hebrew as *ones* and *tinok she-nishbah*. The principle of *ones* (duress) implies that a person who behaves under unbearable pressure should not be held accountable for actions that might otherwise be considered sinful. Thus, the first argument basically says that homosexuality is an involuntary condition that creates psychological duress for which sexually active gays

shouldn't be harshly condemned. The principle of *tinok she-nishbah* refers
to a Jewish child raised in captivity, who doesn't know Jewish law and therefore should not be condemned for violating it. Thus, the second argument
says that homosexuals have been seduced by Western permissive values and
should therefore be treated with leniency.

Greenberg says these strategies may be able to slowly nudge Orthodox
communities into offering greater hospitality to gay members. However, he
also notes that gay people "cannot reasonably be required to internalize the
claims that we are either mentally ill or victims of a debased social milieu."
Most gays must wrestle more deeply with the Bible than the Orthodox traditions are ready to allow.

Rabbi Michael Lerner, PhD, offers a radically inclusive vision for gays
in *Jewish Renewal: A Path to Healing and Transformation*. For Lerner, God
is not a big daddy or grand puppet master in the sky. For him, God is the
force of healing and transformation in history.

Lerner does not assume, as the Orthodox do, that every word of
Leviticus is the word of God. What demented, wrathful sort of God would
condemn homosexuals and demand that they be stoned to death? What
sort of fucked-up God would sanction treating women and children as
chattel or tolerate slavery?

Lerner's vision of Jewish Renewal holds that some of what is recorded
in the Bible as the voice of God is actually the voice of human cruelty mis-
takenly attributed to God. Ultimately, people today are obligated to wrestle
with the texts and separate the voice of healing and transformation from the
voice of pain and distortion.

As Rabbi Waskow says about God-wrestling, reading the Bible must be
both integrative and transcending, a synthesis of love making and war making. Merely trying to understand what the book really says about homosexuality will not suffice; we must actively engage in a challenging process
pointing all people toward God, the force that unifies all polarities.

When gays approach the Bible or other sacred books, we should do so
the way wrestlers grapple with their foes. Becoming like the God that reconciles all opposites, we must turn a legacy of fear and hatred into the freedom of love.

Thursday, September 23

Libra

The sun travels through a part of the sky that is connected with harmony, beauty, tranquillity, and serenity. Libra is the sign of the Scales. The symbol of the Scales is rarely depicted in perfect equilibrium; for although balance is Libra's goal, it is not always its nature. Balance cannot be achieved without first recognizing how one is out of whack. Relationships are the key tool for growth; they allow us to develop higher consciousness of self by learning to take the role of the other. Libra's true aim: self-awareness.

Friday, September 24

In this election season, everyone's talking about politics. Everyone has strong opinions, and mostly they're convinced they're right and everyone else is wrong. When looking at politics, I strive to embrace whatever wisdom can be found, regardless of who's speaking or what party they belong to.

Of course, not everyone can be equally right. Some politics are better, more inclusive, and more enlightened than others. Yet I am convinced of the value of starting by embracing as much wisdom as possible from the widest number of perspectives.

I wasn't always so open-minded. My working-class, Mexican-American family raised me with strong Democratic values. As a child, I asked my parents if they were going to vote for Jimmy Carter or Ronald Reagan. They explained that the Democrats are the party of the poor and middle class and that the Republicans are for the rich.

For many years, I believed in variations on this theme, thinking that donkeys represented compassion and enlightenment, elephants greed and bigotry. Being part of the gay community only intensified my left-leaning tendencies.

I still find myself sympathetic to progressive politics. However, now I see the world through a more complex, independent-thinking lens. I see truth and good ideas among Democrats, Republicans, Libertarians, and Greens. I applauded when Barack Obama said, "We coach Little League in the blue states and have gay friends in the red states."

Looking at the Democrats, I see a party that is concerned with advancing the rights of gays and other minorities, protecting the environment, and bettering the lives of the poor and middle class, especially by making health care more affordable. At their best, Democrats honor the traditions that protect individual liberties and oppose attempts to impose the moral values of a majority on everyone else.

Looking at the Republicans, I see a party that understands the importance of empowering individuals to succeed by creating jobs through free enterprise, keeping America's defenses strong, and maintaining limited but effective government. At their best, Republicans understand that government must protect religious freedoms for all and get out of the way of private organizations that are doing charitable works that otherwise the taxpayer would have to provide.

Truth isn't limited to the parties of red states and blue states. Libertarians understand the value of individual freedom and seem to have figured out that government can't solve all our problems. And the Greens support full marriage rights for gay people and recognize the importance of taking a global perspective on the important economic and environmental issues of our day.

Many of the values and beliefs of the Democrats, Republicans, Libertarians, and Greens are noble, and in my opinion each party has a key piece of the truth. The biggest problem with politics isn't that people don't have the right values. What's messed up is that everyone thinks their values are the only ones worth taking seriously.

Don't get me wrong. I'm not saying that there are no differences between the political candidates or parties. There are important differences. In this election, I believe the Democratic Party is clearly the best option for making America a safer, stronger, more inclusive country.

What separates me from political partisans is that I don't think the sky will fall if the other guy is elected. And I don't pretend to believe that if my guy gets into office America will transform overnight to match the rhetoric of his stump speeches.

To put it another way, I keep an eye tuned to politics because I want to stay connected to the world and do good. I keep abreast of the news and I vote, but my days as a political junkie are mostly behind me. Today I rarely find myself using political intrigue as a drug or distraction.

It is possible to bring a sense of detachment and equanimity to the voting booth. But I must confess, it's not nearly as much fun as being a raving partisan! Part of me misses the days when I could have shouted slogans like "BUSH LIED!" from the rooftops. Ah, how good it used to feel to have a nice, convenient target for projecting my hatred and venting my rage at an unjust world.

I remember my days as a knee-jerk, left-of-center partisan with nostalgia, just like a recovering alcoholic talks about Bombay Sapphires. I could hardly utter the name of Jesse Helms or Newt Gingrich or Pat Robertson without sneering and wanting to start bashing some skulls. I was a hostage to my emotional reactions and had a desperate need to blame others for everything bad.

Self-help author Stephen Covey offers a simple distinction that explains what's changed in my life. In *The Seven Habits of Highly Effective People*, Covey says that an excellent way to become more self-aware is to look at where we focus our time and energy. Everyone has a wide range of concerns, from the personal domains of health, intimate relationships, and work issues to those unfolding in the wider world around us, such as global warming, the national debt, and terrorism. We could draw a circle and put inside it everything in our "circle of concern."

Inside this circle, we could draw a smaller circle. We could identify those concerns that we can actually do something about. We could call that our "circle of influence." Covey says that by figuring out which of those circles receives our largest investment of time and energy, we can be more productive. Gradually, I've begun placing more of my time and energy inside the smaller circle.

Spirituality begins by being present to experience as it arises and avoiding life's tempting distractions. In other words, we must try to stay focused on our circle of influence. We can't "be here now" if we're always analyzing the latest Karl Rove attack ad or mentally solving the crisis in Liberia (unless, of course, we work as a political consultant or columnist).

We grow spiritually by expanding our circle of concern to the widest possible degree. We all start out by caring only for ourselves, and then we grow to care for those close to us. From there, we may grow to care for everyone in the world and for all life. Our heroes are folks like Mother

Teresa and Gandhi precisely because of their universal care and concern for all living things.

Political wisdom is the art of bringing increasing amounts of love and compassion into our circle of influence.

Tuesday, September 28

I just finished the chapter "Reality Omnipresent" in Sri Aurobindo's *The Life Divine*. Aurobindo is a Hindu philosopher credited with introducing the concept of spiritual evolution into Vedantic thought. This is a book hailed by some as the most profound spiritual work of the 20th century. At over one thousand pages, it had better be. ;-)

It's a difficult book but so far very rewarding. Aurobindo's definition of faith is the best that I've ever read. He says that faith is the ground that dissolves all dualities of reality into a higher unity. Here's a taste:

We start, then, with the conception of an omnipresent Reality of which neither the Non-Being at the one end nor the universe at the other are negations that annul; they are rather different states of the Reality, obverse and reverse affirmations. The highest experience of this Reality in the universe shows it to be not only a conscious Existence, but a supreme Intelligence and Force and a self-existent Bliss; and beyond the universe it is still some other unknowable existence, some utter and ineffable Bliss. Therefore we are justified in supposing that even the dualities of the universe, when interpreted not as now by our sensational and partial conceptions, but by our liberated intelligence and experience, will be also resolved into those highest terms. While we still labor under the stress of dualities, this perception must no doubt constantly support itself on an act of faith, but a faith which the highest Reason, the widest and most patient reflection do not deny, but rather affirm. This creed is given, indeed, to humanity to support it on its journey, until it arrives at a stage of development when faith will be turned into knowledge and perfect experience and Wisdom will be justified of her works.

Friday, October 1

On a Conservative Christian's Journey of Faith

Today Scripps-Howard columnist and religion professor Terry Mattingly offered readers of the GetReligion blog a peek into his spiritual journey and conscience formation on the thorny issues involving homosexuality and the Episcopal Church. He posts a link to a poignant 1993 essay called "Liturgical Dances with Wolves: Ten Years as an Episcopalian: A Progress Report."

In this essay, Mattingly tells of attending a Gaia mass at the Cathedral of St. John the Divine in New York City. He describes a church service "complete with chants by timber wolves, a humpback whale (taped, not live) singing the Sanctus, a sermon by Carl Sagan, and a liturgical procession featuring an elephant, a camel, a vulture, a swarm of bees in a glass frame, a bowl of blue-green algae, and an elegantly decorated banana."

The experience was so troubling to Mattingly that he decided not to receive communion at an Episcopal altar. This was the first time he had made such a choice.

"I was not sure what I would be receiving," Mattingly explains.

Not long after observing this mass, Mattingly left the Episcopal Church for the Christian Orthodox Church. He explains the core of his profession of faith: "Simply stated, I believe that Jesus Christ is the Way, the Truth, the Life. Thus, I believe in heaven and hell and that salvation is found through faith in Jesus Christ, alone."

In leaving the Episcopal Church, Mattingly received inspiration from Moses Tay, an Anglican bishop in Singapore. Preaching in Denver in 1992, Bishop Tay took as a text Revelation 2:12–16, in which the exalted Christ says to an angel: "I know where you are living, where Satan's throne is."

Bishop Tay then asked if Satan had set a throne in the Episcopal Church: "Would we be shocked if that is true, that Satan has his throne in some of our churches?" This section of the Book of Revelation offers two danger signs, Tay noted. The first is the presence of corrupt teachers who bring other gods and idols into church life through forms of syncretistic worship. Danger sign No. 2, he added, is compromise on issues of sexual immorality.

Mattingly believed that both of these danger signs were prevalent in some parts of the Anglican Communion, and this brought him shame and sadness. It upset him because it is forbidden in the Bible. Fearing that the Episcopal Church was betraying its essential principles, he abandoned it for a sect with greater doctrinal purity and old-fashioned sexual ethics.

In Mattingly's story of conversion, there is no denying his great fear for the state of the Episcopal Church. He openly wonders if the liberal wing of the church is nothing less than Satan's throne. And the ordination of openly gay persons is, for Mattingly and millions of other conservatives, a key symbol of the Episcopal Church going astray and a vindication of their fear.

If homosexuals are accepted in the Church, conservative religionists fear that the authority of their traditions and scriptures will be impugned. And if the authority is lost, then the faith's definition of God is in doubt and their own personal salvation is at stake. Mattingly asks this haunting question: "Today one issue looms above all others: Who is our God?"

I believe this really is the great question of our times—not just for conservative religionists, but for all people who seek Truth with an open heart and mind. But instead of asking "Who is our God?" I would ask, as Ken Wilber does in *The Eye of Spirit*, "Where do we locate Spirit?" The answer to this question always translates into the political agendas confronting our churches and society. Is God on the side of the West or on the side of the Muslim extremists? Is God with the poor or the wealthy? For whom would Jesus vote?

Do we locate Spirit in a revelation given to a particular people some two thousand years ago? Do we locate Spirit in the traditions of the patriarchy and in romantic times past, when men behaved like real men and women like proper ladies? Do we locate Spirit in a concept of God that is separate from the world, a jealous God who opposes the worship of other gods and smites unbelievers with threats of eternal damnation? Do we locate Spirit in a homophobic God who demands that men who lie with men should be stoned to death?

I suggest that all of those answers are wrong. I suggest that we locate Spirit in the midst of an evolving world, where growth in consciousness has proceeded from partial and incomplete visions of the divine to ever greater degrees of unfolding understanding, rationality, and harmony. I suggest that we locate Spirit not in the revelations given to only one tribe but (in degrees) to the best wisdom traditions of all the world's religions, including pagan and goddess traditions, such as those affirmed by the Episcopal worship service that so upset Mattingly.

I suggest we locate Spirit deep in the heart of the individual, in the midst of relationships as the source of love and healing, and as the force deep in authentic community, nature, and the evolution of life on the earth. I suggest that we see Spirit in the growth of Enlightenment rationality that reveals the historically conditioned, mythic character of "revealed truth." I suggest that we notice the emergence of Spirit within the great liberation movements that ended slavery and that are in the midst of ending the suffering of women and men, gays and straights, and all sentient beings.

There is much to fear in the contemporary world. Many of my fears are related to the rise of radical religious fundamentalism in our midst. And yet there is reason also for hope, when we can look into the hearts of conservative religionists and identify a common bond. We may find ourselves sharing a devotion to the search for Truth and a conviction that there is no question more profound than the matter of where we locate Spirit.

Wednesday, October 6

I'm speaking tonight at the Ken Wilber meet-up in Seattle—7:00 p.m. at the Madison Park Starbucks. The topic is the mythopoetic movement and how mythology fits with integral theory and practice. I will be talking briefly about Robert Bly, Freud, mythic archetypes and the masculine/feminine types of integral psychology, and the mythopoetic men's movement.

Speaking of masculine/feminine types, in a post on his blog today profeminist gender studies teacher Hugo Schwyzer is being criticized by some of his feminist readers for the unpardonable sin of actually using the words "masculine" and "feminine" to describe behaviors and tendencies among the genders! Here's part of what I said on his blog today:

One of your commenters wrote:

I'm out here pulling my hair out at the idea of certain behaviors and stances being labeled "masculine" or "feminine." Gahh!!! Erect penises are masculine. Breastfeeding is feminine. But being outspoken, or aggressive, or liking sports, or . . . whatever . . . is simply human. OK???

Hugo, I hope you don't stop writing about gender issues and using appropriately descriptive labels like masculine or feminine. I think you include more than enough disclaimers, qualifications, and links to background information to explain yourself well. The problem isn't how you write. The problem is that some highly sensitive souls refuse to acknowledge ways of talking about tendencies and generalizations regarding masculinity and femininity that are not oppressive. That's their problem, not yours.

Take the commenter who wrote that liking sports is human, not masculine or feminine. I don't think you ever would claim that all men like sports and all women don't, or that all "real men" like sports, etc. But just the thought of acknowledging that there are tendencies among the genders — women do not, on average, participate in sports or watch sporting events with nearly the frequency of men (ask any sports program director, media buyer, or Gallup pollster) — will send some of your readers into a hissy fit. The more vehement ones may even call you nasty names or try to bully you into silence. Try not to let it get you down.

Wednesday, October 13

Did Jesus Really Rise from the Dead? Part 1 of 3

Did Jesus really rise from the dead? For the first time in many years, my answer to this question is *Yes, I do believe.*

What changed? Part of the answer involves a story of a riddle from my past: a troubling breakdown and spiritual experience at age 30, confinement in a psychiatric ward for a time, visions in a hospital room, and an unexpected sight outside my room. I told this story in my journal (see entries on June 8 and June 15), and I'll have a bit more to say about it. And part of the answer involves a topic I've written much about: my encounter with the integral philosophy. But for now, here's how the story ends: my mind now accepts the reality of the bodily resurrection.

It's helpful to contrast my perspective today with other ways of affirming the reality of the resurrection. Mythic-level Christians and rational-level Christians also answer the question yes, but the mythic-level "yes" means something very different from the rational-level "yes"; and both mean something quite different from my "yes."

At the mythic stage of consciousness, the resurrection is frequently invoked as an apologetic for faith or as the ground for fundamental or foundational theology. God is conceived of as separate and apart from human beings and natural history, and as the source and destiny of a purposeful order of existence governed by moral and social laws. Jesus's resurrection is therefore seen as a supernatural intervention in our history by a divine being. The empty tomb may be cited as historical demonstration of the veracity of the resurrection faith. Omnipotence is an attribute of God, it is said; so why couldn't God raise Jesus from the dead? The texts of the Bible are then adduced as proof-texts for the occasion of a resurrection miracle. And above all, the resurrection of Jesus is seen as both a singular event in history and an event with universal significance. If God raised Jesus, then traditional dogmas are upheld regarding the unique salvific power of Christian faith.

Ultimately, as Christians pass from a mythic-level faith to a rational-level faith, they may realize that traditional understandings of the resurrection are susceptible to Adolf Harnack's ridicule in *History of Dogma*: "[Of] the assertion that the resurrection of Christ is the most certain fact in the history of the world, one does not know whether he should marvel more at its thoughtlessness or its unbelief."

At the rational stage of consciousness, Jesus's resurrection is reconsidered in the light of historical-critical scholarship, transcendental theological method, and/or hermeneutical reconstructions of the biblical literary corpus. Gone is the naive belief that Bible texts can be cited as proofs of a literal truth that requires no interpretation and stands apart from hermeneutical critique. With existential theologian Paul Tillich, God is no longer conceived as a separate being apart from human existence and history but as the Ground of Being. Or, with evolutionary theologians, God may be identified as the Alpha and Omega of the process of evolution in history. Since there is no concept of a God outside of and wholly apart from the world, there is no supreme being who intervened in history to raise Jesus physically from the dead. In respect to the question of the existence of God as a supernatural being, rational-level Christians agree with atheists.

When rational-level Christians look at the resurrection, they may (with theologian Rudolf Bultmann) argue that there was no physiological body that appeared but rather a belief born in faith out of the subjective spiritual experiences of the disciples. For these Christians, the resurrection of Jesus is not an event that can be verified by historical research or that took place in human space and human time, but an event of faith.

When I first started writing this journal, my thinking about the resurrection was colored most by the rational-level approach. I might have said that I believed in Christ's resurrection as a symbol of a poetic truth about the endurance of the human spirit in the face of death, much as the Easter bunny is a symbol of hope for life renewed in springtime fertility. Since then, I have come to believe that the mythic- and rational-level approaches to the resurrection are equally suspect and inadequate interpretations.

In my own spiritual path, I have struggled with the rational level of faith, because it seemed to deprive me of a reason for continuing to be religious. When there was no physical resurrection, why bother remaining a Christian? Why pour new wine into old wineskins? Why not abandon religion altogether and just encourage kindness and love to my fellow human beings? Isn't it enough, I have frequently wondered, to be "spiritual, but not religious"?

Until I found myself coming into a new level of awareness, I had no compelling answer to these questions. It was Sunday, June 6. I had spent the morning and afternoon reading Jim Marion's *Putting on the Mind of Christ*, and suddenly years of belief and unbelief came crashing down all around me. I hurriedly threw up a post on my blog that asked, "Could I have been wrong about so many things all these years?"

I had been spending much time reading books on integral psychology and philosophy. My mind was abuzz with new concepts and terminology. This was something genuinely new. The integral approach offered a way out of the box of liberal and conservative theologies, and gave me a new way of believing in the resurrection. But I would have to dig deeper into the resurrection's meaning than I had ever gone before.

Monday, October 18

Did Jesus Really Rise from the Dead? Part 2 of 3

Did Jesus really rise from the dead? My answer is *yes*.

In the New Testament, Jesus asks his disciples, "Who do you say that I am?" Gradually, I came to believe that Jesus is the Christ, the Anointed One of God. And I also came to understand that Jesus is not God's Son in a way that means that all other human beings are less than Jesus. Jesus knew that he was the Christ. He had Christ Consciousness and a nondual consciousness of oneness with the Father ("I and the Father are One"). And Jesus knew and preached that the same reality is also true for us. We are obliged as Christians to see ourselves in unity with Christ and to see Christ in others, especially among the poor and disenfranchised.

At the rational level of awareness, I was handicapped in what I could grasp about the resurrection. I refused to acknowledge any levels of reality beyond those gross, physical, material realities that are amenable to empirical verification and historical methods of research. But I am beginning to grasp that the universe includes deeper levels of reality than what meets the eye. In short, I have learned a new way of thinking about subtle energies.

The writings of Ken Wilber and other subtle-energy theorists provide a philosophical framework for recognizing the truth of the great wisdom traditions in helping us to understand subtle energies. Reality is conceived by many wisdom traditions as comprising a hierarchy of matter, body, mind, soul, and spirit. The term "subtle energies" refers to the nonmaterial layers of being—soul and spirit—that underlie the mind and the gross physical body (variously called chi, prana, manna, ether, and so forth). Wilber shows how the existence of subtle energies can be reconciled with the research of modern science. Let's leave the details aside for now (the curious should read Ken Wilber, "Excerpt G: Toward a Comprehensive Theory of Subtle Energies" at www.kenwilber.com; you can also google for "subtle energy research" to find bibliographies, abstracts, and other resources on the Internet). I believe that there is an intellectually cogent way of talking about a reality that ultimately cannot be grasped cognitively: the existence of the soul. The soul is not a transphysical entity (existing in an unseen realm), but an intraphysical entity composed of the subtle energies (which could theoretically survive the death of the physical body).

The reality of a soul? An actual spiritual body that underlies the gross physical body and potentially survives physical death? That's right. That's what I had come to accept, both emotionally and rationally. This belief required no leap of faith or absurdly irrational tales about Abraham and Isaac. I didn't have to drag out Kierkegaard or Pascal. I simply understood in a rough fashion the plausible theory of subtle energies and then intuited the probable reality of what we may call a soul.

Once I believed in a soul, it didn't take long to figure out how Jesus of Nazareth might have accomplished the resurrection. If the testimony of the Christian tradition is essentially reliable and the New Testament stories of his life and death are more or less based on historically accurate details, then there is no doubt that Jesus manifested the very highest levels of spiritual consciousness available to human beings. If Jesus experienced reality at God-consciousness, then he completely inhabited not only his gross physical body but also the subtle energies.

What's possible for a being such as Jesus, who is fully attuned to God-consciousness and the gross, subtle, causal, and nondual states of consciousness? Well, I haven't got a very good sense of that. But I can work from the evidence offered by the mystical traditions of the great religions, the record of Jesus's spirituality in the New Testament, and my own experiences in attempting a guess. And I can further refine my thinking by taking into consideration the findings of scientific research into subtle energies. The latter step is crucial to avoid slipping back into superstitious notions that confuse belief in the soul with mythic-level notions such as belief in the reality of Casper the Friendly Ghost.

I surmise that it is, perhaps, possible after death for the body to continue to exist in a higher, spiritual form and that this physical form can even reappear on earth. Marion believes that even the Gospel story of the Doubting Thomas, where the disciple touches Jesus's body, can be reconciled with an integral theory of subtle energies. I want to believe that and perhaps someday I will be so convinced. Marion introduces a theory for the physical resurrection in the last two pages of *Putting on the Mind of Christ*. Upon reading Marion's theory, I intuited the possibility of the bodily resurrection of Christ.

The intellectual framework was in place . . . the philosophical outlook secure . . . suddenly, click! At that moment last June the truth about Jesus finally sank in like an energy flowing from my spiritual body to my mental body and from there descending throughout my physical body. I got it! The resurrection was not merely a myth. The resurrection was not merely a very good poetic tale suggestive of some platitude such as "resurrection means living in the hearts and memories of others." There is, indeed, a good, reasonable, rational basis for belief in the possibility of bodily resurrection — including the reappearance of Jesus at God-consciousness, in the precise sense described by the integral spiritual map as best I understood it.

If I could take a time machine back to Jerusalem and visit the tomb of Jesus, what would I find? I'm still not sure about that. The story of the empty tomb is irrelevant to my beliefs, for it neither supports nor refutes them. If Jesus survived death and was resurrected and reappeared to his disciples, it would not be in a gross body but in a spiritual body. The gross body could still be in the tomb. From this perspective, the empty tomb is not a great mystery of faith but a minor historical curiosity.

Would it have been possible to take a Polaroid of the risen Christ? What would the photo show? I'm not sure, but I think the photo might very well have shown something tangible. But perhaps visual perception of the resurrection appearances required a high state of consciousness on the part of the witnesses? I don't know. I want to stay attuned to the scientific research and integral theory related to subtle energies, and I expect to refine my thinking over time.

Friday, October 22

Scorpio

The sun moves through a part of the sky that has long been considered the deepest, darkest, most intense, and most dangerous segment of the zodiac. Scorpio is the sign of the Scorpion. The penetrating, probing, questioning, and sleuthing attributes of Scorpio can only be developed with minute attention to the realities of the moment. Scorpio rules the mysteries of the taboo, the occult, sexuality, death, and resurrection. Scorpio's aim is the transformation of reality.

Thursday, October 28

Did Jesus Really Rise from the Dead? Part 3 of 3

There was a time not too long ago when I preferred the Gospel of Mark to the other Gospels. Mark doesn't have Jesus physically reappearing to the disciples after the crucifixion; instead, the Gospel concludes with the discovery of an empty tomb. This appealed to a part of me that is afraid of commitment . . . and afraid of being wrong.

I liked that I could read Mark and keep a multitude of options open, including skeptical possibilities. I wanted to hold open as many interpretations as possible, without ever having to make a choice that could be wrong. The tomb's empty. Maybe it means this, or maybe it means that. Who knows. My opinion was the preference of an agnostic.

I have decided that it's time to choose what to believe about some of my own life experiences rather than keeping a lot of options open. I've become willing to risk making a commitment to the Christian faith tradition. I believe that Christ is One with all human beings, if we only open our hearts and eyes to see the deepest and truest reality. A central part of my faith commitment is learning how to honor Jesus's life, death, and resurrection by seeing Christ in all persons.

I have scanned my life for experiences with Christ in other persons, and one experience comes to mind more than any other. In September 1999, I was 30 years old. I had been confined to the psychiatric ward of a hospital for many hours. Although I was physically alone, I didn't feel lonely. There was a companion in spirit whose love and presence offered friendship at a critical time. I believed he was a soul mate, a lover, a best friend . . . someone who knew every inch of my body and soul intimately, a man who had traveled a great distance of time and space to be with me. He was a mystery to me. I did not give him a name. I did not address him by name.

In my spiritual journey, I have become willing to risk the belief that some of my experiences involve not merely prerational or delusional beliefs, but genuinely transrational states. I have been willing to look at the ways in which I have in the past elevated some spiritual beliefs inappropriately, and misunderstood other legitimately transcendent experiences just as badly.

I choose to view my experience with the man in the hospital as an actual bodily visitation of a glorified spiritual being, in body and soul. I choose to give him the name of Christ. I do not know if the entity that appeared to me in the hospital bore a physical resemblance to Jesus of Nazareth or any other particular historical being. I don't know if anyone else could have seen the entity, or if he was visible only to me. I don't really see the point of concerning myself much with such speculations.

My experience with Christ in the hospital burned a memory into my mind that will stay with me until the day I die. That memory is, for me: One who perfectly embodies Love. And, it should be noted, One whose love was expressed erotically from a man to a man. It is because my memory of Christ is connected to an experience with an actual physical being in a physical body—not to a mere apparition or mental picture—that I say I have seen the risen Christ.

I am picturing *The Seeker*, the imaginary movie of my life. In a short scene, Joe is in the midst of sharing his experience in Harborview Hospital with Johnny.

Johnny: "And then? When the nurse took you outside your hospital room—what did you see?"

Joe: "I saw a man."

Johnny: "The one you call the Christ. But how do you know he is the Christ?"

Joe: "Because I fell in love with him—madly, passionately, in love with him—at first sight. He was the perfect embodiment of Love. I felt his love radiating from every pore of his body into every pore of my own body. And I looked deeply into his eyes and felt something I had never felt before: total surrender."

Saturday, October 30

The Meaning of Faith

At this point in my life, faith is not about assenting to religious dogmas. Faith is about acknowledging the reality of aspects of consciousness that I have not experienced, or do not currently experience, and then resting trustfully in my unknowing.

The point of faith is not to answer the mysteries of the universe; nor is faith merely the existentialist's act of copping an attitude of trust in the meaningfulness of life in an indifferent universe. In the past, I have seen faith in those ways. Those are fine ways of talking about faith. But as I see it now, those are ways of thinking that I am in the midst of outgrowing.

Fascinating, isn't it, to contrast the ways of understanding faith that I am outgrowing with the one suggested by the words of Sri Aurobindo. His conception of faith stands at a higher level of development, the integral level. I picture myself as a man with one foot walking the existentialist's earth and the other stepping off into the unknown.

What resonates the most for me about Aurobindo's conception of faith: the intuition that the universe itself is supreme and self-existent Bliss.

Faith seems to me not so much like the existentialist's leap to absurdity, but more like . . . More like what?

An odd thing came to my mind just now: a science fiction novella that I hadn't thought about in many years. Daniel Keyes's *Flowers for Algernon* tells the story of Charlie Gordon, a mentally retarded adult who becomes a genius after undergoing a brain operation. The experiment's success is only temporary. After a while, he reverts back to his previous state of retardation. Keyes tells the story in the form of Charlie's journals.

Found the book on my bookshelf. Here's the passage that I've been looking for—it's the moment when Charlie Gordon realizes for the very first time that the experiment didn't succeed. It's his dialogue with himself—or rather, between Gordon and his archetypal Double, Charlie—in the mirror.

Near the end of the story, Gordon has observed the deterioration of Algernon, a laboratory rat, so he knows what's going to happen . . . or is happening . . . to him. He gets drunk, and then there's this poignant moment:

It's as if all the knowledge I've soaked in during the past months has coalesced and lifted me to a peak of light and understanding. This is beauty, love, and truth all rolled into one. This is joy. And now that I've found it, how can I give it up? Life and work are the most wonderful things a man can have. I am in love with what I am doing, because the answer to this problem is right here in my mind, and soon—very soon—it will burst into consciousness. . . .

I saw Charlie watching me from the mirror behind the wash-basin. I don't know how I knew it was Charlie and not me. Something about the dull, questioning look in his face. His eyes, wide and frightened, as if at one word from me he would turn and run deep into the dimension of the mirrored world. But he didn't run. He just stared back at me, mouth open, jaw hanging loosely.

"Hello," I said, "so you've finally come face to face with me. . . . I'm not your friend, I'm your enemy. I'm not going to give up my intelligence without a struggle. I can't go back down into that cave. There's no place for *me* to go now, Charlie. So you've got to stay away. Stay inside my unconscious where you belong . . ."

Faith is the warrior's scream: Unconsciousness! I'm not your friend. I'm your enemy.

6 Bridge of Light

In the beginning was the Word, and the Word was with God, and the Word was God. He was with God in the beginning. Through him all things were made; without him nothing was made that has been made. In him was life, and that life was the light of men. The light shines in the darkness, but the darkness has not understood it.
—JOHN 1:1–5

Monday, November 1

I voted a day early. Vote and do the least harm seemed to be the best available option today because no candidate in the race is without major flaws.

Democrats John Kerry for president and John Edwards for vice president earned my vote (despite my reservations). I supported the Seattle monorail and voted against bringing slot machines to bars and restaurants. I supported a Washington State Supreme Court nominee who is a friend of the gay community. I voted against lowering property taxes and against raising the sales tax. I had long planned to abstain from the vote for governor because the candidates were highly unappealing, but at the last minute decided impulsively to cast my vote for the Democrat.

Thursday, November 4

After the Devastation, What?

Devastated. Depressed. Fearful. That's how I'm feeling after the election of a president who won Ohio (and therefore the presidency) by a relatively modest margin. Anyone remember the flyers passed out by Republicans that warned Christians that if John Kerry gets elected, he and the homosexuals would try to ban the Bible as hate speech? Well, it looks like these dreadful scare tactics may have worked. Exit polls suggest that Karl Rove may have won states like Ohio for Bush by appealing to the worst impulses of religious conservatives.

At the same time, antigay constitutional amendments were victorious in nearly a dozen states. Some of these laws not only made gay marriage illegal but also deprived same-sex couples of other legal rights, such as domestic partnership agreements.

This is a bad day for democracy. I will not spout platitudes about despair not being in the American character; nor will I reassure you that I still have faith in democracy even in this dark hour. At the moment I have precious little faith in the whims of the majority. If only I knew of a better alternative to the theocratic majoritarianism that rules America today! If I knew of a better form of government, believe me, I would be getting to work.

Time will heal the heaviest wounds from the election of 2004. But I have deeper doubts and frustrations about what's transpired that cannot simply be dismissed. When democracy produces oppression of a minority by a majority and denigrates our human rights, something major is broken. But how do we define this problem? And what is the solution?

On his weblog yesterday, Andrew Sullivan placed his hope for the future of gay marriage in federalism. He writes: "[T]he inherently totalist nature of religiously motivated politics means deep social conflict if we are not careful. Our safety valve must be federalism. We have to live and let live. As blue states become more secular, and red states become less so, the only alternative to a national religious war is to allow different states to pursue different options." Emphasizing that gay marriage is an issue best left to the states can help us avoid a federal constitutional amendment, he says, which will allow us to "live to fight another day." Certainly that's part of the solution. Yes, gays should work at the state level to bring legislation forward to their legislatures.

But what hope do such efforts have, when the consciousness of the country is still mired in severely limited ways of thinking about gays? And what hope is there for the gays in the 11 states (including Oregon!) that have now enshrined bigotry in their constitutions. Not everyone can move to Massachusetts! Praising the importance of states' rights is fine, but let's be honest. It's not exactly an inspiring message to bring home to the boyfriend and the beagle. Even when gays score a few court-directed victories in states like Massachusetts, fundamental human rights at the federal level will continue to be denied to us. We will continue to be second-class citizens in our own nation for many years to come.

I suggest that when the immediate pain is over, we lick our wounds and recommit to the grandest principles of the gay movement, all the while reexamining our strategies for making progress. We are spending millions of dollars to fight back antigay legislation and losing badly. Whatever our activists and politicians and all the rest of us are doing now, it should be clear to everyone that it's not working. We have some serious work to do.

We in the gay-rights movement need to be willing to look deeply into our own souls and into the soul of American culture at large, if we are to have any hope of overcoming the losses we have been dealt. We need to find new strategies for success that are able to bring more Americans to a more compassionate and fair-minded consciousness of the issues close to our hearts.

Gays no longer have the luxury of ignoring the role of spirituality and inner transformation in accomplishing the objectives of our movement. Our rights and loves and lives depend upon it. I'm putting my faith not merely in federalism, but in a spiritual revival.

Friday, November 5

Andy Warhol and the End of Camp

In 1964, a *Village Voice* editorial criticized Andy Warhol's filmmaking as "films shot without film, films shot out of focus, films focusing on Taylor Mead's ass for two hours, etc." There was, in fact, no two-hour film of Taylor Mead's ass.

So Warhol promptly created one. A 70-minute film entitled *Taylor Mead's Ass* followed the stinging editorial. In the film, Mead pretends to remove items from his anal sphincter including vacuum cleaner accessories, a mannequin's torso, and a picture of Rhett Butler and Scarlett O'Hara from *Gone with the Wind*.

The making of *Taylor Mead's Ass* fits with Warhol's habit of embracing the very terms of ridicule that his critics used to clobber him. In a similar vein, Warhol's series of Rorschach paintings in 1984 were a reply to a *New York Review of Books* article that compared Warhol's work to a "Rorschach blot."

Such bravura moments reveal Warhol's distinctive style of camp as a kind of "psychological electricity," a way of setting sparks flying and snapping people to attention. So claims University of Maryland professor Kelly M. Cresap in the new book *Pop Trickster Fool: Warhol Performs Naivete*.

Andy Warhol, of course, is the queer pop-art superstar whose output most famously included silk-screened images of Americana such as Campbell's Soup cans. Of Warhol's relation to camp, Cresap writes, "He didn't invent it, but he refined and disseminated it with amazing industry and dexterity."

In *Pop Trickster Fool*, Cresap looks at camp as a form of queer parody that attempts to "transform and undermine the effects of baleful experience," in ways that aren't always straightforwardly positive. Previous scholars looking at camp have tended to emphasize only camp's virtues or vices but not both simultaneously.

Positive views of camp extol the sensibility as a latter-day reworking of Emerson's injunction to "wonder at the usual." They see camp as an excitement of the imagination, a social rallying point, and a form of psychological validation.

Cresap writes: "Camp converts oppression, particularly queer oppression, into a nucleus of self-affirmation. Its ironic laughter acts congenially within the psyche, creating buoyancy where before there was the bewildering weight of misunderstanding and grievance."

However, camp remains divisive. Susan Sontag wrote, "I am strongly drawn to Camp, and almost as strongly offended by it." Other scholars have frequently derided camp's offensiveness. These critics attack it as misogynistic, derisive, self-loathing, cynical, morbid, and decadent.

Cresap finds insight into the controversy over camp by looking at the life and work of Andy Warhol. Cresap also discusses the presence of camp in recent pop culture such as *Will & Grace*, *Queer as Folk*, and films such as David Lynch's *Mulholland Drive*.

Cresap's willingness to look at the dark underbelly of camp is particularly daring when considered in the light of other recent gay scholarship. Cresap observes: "To speak only about the benefits of camp is to promote a kind of liberation theology that makes no place for the problem of evil."

In Warhol's life, Cresap argues, camp served not only self-rejuvenating functions but also the role of keeping the artist stuck in a juvenile sensibility. At times it signaled solipsism, an inability to relate to things outside the self as they really are. Warhol frequently spoke in a childlike fashion, begging others to allow for his lack of maturity.

In a book titled *The Philosophy of Andy Warhol*, Warhol wrote: "I think I'm missing some chemicals and that's why I have this tendency to be more of a . . . mama's boy. A . . . sissy. No, a mama's boy. A 'butterboy.' I'm missing some responsibility chemicals and some reproductive chemicals."

Warhol's juvenile outlook sometimes manifested with a streak of sadism or indifference toward suffering. He once avoided a friend at a party because he had AIDS, and he reacted to the news of a friend's suicide by saying that he wished he'd been told beforehand so he could have filmed the event.

Warhol also was not upset to hear of John F. Kennedy's assassination. According to Cresap he wrote, "It didn't bother me much that he was dead. What bothered me was the way the television and radio were programming everybody to feel so sad."

The pop artist was not known for strong feelings. He once said, "I've never been touched by a painting. I don't want to think."

At its best, camp is a "retro" sensibility that expresses genuine affection as it finds a new use for something old. But today it has often come to epitomize the urge to shed any value or belief that gets in the way of juvenile self-expression.

Cresap shows genuine affection for Warhol, including compassion for his humanity and admiration for his work in the vanguard of the development of queer consciousness. Far from merely denouncing Warhol as a moral relativist or libertine, Cresap credits the artist for breaking taboos in genuinely empowering ways.

Cresap's approach is exactly the complex balancing act needed not only in making appraisals of Warhol's legacy but also in rejuvenating our culture's attitude toward camp. What is desperately needed is the embrace of camp as a technique for transforming suffering while acknowledging its inherent limitations.

Cresap suggests that we can imagine a culture that moves beyond camp as a vehicle for denial and formalized social relations. What does a queer culture beyond camp look like? Cresap urges his readers to recognize and enjoy a camp outlook but then transpose it into an aesthetic that refuses to laugh off pain from a safe distance.

A postcamp queer culture allows for self-transformation, seriousness, and social consciousness in appropriate measures. It delights in surfaces and ironies but does not refuse depth. A phrase that comes to my mind to describe this culture is "soulfully gay."

Saturday, November 6

The Revealer's Challenge

Jeff Sharlet of New York University's The Revealer weblog recently issued a challenge to his blog's readers to explain why so many people build their understanding of the world around opposition to homosexuality. Sharlet conducted hundreds of interviews with religious folks in America. Not just Christians, but Jews, Muslims, Hindus, Buddhists, Sikhs, New Agers, Santeria practitioners, and Wiccans. And everywhere he asked, he heard how wrong homosexuality is.

Here's his challenge:

So I'm proposing a story for some brave journalist, or novelist, or scholar, or filmmaker. Tell us why so many of us build our understandings of the world around opposition to homosexuality. We'll want to know about the various theologies. We'll need to know about psychology, biology, sociology. But what I'm really waiting for is a full account of the faith that underlies this opposition. It's neither simple nor shallow. My travels—and this election—suggest to me that it is deep, profound, and made up of many meanings, spiritual, physiological, political, metaphorical.

And here's my response. Not the full account Sharlet's looking for, but a hint at the answer that I believe best makes sense of the current of homophobia and heterosexism in the world's religions.

The world is the unfolding manifestation of an ineffable Great Mystery that goes by names such as Spirit or God or Absolute Reality. And the history of the world is the unfolding evolution of Spirit in our midst: waves of cascading growth in consciousness from archaic to magical to mythic to rational and transrational modes of awareness. And these stages of consciousness have roughly corresponded to stages of socioeconomic structures that may broadly be categorized as horticultural, agrarian, industrial, informational, and postinformational. As Spirit unfolds in history, there are greater and greater degrees of emerging depth, love, sensitivity, compassion, and awareness of an underlying unity to all reality.

In this context, note that the world's major religions that today condemn homosexuality arose at the mythic/agrarian stage of the world's evolution in consciousness, approximately five thousand years ago. At this stage, also known by feminist scholars as the rise of the patriarchy, gender roles were rigidly defined and oriented toward male dominance of the public sphere. Early in the history of consciousness, body, mind, and spirit are undifferentiated (in the mythic/agrarian stage); but with the rise of modernity they are differentiated (at the industrial/rational stages), and finally they become increasingly integrated in the postmodern world (in the informational/pluralistic/integral stages). As Spirit unfolds in history, humankind grows in awareness of the complex nature of our sex and gender, and of the ways that the diverse forms of all human beings, including gender and sexual minorities, reflect the divine.

So now we can turn to Sharlet's question: how shall we explain the omnipresence of homophobia? There are many relative levels of explanation, and for these we can turn to psychology, biology, sociology, and literature. However, the most general explanation for the prevalence of homophobia in the world's religions is a spiritual one: it is because many people haven't yet evolved to a higher, deeper level of awareness—one that transcends opposition to homosexuality—that so many religious people are homophobic. In general, the greater the consciousness that develops in a human being, and the more spiritually enlightened one becomes, the deeper the sympathy for homosexuals and the sensitivity to our common humanity.

Homophobia is real. It is nasty, it is unseemly, it is ungodly, and it is present only at the lowest levels of human development. To put it bluntly.

The way that I explain this nearly uniform condemnation of homosexuality by so many religions is to note that in virtually every religion under the sun there are homophobes and then there are persons who are nonhomophobic. Then I note that religious homophobes generally fall at the lower end of the ladder of consciousness. It is not of the basic nature of religion to condemn homosexuality. Rather, it is religion at primitive, childlike levels of development that does so. It is not an intrinsic quality of theology to justify antigay attitudes. Rather, heterosexist and homophobic theologies derived from lower levels of development will do so.

To cite one example: the Christian religion is absolutely not a heterosexist religion per se; however many Christians in the U.S. are at or below a mythic-level stage of development, and most of them have beliefs that are properly said to be homophobic. They probably don't think of themselves that way; they just think they're being old fashioned and upholding good "family values." That's the complexity that Sharlet's talking about. Of course, this is largely a delusional way of thinking. But it is not helpful to speak of such folks as merely bigots and hate-mongers. Let's save that talk for the most extreme religionists, like Reverend Fred "God Hates Fags" Phelps, who really are vile bigots.

The truth is more complex. Persons at the lower rungs of the ladder don't recognize that there are steps on the ladder or even that there is a ladder at all. If they hear it said that there is a ladder of development and that they're on the lower end of it, it's easier for them to attack the idea (and those who bring it) than to absorb a damaging blow to their self-esteem. Belief that homosexuality is sinful may be a perfectly appropriate and healthy expression of gender beliefs at lower levels of human development. But when people act on their view that homosexuality is sinful by stigmatizing, humiliating, or persecuting homosexuals, or by using violence against them, this constitutes a social pathology even at the homophobe's own low level of development.

If they hope to be successful, attempts to unravel the "many meanings, spiritual, physiological, political, metaphorical" of homophobia will require not only efforts to understand the religion of the homophobes but also research into the various stages of consciousness of the religionists. More research should be done, and good journalists should write about it.

Feelings about homosexuality are frequently intense and justified in multifaceted ways. But I disagree with Sharlet that there's anything "deep" or "profound" to be discovered about the opinions of homophobes. Smart, well-intentioned people can be very low on certain lines of psychological and moral development. Interview thousands of homophobes, if you will, but wisdom and truly deep thoughts you will not find at the end of the journey.

Sunday, November 14

Urban Spirituality and Democratic Renewal

In "The Urban Archipelago," Dan Savage and the other editors of my hometown progressive weekly, *The Stranger*, present an important vision statement for the future of progressives, liberals, and the Democratic Party. The piece urges Democrats to make a renewal of urban life and urban values the core of their vision for America's future. Their conclusion includes this startling sentiment: "The fight is largely spiritual; it consists of embracing the reality that urban life and urban values are the only sustainable response to the modern age of holy war, environmental degradation, and global conflict."

They clearly think of their program for progressive reform as nothing less than a spiritual vision for America. What new breed of spirituality is this? The first thing worth noting is that there is a lot of righteous anger and resentment. Here's a small taste of the hot rhetoric:

Rural, red-state voters, the denizens of the exurbs—are not real Americans. They are rubes, fools, and hate-mongers . . .

We [progressives are] everywhere any sane person wants to be. Let them have the shitholes, the Oklahomas, Wyomings, and Alabamas. We'll take Manhattan . . .

From here on out, we're glad red-state rubes live in areas where guns are more powerful and more plentiful, cars are larger and faster, and people are fatter and slower and dumber. This is not a recipe for repopulating the Great Plains . . .

Country, an archaic synonym for stupid, . . . should be revived in our post-2004 election world . . .

According to *The Stranger*, conservatives have vilified liberals for decades, and so it's about time for liberals to paint their enemies with vitriol and venom. Attacking the red-state conservatives as rubes, fools, and hate-mongers who are fat, slow, and dumb and live in shithole states is all part of partisan politics. It's part of a rhetorical strategy for turning "conservative" into an epithet, just as conservatives have done to the word "liberal."

In *The Stranger's* political theology, there's a positive but limited place for religion. "We're for a freedom of religion that includes the freedom from religion—not as some crazy aberration, but as an equally valid approach to life," they say, while articulating a positive place for liberal values, morality, and an unspecified sort of spirituality. They even praise "a basic Christian tenet": "greed is bad, sharing is good."

Cities are the core of the progressive's spirituality, they say, because of the changes they produce in the people who live in them. People become more cultured, tolerant, and even interdependent. If the authors were developmental psychologists, they might have claimed that the average stage of consciousness development is higher in cities than in rural areas.

The Stranger's political theology is also noteworthy for its reimagining the role of the federal government as a source of reason and enlightenment. During the civil rights era, the federal government was viewed as an "enlightened center from which reason and justice emanate" and the source of a "transcendental order." Unfortunately, *The Stranger* says, "the federal government is no longer the enforcer of reason, the cities are, we urbanites are."

In *The Stranger's* manifesto for a progressive America, I see a rough attempt to wed progressive politics with both rationality and spirituality. Very rough. The *Stranger* should be praised for making room in their vision for affirming an explicit set of cultural values and for including both religious and secular alike. Unfortunately, the *Stranger's* essay is hampered by three major flaws.

First, their reference to some sort of spirituality is encouraging but too vague to be taken seriously. Is this spirituality just some sort of sentimental platitude, or are they willing to take a long, hard look at Spirit? I will return to this point in a moment.

Second, *The Stranger* fails to take seriously the moderate and progressive strains of religion to see how they might contribute positively to a vision for the future of progressive politics. They don't distinguish between bigoted hate-mongers and religionists who, say, disapprove of all nonprocreative sex on religious grounds and yet support gay rights. There is a great diversity of attitudes toward homosexuality, abortion, and stem-cell research among religionists. Therefore, it is impossible to simply divide them neatly into idiotic rubes and enlightened sages.

It makes no sense for *The Stranger* to imply that there is a spectrum of evolving cultural sensibilities from idiotic conservatives to enlightened progressives while at the same time refusing to articulate a theoretically coherent vision of the nature of consciousness or the ways in which cultural outlooks grow from lesser to greater stages. Unless a model of consciousness is based on validated empirical research into human development, then such talk is merely the worst sort of detestable liberal elitism.

Third, by ruthlessly attacking conservatives, the editors of *The Stranger* fall into the trap of implying that there are no conservative values worth taking seriously. Positive conservative values include personal responsibility, self-control, self-discipline, and strong families. I didn't know that "country" was once a synonym for stupid, but I certainly wouldn't advocate resuscitating rank bigotry against rural folk as these "progressives" advocate.

The harsh antireligious rhetoric used by *The Stranger*'s editors also feeds into the knee-jerk rejection of religion that has cost elections and support among moderate and progressive religionists. I think it is crucial to recognize that the true target of progressives' ire should be bigotry, hatred, and other nasty business. It's wrong to target simply the religious versions of those pathologies of consciousness or the religions that sometimes serve as vehicles for pathological values. Secular-minded folks can also be intolerant, stupid idiots. God-minded folks can be tolerant, intelligent, urbane sophisticates. Let's not detract from our true aims by making religion the focus. That would be a terrible distraction. And let us not label antireligious bigotry as spiritual. That would be most disingenuous.

The weakest part of the essay in *The Stranger* is its failure to articulate a coherent theoretical basis for proposing a major initiative of urban renewal. I believe that a spiritually informed evolutionary philosophy is uniquely able to provide the basis for a progressive politics of urban renewal. Indeed, spirituality suggests the actual meaning and end of "renewal" itself. A progressive spiritual philosophy must make room for all varieties of belief and unbelief and include folks from a diversity of religious and political orientations. It must be able to adequately explain, on a spiritual level, the gulf between the conservative religionists, the liberal secularists, and the progressive spiritualists. The philosophy behind a truly progressive politics must affirm Spirit (by whatever name) at the heart of liberal values.

Without bringing a philosophy of human nature and development into the picture, *The Stranger*'s essay falls apart as intellectually incoherent. How does it make sense to speak of government providing a "transcendental order" without defining the nature of transcendence? It doesn't. It doesn't work to speak of secular humanism and religion as "equally valid" approaches to life, as this essay does, without addressing the nature of secular and religious truth . . . or specifying what it means to have a "valid approach to life" to begin with. It's rhetoric that ultimately rings hollow.

Despite its many very serious flaws, *The Stranger's* call for a renewal of attention to urban life and values will likely resonate with many people, because it speaks to a genuine and neglected impulse. Cities have long been regarded as the home of the marginalized and economically disadvantaged. But they are also beacons for hope, places where people go to build on their dreams and find new opportunities. The genuine impulse that we should honor is a call to reclaim urbane, cultured, and ordinary ways of interacting with the sacred that are compatible with modern city lifestyles. The hardships of city life, such as crime, poverty, and pollution, must be balanced in the human spirit by sources of hope and faith greater than the threats to life. It is from cities alive with hope and faith that true democratic renewal can spring.

Friday, November 17

A Time for Renewal

I met Camilo Delgado earlier this year at the Gay Spirit Culture Summit in Garrison, New York. After the November 2 election, in which Republican George W. Bush won by a narrow margin, we spoke by telephone about spirituality and this challenging time for gay and queer Americans.

Cami is a psychotherapist in private practice in Miami, Florida. He has also been a pioneer of AIDS care in Dade County, having been involved in community activism since 1982.

Joe: Cami, what does spirituality mean in your life?

Cami: In my life, spirituality has meant different things. Usually it has meant being around things that charge my inner battery—music, nature, and friends. It's about making conscious choices to include energies in my life that feed my soul.

Spirituality can look like going to a church or a temple or a meditation group, but it doesn't have to. It has to do with tapping on an inner source of strength. Different people use different words for Spirit, and I don't care what you call it as long as it fuels your life.

Joe: How is music a spiritual practice?

Cami: Music has seen me through many tough times. For every breakup I've had with an ex-boyfriend there has been music to sustain me. The music I get the most out of is show tunes and opera. I'm a gay man and, yes, that's the stereotype!

Show tunes are medicinal for me. I find a powerful song and play it to boost my spirit. Other songs will work for others. The point is people need to search for the music that works for them, then music becomes a practice of spirit that moves the energy of our soul.

I also sing with the Miami Gay Men's Chorus. That's powerful medicine. To me it's no less spiritual than a church choir. Fifty gay men singing together can stir the soul of an audience. Being in community and lifting up our spirits together is the sort of thing we need to do more of now.

Joe: Tell me more about nature and friendships as part of a spiritual practice.

Cami: A spiritual practice doesn't have to involve candles and incense. It can be spending time in nature or reaching out to other people to empower each other.

I have a view from my balcony that overlooks Biscayne Bay. Simply stepping onto my balcony charges my soul. There's something in nature that renews us and gives us strength. Nature can cleanse us inside, remove negativity, and help us get centered. It's like taking a spiritual shower.

My belief is that we human beings are created to do well when we are in contact with each other. It's not neediness; it's being human. Join something. Find out what your community offers. Spirit is awakened and brought out by being around the right people. This is a time for a new solidarity and a new sense of cohesiveness.

Joe: There was solidarity years ago with the AIDS epidemic . . .

Cami: I did volunteer work for many years and spent time with friends who were living with the virus. I had a partner who died of AIDS. I've also dealt with it professionally as a psychotherapist for the past 15 years.

I was submerged in a world impacted by AIDS. I witnessed ordinary people doing extraordinary things. I witnessed gay men and lesbians performing acts of love and care that I have never seen before. In the middle of the crisis, a spiritual force within us emerged and was awakened, a powerful, dormant force that propelled many people to do great things.

Those wonderful HIV meds that are out there happened for a reason. Gay people with purple lesions handcuffed themselves to federal buildings. They could barely walk. They weren't muscle boys, but they had the strength of spirit. I saw them. I was there. They were heroic. They were spiritually awakened men and women.

Joe: You've said that the situation today is another crisis.

Cami: Yes, I believe that the elections were a jarring alarm. Let's wake up. I know this new crisis can awaken a powerful spiritual force within us. This is a time for renewal and restrategizing.

Spirituality takes on a whole new relevance now. We have to get over our knee-jerk rejection of spirituality. We have disempowered ourselves in relation to this source of strength. We cannot afford not to tap into it. We have to get over our allergies to words like soul and spirit. Spirit is the ultimate strength.

Joe: What do you think about the role that "moral values" played in the election?

Cami: In this election, religious rhetoric was used for political gain. What I heard was the sanctification of hatred. Some churches are sanctifying hatred. However, I think we need to reclaim the phrase "moral values" and define it in new terms. It is moral to save and protect the environment. It is moral to have universal health care for everybody in America.

We need to redefine "liberal." Liberal doesn't mean licentious. It is the liberals who abolished slavery and who fought for women's rights. A liberal is a very moral person. We need to have no shyness about those words, and others like "family values."

Joe: I was surprised that after this election there weren't more candlelight vigils or protests. Did that also strike you?

Cami: I think people are still in the shock stage. It was a rude awakening, but something new is gestating. My optimism is not fluffy optimism, but the down-to-earth optimism of a man who witnessed the spiritual power of gay men and lesbians in motion.

I know we can rise, because I saw it happen before with my own eyes. This is the time to call forth the energies of Spirit once again.

Monday, November 22

KramerVision

Author and activist Larry Kramer recently gave a much-noticed speech called "The Tragedy of Today's Gays." It presents a post-2004 election vision declaring that gay rights are "officially dead," most gays are too preoccupied with sex and drugs, and AIDS is part of a government plot to murder homosexuals.

Whatever else you want to say about this speech, you've got to admit that it's got an interesting spin on "the vision thing." The ACT UP founder has got a view of what's wrong with gays in America and a few ideas about how to fix the problems. His vision of what's wrong can be summed up in three words: hate, hate, and hate. He uses the word about twenty times. A "huge portion" of our fellow Americans actively hate us, he says. A hateful cabal of power lords deny us our rights and aim for our eradication. (In contrast, Martin Luther King, Jr.'s "I Have a Dream" speech attacked racism without once using the word "hate.")

Gays share the blame for what's gone wrong, says Kramer. By virtue of our sexual practices and drugging with crystal meth, we are killing each other. He asks: "Has it never, ever occurred to you that not using a condom is tantamount to murder?" Kramer says that he has come to believe that gays are "tragic people."

The first step toward an answer to these problems, he says, is to have a discussion. Kramer says that we must resist the temptation to affirm everything that gay people do as good. Instead, "we must have an honest discussion amongst ourselves about what's good and what isn't." In other words, we must talk frankly of values, morality, and personal responsibility.

Kramer imagines that following such a conversation, gays will be able to come together to fight again in a united way. He said: "We must find a platform that all of us can support without divisiveness and shame and guilt and all the other hateful weapons they will club us with. . . . How do we frame this issue? How do we claim the God that they have subsumed into their own ownership?"

In the December 15, 2004, issue of *The Village Voice*, Kramer was asked, "don't you also need a long-range vision?" To which he replied:

"Honey, to be free and have equal rights. You don't need any more long-range vision than that."

I won't pretend that I have all the answers to the difficult issues that Kramer courageously tackles. But I will say this much: when it comes to "the vision thing," Kramer's vision is a start. However, gays can—and must—do much better. It's not so much that gays are tragic people as it is that we sometimes allow ourselves to be led by leaders with a tragic vision.

Certainly, many Americans hold conservative positions on the political issues that most impact gays. However, I don't believe it's true that gays are actively hated by huge numbers of heterosexuals. A 2003 Pew Forum survey showed that 76 percent of Americans say they are comfortable interacting socially with homosexuals. Also, from what I've heard, many gay Republicans say that they get more hatred from liberal gays than from other Republicans.

I'm sure that such a distorted belief as Kramer's can seem very real to many gays, especially those who have suffered badly from the homophobia they perceive to surround them. But the views of Krameresque gays show the same signs of irrationality and rigid defensiveness as the beliefs of religious fundamentalists. Antigay sentiments are a fact of life; in the worst cases, they include hatred. Homophobic beliefs never go away overnight. As most of us know quite well from our own coming-out journey, they must be outgrown. For many people, this outgrowing can be a long and complex process.

Homophobia is not a masquerade for hate but an attitude present at certain early and less mature stages in human development. In fighting it, we must develop strategies consistent with the best methodologies for encouraging growth. As people grow in consciousness—that is, as we become more spiritually mature and develop integrally—we become less homophobic.

Religion isn't the enemy. The battle against homophobia is the struggle of more mature forms of being human against immature expressions. We all have parts of ourselves that are more or less mature, so the struggle for gay freedom can't be separated from our individual and collective efforts at growth.

The battle at the heart of the struggle for gay equality is the imperative to grow the consciousness of all, and to do so simultaneously in individual, cultural, social, and political dimensions. Failure to understand this fact results in bizarre notions such as Kramer's nightmarish vision that the gay movement is torn between self-loathing, murderous gays on the one hand and hateful, murderous heterosexuals on the other.

HIV-prevention efforts in public health have recently begun to recognize the importance of encouraging responsibility. The idea is to place the responsibility for the health of gay men squarely on their own shoulders. And these efforts seek to encourage HIV-positive men to take care not to spread the disease to others.

Some liberal critics of these efforts say the best way to stop AIDS is to nurture a gay man's self-esteem by never casting moral judgments against gay sex. These critics want to focus exclusively on external causes of the problem and ignore the inner causes, and they don't see the perils of encouraging an "anything goes" culture.

Sex is certainly a wonderful source of pleasure, but as adults we must be mature or face the consequences. We need leaders who will speak the truth: gay men should treat each other as sacred, not merely as disposable sex objects. We also need leaders who can encourage maturity without crossing the line into counterproductive rhetoric and Krameresque distortions.

Kramer's speech is certainly worth reading, if for no other reason than to see one of our great agitators grapple with the dreary state of gay activism today. Although his diagnosis is faulty, his medicine is more promising. Conversations aimed at finding a united way to approach our shared struggles are a good way to start.

As we look forward, I suggest that no vision for the gay movement will be complete unless it attends to the challenge of expanding consciousness in all dimensions. We must bring healing from the antigay fear, shame, and hatred buried within the heart of every person, transmitted in the very fabric of our families and culture, and institutionalized in our laws and other social structures. Our liberation must make us vessels of healing and transformation in the world, and our soul searching must take us to the Source of All.

Wednesday, December 1

Proposing a New Queer Winter Holiday

A review of the major holidays celebrated in the United States reveals that not a single one is focused specifically on the growth and development of

GLBT people. Here's a proposal for the creation of our own distinctive holiday tradition, starting this month.

Gay people are noted for their love of merrymaking. We are celebrated entertainers, gracious hosts, and unsurpassed in the art of throwing a fabulous party with style. However, many of us are disconnected from the winter holiday season because of strained relationships with our families or a feeling of alienation from the season's religious symbolism. Therefore the holidays can be a source of pain and loneliness.

Dr. Maulana Ron Karenga first celebrated Kwanzaa, the African-American cultural holiday, in 1966, and today it's celebrated by millions throughout the world African community. However, so far as I know, nobody has ever celebrated a distinctively queer winter holiday. We can all dream that someday such an observance may bring festivities to our homes, churches, temples, mosques, schools, and workplaces.

This year, I will be celebrating a new queer winter holiday called Yuletide. And I'd love company. I propose that a festival be created with the specific purpose of protecting and advancing the distinctive cultural traditions associated with the GLBT community.

Yuletide will be a winter holiday that affirms a connectedness to gay cultural identity and provides a special focal point for our holiday gatherings. I don't intend this to be a commercial holiday. More than anything, Yuletide should be an opportunity to reflect on GLBT heritage and the principles that have sustained folks like us throughout the ages.

"Yuletide" means Yule greetings. What is a yule? Like many terms now associated with the Christian nativity, yule actually dates to pagan traditions. According to *Merriam-Webster's* dictionary, the word "yule" comes from the Old English "geol," which came from the Norse "jol," a pre-Christian pagan festival at the winter solstice. It is a celebration of the cycle of nature and an affirmation of the goodness and continuity of life.

Although the name has connections to both pagan and Christian religions, Yuletide will be a nonreligious holiday. Celebrating the holiday will be open to persons of all religions and spiritual paths, including secular ways of thinking.

I don't pretend to be a linguist, but I have noticed a queer way of looking at the "Yule" name. In Middle English, the word "faggot" originally meant "bundle of twigs bound up." And "Yule" is commonly found in the term "Yule log," a large log traditionally put on the hearth on December 24 as the foundation of the fire.

Like Gay Pride celebrations in June that commemorate Stonewall, the Yuletide holiday will allow us to celebrate the goodness of life without shame in who we are. However, the holiday gives us an opportunity to move beyond pride to affirmation of a healthy, positive identity based on creativity, community, integrity, self-reliance, compassion, and faith.

I propose that Yuletide shall be a six-day celebration to be held beginning on December 19 and continuing through December 24. There is one day for each color on the rainbow flag. Each day of the observance shall be linked not only to a color of the rainbow but also to spiritual principles of special relevance to GLBT people.

Day 1. Creativity. Tonight we light a purple candle to honor Creativity. This principle affirms the vital life force of the universe and our connection to Eros. We especially honor queer artists, musicians, and all who create and protect beauty . . . and the creative principle within each of us.

Day 2. Freedom. Tonight we light a red candle to celebrate Freedom. This principle affirms our individual self-respect and collective power, and the pursuit of joyful self-expression in community. On this evening we honor freedom fighters, activists, and heroes . . . and our own warrior impulse.

Day 3. Integrity. Tonight we light a blue candle to affirm Integrity. This principle stresses the value of looking within to search for meaning and purpose in our lives and of recognizing our responsibilities and duties, honesty and accountability. Gay and lesbian parents, teachers, and mentors are especially honored this evening . . . as well as our own impulse toward authenticity and wholeness.

Day 4. Self-Reliance. Tonight we light an orange candle to celebrate Self-Reliance. The principle of Self-Reliance reminds us of our need to define our success in terms of bringing our individual interests into harmony with the common welfare. We especially honor our scientists, inventors, and business people . . . and every person's drive to self-determination and spirit of innovation.

Day 5. Compassion. Tonight we light a green candle to embrace Compassion. This principle focuses on cultivating sensitivity, kindness, acceptance, and living in harmony with the earth. This evening we honor all peacemakers and affirm the goodness in the diversity of our world.

Day 6. Faith. Tonight we light a yellow candle in recognition of Faith. This principle honors each person's childlike curiosity and gratitude about being alive. We honor everyone alike in the spirit of unconditional love, and we share our stories of hope and wisdom. We honor the spirit of truth in our religious and wisdom traditions.

So there you have it—my proposal for Yuletide, a new queer winter holiday. Through our celebrations, we can honor all those who have gone before us and on whose shoulders we stand, and the queer generations yet to come. Merry Yuletide to one and all!

Wednesday, December 8

I had a liver biopsy today. I was sedated through the whole procedure. The only sign that there was a needle stuck into my liver is a small bandage on my abdomen. My liver continues to be highly inflamed, and the biopsy is intended to rule out some possible causes of the inflammation.

I want to resume antiviral medicines, but the risk of liver toxicity is high with most of the available drug treatments. If I begin a medication that causes a toxic effect, the risk is clear: I could die. On the other hand, if I don't resume medications, my HIV disease will continue to progress. My T-cell count has already fallen to 86. Without medications, the life-expectancy at this stage of AIDS can't be good. It's a tough situation.

Friday, December 10

Outing: A Spiritual Dilemma

Have you ever received a private e-mail and struggled with whether it would be okay to forward it to others? When I faced this dilemma recently, I made a choice that helped me understand the spiritual dimensions in the debate over outing.

I had attended a men's retreat where I was the only openly gay man among all the participants. A controversy arose, and I spoke out about an incident of heterosexism that I had witnessed. Afterward, the participants of the retreat discussed the controversy by e-mail.

One heterosexual man sent me a couple of private e-mails that I saw as containing rude and heterosexist remarks. I knew I was in trouble when I read the first paragraph of his e-mail. It began with the telltale sign of the homophobe: "I am not at all homophobic," he said, before telling me about how many gay friends he has.

I wanted very much for this man to send his e-mails not only to me but to everyone who attended the retreat. I thought it would raise a healthy discussion. However, the man declined to give me permission to forward his e-mails. Perhaps he was afraid of being judged a homophobe or bigot.

I faced a fairly common ethical dilemma involving privacy. On the one hand, I felt offended by this man's insensitivity and rudeness, and part of me wished that I could expose his beliefs to everyone. I rationalized that sharing his e-mails could raise consciousness about the heterosexism that gay people face every day.

On the other hand, I wanted to respect his privacy, since he clearly didn't want his beliefs known. If I exposed him without his permission, he would be hurt and would probably respond with anger. Moreover, other people might begin to feel sorry for him and then lash out at me because I had exposed something that he wanted to keep secret.

As I wrestled with my decision, I thought of the current controversy over outing. Recently, debates have raged regarding conservative Republican politicians such as Congressman Ed Schrock of Virginia. Is it okay to reveal the secret homosexual orientation of those who oppose our political agenda?

I have mostly been sympathetic to the folks who "out" politicians, because the politicians are public figures and are behaving in a hypocritical manner. I have believed for some time that outing such politicians can be defended as serving the public interest.

However, a recent editorial by Andrew Sullivan in *The New Republic Online* raised some troubling questions in my mind. Sullivan acknowledged that outing politicians who are obviously hypocrites seems justified. However, he pointed out that gay men who live secret lives have complex psyches, and it is difficult for outsiders to judge them accurately.

It is impossible to truly know the hearts of those tortured souls, Sullivan implies. He adds: "But what I do know is that forcing this man [Schrock] to cope with all of this in public, as an exercise in public humiliation and disgrace, is simply and manifestly cruel. And if the gay rights movement is about anything, it should be about the abatement of cruelty. Especially when directed by one gay man toward another."

Sullivan claims that the gay movement should be about the abatement of cruelty, a vision that I applaud. This conception of the gay movement signals the deeper spiritual dimensions of our collective struggles. It holds that our purpose as a community goes beyond our social life and political agendas into healing the hurts of our souls, which have been scarred by homophobia.

The notion that the core purpose of the gay movement is the abatement of cruelty—and, more generally, of suffering—brings our struggles into harmony with the best insights of the wisdom traditions. Jewish and Christian liberation theologies identify the essence of religious practice as solidarity with all who suffer and locate God's presence in the world as the force of healing and reconciliation.

Sullivan's opposition to outing is in essence a spiritual argument. Outing means playing God. Who are you . . . who am I . . . to cast a judgment on a man that will cause him and his family to feel pain and suffering? Such arrogance can only backfire, spirituality suggests. "Judge not, lest ye be judged," says the Bible. Have mercy on the hypocrites, and we may hope to receive mercy for our own shortcomings.

A loving and compassionate gay culture will use outing only rarely as a political strategy, if at all. But is it true to say, as Sullivan does, that outing is simply and manifestly cruel? I think this is going too far. There are some public figures whose work causes great harm, and outing them could be an act of tough love that actually alleviates suffering in the long term.

When facing this dilemma, we should choose the act—outing or not outing—that results in the greatest abatement of suffering for the greatest number. We may not be able to perfectly predict the consequences of our actions, but we should try to anticipate them.

Although Sullivan's argument against outing does not hold as a universal moral requirement that outing is always wrong in every circumstance, the guideline that outing should usually be avoided is a good rule of thumb. We can choose to reject the "eye for an eye" mentality.

I encountered this spiritual lesson myself with the man who offended me by e-mail. I decided not to forward the messages without his permission or reveal his identity to others. If I had treated the man with harshness, I fear I would only have created a backlash of meanness in which others would treat me with the lack of mercy that I had shown to another.

Let us work to cultivate a political climate based on respect, love, and diminishment of suffering. Our goal should be to make outing unnecessary and rare.

Saturday, December 18

I hung out at The Cuff earlier tonight and had a few drinks. I dressed in the standard black and blue attire: jeans, black T-shirt, black leather jacket, and White Sox cap. There was a young man with many tattoos and piercings who wore a T-shirt with George W. Bush on the front (the back read, "Shit Happens").

I enjoyed the sight of beautiful men and the energy of a stimulating atmosphere, but I was feeling lonely. I flirted with one or two men, but nothing came of it.

There was a gorgeous Seattle Quake rugby player there. His look in a black cowboy hat took my breath away. I really wanted to meet him, but my shyness got the better of me. He spent most of the evening hanging out with his teammates, and I didn't have the balls to introduce myself.

I was admiring the rugby player when a man walked by, stopped in his tracks, turned to me, and said: "Damn! You sure got a Tim McGraw thing going on.

"Do you get that a lot?" he asked.

I started to say something, but he quickly disappeared into the crowd.

I do hear the Tim McGraw remark from time to time. The first time was with a punk musician I met a few years ago. Ricky had a huge crush on the country music singer and thought I looked just like him. He wanted to take me home in order to live out some sort of twisted Tim McGraw sex fantasy. And I don't even own a cowboy hat!

I have ambivalent feelings about the attention I get for supposedly looking like somebody else, but mostly I just have fun with it. I seem to recall reading a clever axiom somewhere on the topic of people who look like celebrities. There's an immutable law of the universe dictating that whenever somebody says they resemble somebody famous, there is nearly a 100 percent probability that they're the less attractive version. Someday integral theorists will discover that a very general version of this law is actually the 97th tenet of all holons.

Sunday, December 19

Today was my first time at Dharma Buddies, a Buddhist meditation club for gay men. I felt very comfortable meditating there, just being in a room with others with whom I felt no disharmony. I've also been checking out other spiritual and religious groups for Seattle gays, including Metropolitan Community Church and Integrity, a service for gay Episcopalians. The Integrity service at Saint Mark's Cathedral was okay, but the stuffiness of the hymns and the heavy ritual hit me as cold. The MCC service was much warmer and friendlier. None of the groups were especially well attended, with no more than one- or two-dozen folks at any of them.

I've decided that for now I don't need to select one religious community in which to participate. There may very well be several groups that have something to offer me and to which I have something to bring. I expect to be returning to MCC, Integrity, and Dharma Buddies, as well as exploring other groups. Perhaps one day I'll formally join one or more of these groups.

For the past year I have been seeking a church to fill the void created by my departure from the Roman Catholic institution. However, I think my longing for more joyful and abundant social contact is not primarily a religious impulse. Joining a sports team or social club or volunteer organization is probably a better way for me to satisfy my social needs.

I am growing to recognize that my spiritual longings may not be satisfied in conventional Christian or Unitarian worship services. I will increasingly be seeking opportunities for instruction and fellowship in transformative practices such as that offered by Buddhist Vipassana centers, Dharma

Buddies, or the Episcopal Church (which offers centering prayer, a form of Christian meditation). I will also continue my involvement with Seattle Integral and in the men's-work community.

Monday, December 20

The First Yuletide

Yesterday I got together with a small group of friends in my home for a Yuletide potluck gathering. The six of us hung out, ate festive snacks and dinner, and drank eggnog. We all had a great time. Somehow a simple gathering of friends seemed most appropriate for this, the world's first Yuletide party.

There were several sets of six colored candles on the fireplace mantel, each arranged in the order of the rainbow flag: purple, blue, green, yellow, orange, red. When the time arrived for the Yuletide candle-lighting ceremony, I asked one friend to give a blessing over the candles and another to light the candle when signaled.

I introduced the holiday and read a short piece from the Yuletide vision statement. Roger delivered a blessing over the candles, and then David lit the purple candle. Finally, we went around the circle and participated in a spiritual exercise specially designed for the occasion (one inspired by a Chanukah exercise written by Michael Lerner). We each shared our Yuletide visions, in which we imagined how things could be if they were the way they ought to be in the world . . . and how we might each participate in the realization of the dream.

We listened without criticism as each man shared his hopes and dreams for the world, as well as the role he saw himself playing in the future. Several men, including a school teacher, spoke of creating a world safe for gay youth in schools. Others spoke of world concerns such as the need for better access to health care and food. Others spoke of changes in becoming more whole and healthy in their own lives, free from shame and all that limits full self-acceptance.

I spoke about one of my reasons for hoping that Yuletide becomes a traditional gay holiday event. I explained that I love Gay Pride celebrations in

June. I enjoy their wildness and festiveness. But let's face it: they're not exactly a public relations coup for the gay community. Thanks to culturally conservative folks all too willing to exploit the Pride celebrations for their political advantage, the event allows our enemies to portray the gay community in its most outlandish, outrageous, over-the-top, and sexually supercharged aspects. Gay Pride can be perceived as a freak show, and yet it is the primary event that defines the gay community's image in the eyes of the rest of America. But what if there wasn't just one event that defined the gay image, but two—Gay Pride in the summer and a winter holiday like Yuletide?

After sharing our visions for the future, my friends and I discussed our visions for how the holiday might develop over time. We talked about whether the name of the holiday should stay or go. Rejected names: Queermas, Lesbigayikkah, and Holagay. Someone suggested an alternative spelling for the name: Yooltide. The name Yule-Pride was offered by one man. Someone even suggested a variation of Yuletide for the leather community: You'll-B-Tied! LOL.

On a serious note, I explained that I had received some feedback critical of the Yuletide name. It's a synonym for Christmas, said some. Too Christian said another. Too close to the pagan holiday of Yule, said another.

Ben joked that if the cultural tradition takes off, then I might affectionately be known as Father Yuletide. I hated the sound of that and told him sourly not to even joke about it.

After my friends left, I stood for a while next to the fireplace just staring at the six candles. They stood in a row on the mantel. *This isn't right. The colors of the rainbow flag are too flat. The candles aren't in a straight line; they're in the shape of a bridge. And the candles must be lit not in a row but in a Spiral: purple to red, red to blue, blue to orange, orange to green, green to yellow, falling and rising, zigging and zagging, descending and ascending, like evolution and involution, like . . . something else.*

Wednesday, December 22

I'm emotionally exhausted, but I feel great. Cleansed. Open. Serene. Loving. Peaceful. Energized. Confident. Ready for life.

I did a nice piece of work in one of my men's groups tonight. I often feel this good when I've gone a little deeper in my work than ever before. I bet the process lasted at least 30 minutes. Now that I think about it, I don't know how long it took. I totally lost track of the time.

Tonight's work came after our check-ins and all the other stuff that we do to create an atmosphere of emotional safety. We call the preliminary stuff "building a sacred container." It gets us ready to move past the head trips, storytelling, and other defenses that we use to keep ourselves from being more fully alive. Creating sacred space allows us to deeply enter into whatever shadowy places a man needs to go. In terms of the symbolism of the *Iron John* story about the adventurer and the Wild Man, safety allows us to give a man a bucket so he can go to the deep pool in the dark, forbidden forest of the psychic underworld.

Shadow isn't all about pain and misery. There's golden shadow, too. That's the part of ourselves that's so magnificent, so beautiful, so sexy, so glorious, so courageous, so powerful, and so divine that we have to hide, repress, and deny it. Think of the inner golden child whose parent slaps him and says, "Wipe that smile off your face!" That's a hint of the sort of thing that golden shadow is all about: it's about bringing the smile back.

If it's done well, mythopoetic shadow integration work isn't just about woundology, the Caroline Myss coinage that refers to the potential for people who suffer to become immersed in their traumas and to define themselves in terms of their wounds. Integration work can be a way of contacting our highest Self or soul. Reclaiming the golden shadow is much more difficult work than reclaiming the dark shadow, at least for me. It can take years and years . . . and my own journey continues.

In the first round of check-ins, I gave the men an update on my health status. I told them how worried I was. I told them I was pretty confident that I would make it through this okay. But my deeper truth is that I am more worried than I have ever been in 10 years. I'm worried that this could really be the end. I told them so.

My friend Steve Tracy helped to facilitate a process for me. He began by asking me, "Joe, do you know what your work is this evening?"

I took a moment to become aware of my resistance to being fully and completely who I am. Resistance is a sure sign of the shadow, just as much as white shit on my car is the sign of pigeons or seagulls.

"Yes," I said. Then I spoke with the greatest clarity and conciseness that I could muster. "If I were to work tonight, I would look at my resistance to being with my fear of death, and my resistance to asking for support."

"Okay," said Steve. "Do you know what your work would look like?"

I said, "I can almost picture it."

"Close your eyes and breathe," Steve suggested. "Allow yourself to sink into your body."

I stood on the floor in the center of the circle. As music began to play, I grasped my knees and began to sink down as I felt the vibrations beginning to stir the feelings in my body . . .

Thursday, December 23

The first Yuletide endorsements have started to trickle in from the men who attended the Gay Spirit Culture Summit. Toby Johnson made a great suggestion that I'm considering very seriously: changing the focus of the celebration from the solstice to the New Year.

Toby remarks: "I think the secular new year is what we should actually be celebrating these days . . . it is virtually universal. Almost everyone on earth uses or at least is aware of the Western secular calendar. It's the dating system of the Internet and modern science."

Toby and I are discussing possible names for the Gay New Year. I doubt that gay would go over very well as part of the name—look at all the attempts in the queer community to come up with an inclusive term like GLBT. We both think there's potential in using the term "rainbow"—for as trite as it can be, it is the symbol most universally known and accepted as a depiction of the gay movement. Tentatively, I like the idea of calling the new holiday something like Rainbow New Year.

Saturday, December 25

Today I spent a quiet Christmas with my family. My sister prepared a delicious prime-rib dinner with garlic mashed potatoes and all the fixings, and afterward we all played card games.

Monday, December 27

"Something about you is different," said the nurse.

"Is it the hair? The sideburns? The scruffy beard?" I said. "I've been trying a different look."

I weighed in today several pounds lighter than just two weeks ago. How surprising that I lost weight over the holidays, she said. I haven't been doing anything in particular to lose weight, so it was a bit odd. Perhaps my appetite has been a little off, but I hadn't really noticed.

Afterward, I saw my doctor to go over my new HIV-medication regimen and the results from the liver biopsy. A few more things are ruled out by the biopsy, but there really wasn't much useful information to help us to understand the cause of the problems with my liver.

"You're an enigma," she said.

Medically, it looks like I have to choose between the rock and the hard place. I've decided to go with the HIV medications, for now, and to monitor my liver closely. Just in case, I think it's a good idea to start to prepare for the worst-case scenario.

Tuesday, December 28

I had trouble sleeping again last night and was still awake at five o'clock in the morning. Finally, I closed my eyes and began to enter a restful state. That's when the visions started to come. At first, I could see nothing well formed, just the most rudimentary of shapes and textures. I was still quite awake and lucid.

One of the images was a brilliant shooting-star field. Stars floated in my vision, looking like the hypnotic, brilliant lights that appear on the viewing monitor on the bridge of the Enterprise in *Star Trek*. I could poke at the stars with my mind and they would move. I tried to see if I could reverse the motion of the stars, but their force was far more than I could control. I relaxed gently into the images that came before me and allowed them to simply be in my awareness. Soon I drifted off to sleep.

Then I started sliding through a twisting realm of existence quite different from ordinary reality. It was like being in the starring role of *The Seeker*, the imaginary movie of my life. I was watching Joe Perez on the screen, but it wasn't me. It was an actor. I would run into people who couldn't possibly be there. Who's that man in the disguise? Is that Andy Warhol? I don't know. What I was looking at was clearly nothing but a massive projection screen. But where are all the projectors? As the movie rolled along, I remained conscious as I perceived fascinating and bizarre sights and sounds. I felt absolute delightfulness and playfulness, like a boy suddenly realizing that he's been turned into Harry Potter or a teenage girl becoming Britney Spears. It was better than being a wizard or a superstar; it was like being a powerful god or goddess. It was totally rocking cool. I loved it!

Then my enthusiasm evaporated, and in its place came fear, disgust, and dread. The movie was also filled with disturbing images of cruelty, hate, pain, violence, and insufferable boredom. It was like walking through the world's most twisted fun house from a horror flick with evil clowns.

I remember a scene set in a dining room. Someone is speaking on integral philosophy from another room. The Joe Perez actor can hear the voice while seated at the dining room table, but he can't see who's speaking. Someone in the kitchen (off screen) says: "Evil is a tricky problem for integral philosophy, because it's ultimately nondual."

The actor playing me says: "That sounds great in theory, but how do you reconcile it with Kosmic Terror, Kosmic Horror, Kosmic Evil?"

And a voice says: "Good and evil, angels and devils, Christ and Antichrist—they're already coming together. You're just becoming more conscious of the nonduality."

Joe: "People say that the goal of spirituality is to 'be here now' and to be 'one with everything.' But that's not the road to heaven. It's the road to hell! First there was suffocating, blinding white light and then everything collapsed around me. Blades and spinning razors and shards of glass, the walls of my hospital room, bodies mangling, crushing, tearing, being trampled underfoot . . . there was no breath, no air, life was going out everywhere . . . only blood, steel, and fire remained. Fire and my awareness . . . perception and causation were not separate . . . and there was pain, perfect cruelty for absolutely no reason whatsoever, agony without end in a reality without death, an obsessive/compulsive loop of Kosmic Torture . . . from the insufferable boredom of the primordial void until the frozen numbness after the Sun's last heat was spent . . ."

I screamed and threw myself onto the table.

Then I stood, yanked the tablecloth off the table, and sent dishes flying and shattering everywhere. I grabbed a knife and screamed: "I'M NOT GOING BACK!" Suddenly, the lights go out. Then I ask, "Where am I?"

A deep, malevolent voice says something unintelligible.

I'm back in the dining room—curled into a fetal position on the table— my flesh is charred, my body twisted in knots, and my clothes are covered with blood.

A woman's voice says, "I'm sorry, but you're still asking the wrong question."

I wake up. I look about and see myself lying on my bed in my own room.

I hear an older woman's voice in my head. She says, "You're Ivan."

Then I whisper out loud: "Ivan the Executioner." Why did I just say that? I don't know.

The woman's voice says, "You're going to drink yourself to death, Ivan."

I turn over in bed. There's a horrible stench in the air; it's a smell like rotting meat. I don't like where this movie seems to be going, so I plug my nose, fluff my pillow, turn over, and hope to fall into oblivion.

I must be dreaming lucidly again, because a new movie begins.

Now I'm acting in a scene where I'm trapped alive inside some sort of coffin. I kick open the coffin lid, and an avalanche of small, bloody, fleshy things comes crashing down all around me. In a glimmer of light, I see myself covered in blood. I hear a pulsating drum beat and a sound like an electric razor. I am savoring the taste of blood in my mouth.

I hear chanting: "Feed us! Feed us!"

I go unconscious. *Forgetting . . . forgetting . . . forgetting . . .*

After a while, there's a scene where I'm in an abyss of darkness. A devil appears, first as a wisp of light and then as a horrible, bloody face. A devilish voice says: "Who, me? There's no ME here. You're looking in a mirror."

A new roll of film got put into the projector. This time I am the movie director, and I'm watching myself coaching a handsome actor. But I'm not really the director. I don't have control over the show. I could push things around a bit with my mind but I can't say cut.

I say, "This is not a typical Jesus movie. It's a very tricky part. You have to play the role as if you were half of an archetypal Double."

Then the actor is stripped naked and blindfolded, perched on the edge of a tall tower. He is surrounded by menacing cloaked figures.

Now I am coaching the cloaked figures. I say: "Your line is, 'I don't love you.'"

Many voices: "I don't love you."

Then I say: "Your line is, 'Fall back!'"

Many voices: "Fall back!"

Then the actor falls from the tower onto the ground below and breaks his neck. That's not how the scene was supposed to go! Where was the stunt crew? Where were the cushions? That wasn't what I had in mind. I stare at the actor's twisted corpse, and there's something about his olive skin and dark hair that looks strangely familiar. I feel sad, but I don't know why.

I hear a man's voice in my head: "You're my executioner."

No! It can't be true. I wasn't really the director! I'm not the director! I wanted to say cut. I wanted to stop shooting the movie, but I couldn't. It wasn't me. It's not my fault.

The movie was too much. It was far more than I wanted to experience even for another moment. Nevertheless, I was helpless to stop another movie from playing. This time it was like I was the producer watching the director filming the actor.

I say: "I would close my eyes to shut out these visions, but I can't feel my eyelids."

The director says, "Stop time! Voice-over dialogue."

I say, "Time is paused. Freeze frame, stop motion."

The Joe Perez actor is in a Mexican restaurant with his family, and they're being covertly watched by a beautiful waitress with long, flowing black hair. The director is listening to the Joe Perez actor giving this line: "Everything is so still, except the tip of that waitress's pencil. It's moving so fast! I can't take my eyes off it. Has she been recording everything I say in shorthand? No, not everything I say. She's recording everything I THINK. She just wrote that down on her pad!"

The director says, "More terror, more surprise! You know where this is going, you've seen it before. She fascinates you, but she's your worst nightmare; she's the Dark Goddess."

The actor screams hysterically: "No, save me! It's true. Space and time and thought: they're collapsing. History's all scrambled up. What have I done?"

Then the director says, "No, that's not it. Not yet. Your line is, 'We're still in the restaurant. Then there's time.'"

There's an actress in a blue dress playing my mother. She speaks to the Joe Perez actor: "*Diese Männer sind hier um Dir zu helfen.*" ["These men are here to help you."]

Get me out of this nightmare! I see a door open, and paramedics burst into the restaurant. There's something peculiar about their faces, their uniforms. They sport a Seattle Police Department patch, but there's another symbol as well: a swastika. Nazis in Seattle.

"The Holocaust never ended," I say.

Oh my God! What has happened? What have I done? And then I went unconscious. *Forgetting . . .*

Then I was the projectionist in the movie theater. From his perch in the back of the theater, he is watching a Nazi propaganda film. He secretly splices a scene from *The Seeker* into it. There are Nazi storm troopers carrying a man in a prison uniform and a straitjacket off to jail. *Forgetting . . .*

The projectionist inserts a scene of the Joe Perez actor pulling a ribbon of toilet paper out of a hat. The message on the toilet paper says: "Kill him."

No more! No more! I've seen the death scene before. I must have. I remember the knife. I'M NOT GOING BACK! I can't bear it. I want out of this movie. Stop!

On the movie screen, there's a man riding a motorcycle along a deserted highway. He's carrying an urn full of ashes. The projectionist is humming and singing a ditty that goes like this: *A he a he a he a hoo a he a he a who. A he a he a he a hoo a hee a hee yahoo. Chigga-chigga. Sweet angel baby!* Repeat, over and over, with variations.

"What are you singing?" I ask.

"It's called Moses Lake," says the projectionist.

"Islam is the knife," I say. Why did I say that? I reach into my pocket. There's nothing there.

Then I became all the people in the movie theater. On the screen, we are watching Joe Perez driving a blue car on a stormy night. Ken Wilber and Harry are there, too. They're in the backseat.

When the Ken and Harry actors communicate, they express the same thought out loud simultaneously. The lips of both men are moving, but only one deep, eerie voice comes out. They say: "Be present. Stay calm. What is going on here, Joe? Where are you?"

The Joe Perez actor delivers this line: "The sign says the West Seattle Bridge."

Ken and Harry reply: "That's not what we meant."

Joe: "Perhaps this is the Dark Night of the Soul . . . and I've gone insane. Can you help me?"

Ken and Harry look at each other and say: "He thinks he's driving."

"You're not where you think you are, Joe. You're in bed right now. In your own room. You must think about this problem calmly and rationally. You can wake up anytime you want."

The people in the movie theater shout at the screen: "We want to go home!"

I'm still watching *The Seeker*. Then I see a short clip of film spliced into the car scene. There's a small blue room with cinder-block walls, and my awareness floats over a stainless-steel toilet filled with urine. I hear the projectionist's voice saying: "I'm not going back. I must drown myself in my own piss."

Joe: "The gravity clock in my old apartment. It was broken. Someone set it to the wrong year! This hasn't happened yet."

Ken and Harry: "You're talking incoherently, Joe. Quiet your mind and listen. You must trust us. You can trust. Surrender control. Let go."

Joe: "I'm so sorry. It was the only way I could stop the cycle. I had to drink my own piss and eat my own vomit. So much depended upon it."

Ken and Harry: "Not to worry. Just let go of the wheel."

Joe: "But I'm driving!"

• • •

Now I'm back in the movie theater. I am wet, shivering, and naked. I see a man standing behind the concession stand. He has spiky blond hair and a tattoo on his arm: a cross. His name tag says John. When I see him, I feel calm and glad.

I ask, "Johnny, where am I?"

He says, "King County Jail."

Then I laugh and say, "I believe you!"

I ask: "Who am I?"

He wraps a blanket around my shoulders and looks me in the eyes. Then he reaches into his pocket. He puts a TV remote control firmly in my hand and presses it to my heart.

That's when I woke up.

Wednesday, December 29

After my dream last night, I checked the time. It was seven o'clock in the morning. That was the most bizarre dream of my life! And yet the state of consciousness that I experienced in the dream is something I've known before. Perhaps it's like swimming, almost drowning, in the subtle energies. But when I experienced this state before, I wasn't sleeping or meditating. I was wide awake. It was more than five years ago. The memories are starting to come back to me now.

The scene: interior view of a Mexican restaurant in Seattle on September 3, 1999. The cast: Joe Perez, his mother, sister, brother, stepbrother, niece, and nephew. A Mexican busboy. Seated at the next table is a family with young children. We're filming the evening that Joe's nervous breakdown officially began; it's only minutes before he is taken in a straitjacket by ambulance to Harborview Hospital. Let's open with the moment when Joe tries to enlist his family's aid in building a new Internet company. Action!

Joe: "We need to register the domain name. The one I mentioned earlier. Wired. No, that's not it. It's Weird. Don't you see?

"W-E-I-R-D, that's queer. W-I-R-E-D, that's the Internet. They're the same, except the letters are scrambled. I can't believe I didn't see that before. It was all plain as day, right there in my journal. It's what I've been writing about for days. I just hadn't seen the connection until just now.

"And it's not dot com, dot net, or dot org. It's none of those three. There aren't three domains. There is only one domain."

Joe makes typing motions in the air, and clicks an invisible Enter button.

"It's done."

"Done?" his perplexed brother asks.

"Yes, just now. It is done. The domain name that we need. It is registered."

"OpenBot?" asks the brother.

"No, not OpenBot. Something else. I don't know what."

"Slow down, Joey, eat something. You're not eating enough."

Joe: "You're right, Mom. I should slow down. But I'm just not hungry. Does anyone want my menudo?"

Joe gets up to look at a piece of art on the wall.

Joe: "It's glowing . . . the painting, the colors are on fire."

Joe takes a seat, and a Mexican busboy approaches the table. Joe abruptly stands up and draws his face near to the man's and begins to give him a kiss. The busboy is stunned. An instant before their lips touch, Joe sits back down.

His family reacts in horror, and they talk of leaving the restaurant immediately.

"No, wait! Please, wait!" Joe pleads.

"Mom, sister, brothers . . . I can't do this alone. I need your help!

"The Internet's a mess. It's chaos. It's impossible to find anything. There's no order, no structure, no hierarchy. We need to link everything together, but in a new way. The other dot coms, they don't get that. They think that the Internet will get organized by computer algorithms, but they're wrong. It's not computers that are the key; it's the people. That's what AltaVista and Lycos and the other search engines don't understand. The Internet will never get organized that way. People have to do it. There's no other way. The other companies, they're clueless. They will fail. I see what they don't, and I will show you the way. We will succeed beyond all measure."

"People organizing websites? It sounds like what you're talking about is a WebRing," says someone.

"WebRings? No. They're awful. They're not going anywhere. All linking, but no ranking. It's all wrong."

"How then?"

"In here," Joe says, pointing to his head. "That's what needs to be organized, where the links need to be added."

Joe pauses and looks upward, mouth agape.

"Joey?"

"We're going to compile an Internet directory of people. Not just people: there will be businesses and organizations, too. But our main focus must be people. That's where we start. We must find them and add listings into the directory."

"Who?"

"All people. No. That's not it. Too big. There's no need. Most of the world isn't online yet. More than ninety-nine percent of the population doesn't have a web page. There are only tens of thousands of personal web pages, not hundreds of thousands. That is the reason that it's possible. We start with the people who have live web pages, and get them all listed in the directory. Then as new people go online with their web pages, they are drawn to add their listings, because there's already a critical mass. They see how great the directory is, and they will be drawn as if by a magnet to its radiance."

"Joey, you are talking too loudly. Lower your voice."

"There are a few other Internet directories compiled by humans, but they overreach. They try to shoehorn everything into one structure. They are too egalitarian. They organize categories of information like library card catalogs. But that will never work. They think they're being comprehensive, but they're not. We need to go deep and focus like a laser beam on this one area. People are the key.

"We need to go deeper, because—Listen to me carefully: there can only be one directory. Listen to me carefully: there can only be one director . . . One dir . . . *What is happening to me?! Did you see that?!*"

"See what? Joey, are you feeling okay?"

"My head is spinning."

The people at the next table are frightened. They are talking about what to do.

"Joe, lower your voice," says someone.

"Where's our waitress? We need the check," says another.

Joe whispers something inaudibly.

"Say again?"

Joe says, "You must trust me. It is not time. You may be asking yourselves: How can we do this, when there are so few of us? Know that you are not alone. There are more, right now as I speak."

Joe laughs and smiles. "Not many, but some. Some even whose names would surprise you. They are our friends."

"Other people are making a directory of home pages?"

"No, that's not it. I don't think so. I don't know. We must do this work, that's our role. Focus on collecting the web pages with the most pleasing designs. The beautiful ones, that's how you will spot them."

"Shhhhh! Please Joey, you need to go home. Keep your voice down! Don't you understand? You're not feeling well."

"Yes, that's a very good idea, Mom. It's not safe here. There are enemies here."

Joe's eyes widen, and he brings his hands to his mouth as if to block a scream.

He whispers softly to himself: "The patterns, the patterns are repeating. *They will call me the Antichrist. They will crucify me.*"

Joe looks around frantically, confused and disoriented. Through tears: "We're . . . we're still in the restaurant. Then there's time. Mother . . . you must save toilet paper."

"Toilet paper?"

"Yes! There is no paper here. They've cut down all the trees, and they have taken all the paper! They have unplugged the Internet! It is all dark.

"Hide it NOW . . . hide the toilet paper. Don't let them see it. They forgot to take the toilet paper. We can use it. That's how we will outsmart them. Do you understand, Mother? It is very important. I don't know how much time I have left."

"Joey, you are talking crazy. Please, let's go."

"Save toilet paper, Mother!"

Joe gives his brother a computer disk.

"You will need this. Keep it safe. These are dangerous times, more dangerous than you know. There are men coming to ask you questions about me. Do you understand? Something will happen soon, something terrible. They will try to take things of mine. Do not trust them unless they are those whom I have sent. And do not believe them when they say that I have sent them. Ask for their credentials. Be careful. You don't know who can be trusted. We must all be very careful now. Our lives will never be the same.

"Mom, you must take the package that I gave you, the one with my journal. The journal is very important. It's the key. It's the only one; there is no copy."

Joe whispers: "There's something else in the package: results of my bloodwork. Two nights ago I went to Swedish Emergency. They drew my blood and ran some tests. I asked the front-desk receptionist if she would give me a copy of the lab report, and she did. The results were strange. They found something that shouldn't be there. I can say no more. I don't know what it means, but I am certain that it's important."

Joe whispers something else, but it is inaudible. The only word that can be heard is "Vatican."

"What did you just say?"

"Nothing, Mother. I am going away soon and cannot do this. You must do this for me. So much depends upon it.

"You must send the package to my friend, the man whose name I gave you earlier. Do not speak his name aloud here. You must call him and ask for his mailing address. Do not use the post office. You must use Federal Express. He can be tr—"

"Joey! We have to go! The manager has come."

Thursday, December 30

The thunder and lightning disturbed me. No! *This shouldn't be happening! I shouldn't be hearing this. This isn't happening. This can't be happening.*

I wanted to scream but felt cut off at the throat. My breathing quickly reached a rapid boil. I would hyperventilate at any moment. I pulled the blanket over my head and curled up into a ball in my bed.

I heard the thunder again and then slowly started to relax. *I don't hear rain or wind, but there must be a storm coming. There must be. I'm not going crazy. There must really be thunder outside. Or maybe, maybe it was all in my head. Or maybe . . . Shhh! Don't go there. Too risky.*

I looked over at the clock. It was 5:42 a.m., and I'd been awake in bed for at least an hour, meditating because I couldn't sleep. With my eyes closed, I looked straight ahead to the patterns that appeared before my eyes. I directed my attention to the shapes and forms that appeared from out of the patterns in the background. There was movement and change. The images started to transform and rearrange themselves. And then I relaxed into the flow, steadied my breathing, and directed my attention to the sights.

They're occasionally breathtakingly beautiful, like watching the world's coolest kaleidoscope. But usually they're about as exciting to look at as a plateful of worms slowly slithering in circles. Sometimes fully formed images come to my mind as if from a dream. And once in a while, the images begin to form ghastly, frightening, ghostlike pictures (that's when it's most difficult to relax).

I'm relaxed now. There was thunder earlier . . . and lightning. I heard it. I saw it. It was real. When I heard the thunder, a memory came back to me. It's 1999. Harborview Hospital. The psych ward. I've been in the hospital for a few days. They've been moving me from room to room since I arrived. My restraints are gone, but the doors are locked. I am lying on a bed in a hospital gown.

I am awake, not sleeping for even a moment. My eyes are closed, and I am watching shifting patterns all through the night. I am breathing deeply and continually unwinding the tension in my spine and every bone in my body. I am tapping the theme from *Close Encounters of the Third Kind* on the bed with my fingers. I am following the lights before my eyes and they are shooting like stars and shimmering like the surface of a lake. Now they are swimming like sperm, thousands of tiny little tails flittering into an endless stream. No, these really are sperm that I'm seeing. *Actual memories of swimming sperm! How cool is that?* Some of the images are of scenes that I couldn't possibly have ever encountered before. Scenes of friends and of celebrities and people I've never met. That's Ellen DeGeneres in the role of the Harborview nurse! There's a police station and a boxing match and a cowboy yelling "yee-haw." I can see the images and feel their substance with the clarity of actual memories.

I turned over in bed and let out a big sigh. I'm still back in 1999. I feel myself regressing . . . I'm an infant now playing with my pee-pee . . . now I'm even smaller . . . I see lights crawling like armies of insects on my skin and through the hairs on my eyelashes. No, I'm actually seeing tiny creatures on my eyelashes. *I've seen pictures of these things before on TV. Maybe they're dust mites. Scary-looking!* I can feel them moving on the hairs, like ants marching on blades of grass. Now the lights are racing me through wormhole tunnels to another galaxy. They're bouncing up and down on the surface of a planet that looks like an old typewriter ball. The lights are dancing on the letters, and a message lights up. I am reading the words and making them rhyme. . . . I'm rapping a lewd, nonsensical song that is coming to me on the fly, tapping my hands and feet, and moving my body to a tribal rhythm. *I like to talk and I like to fock and I like to sock mayonnaise . . . I like to crock and I like to rock and I want to fock a bock/sock!* Now I'm dancing on the typewriter ball myself, jumping from letter to letter on the surface of the planet like Michael Jordan flying on a basketball court. As I skip over the letters, images of the letters fly overhead and arrange themselves into a sentence in the sky.

"The Meaning of Life is a 1976 IBM Selectric typewriter ball."

Q: "Actually, 42 of them, to be precise."

Goddamn it Q, this isn't funny, shut up you motherfucker!

Hours have passed since I began the voyage. Now the lights are smaller, much finer, arriving in all shapes and textures and directions, spinning and twirling. There are few colors here (it's like a black-and-white movie), but when they do appear they are magnificent. *Typewriter ball . . . typewriter ball . . . typewriter ball . . .* What am I looking at? Is this Jung's collective unconscious, perhaps? This all exists in my imagination . . . but what is the imagination, really?

That's when I heard the thunder outside the hospital room, repeatedly. Astonishing! I also heard rain and wind and the sound of breakers on a beach. And with my eyes still closed I could see a trail of energy leave my lungs and flow out of the room and into the sky. *I created the lightning! I created the thunder! . . .* As I breathed, I could feel the clouds billowing in the sky, as if the heavens were giving out a long rolling sigh. *I am taking in stars with my breath and exhaling the clouds in the sky.* Somehow I knew that the earth and seas were rejuvenating and healing as I breathed in and out. *I hear thunder when I close my eyes and see lightning when I blink. I am the thunder. I am the rain. My shit is the earth.* With my eyes closed, I saw a trail of sludge/excrement that seemed to stretch out for miles. I tried to relax my anal muscles to allow the excrement to leave my body. *HIV is Death.* And paradoxically, it's life at the same time. I can see it as a chain that stretches through all life, all across the earth. *I AM the typewriter ball. I am Everything.*

Is this Enlightenment? Is this Godhead? Buddha nature? God-con-sciousness? Do the sages and mystics actually *hear* the thunder and *see* the lightning? Do they *feel* themselves as the Creator like a child feels mud on his hands when he builds a sand castle? Because I do. Or is this not Enlight-enment at all, but something more primitive and primal? Or perhaps it is both primitive and highly evolved at the same time. I don't remember read-ing about this exact state of consciousness in my many stacks of religion and philosophy books. Close, certainly, but not exactly like this. I think I can lo-cate it on the integral map, but I'm not certain.

The enlightened ones often say that the pinnacle of Spirit is a peak you can climb, like scaling the Temple of the Sun to bask in the glory of the light. But if you tunnel into the deepest layers of the soul's catacombs, where the insanity and the delusions and the shadows dwell, is there an exit at the end? Did I escape the maze five years ago and pop my head out a trap door into the clear, formless darkness of the Temple of the Moon?

If I am Everything, then I am responsible for everything. Perhaps being God is having the awareness of all the victims and all the perpetrators in the Universe at the exact same instant in time. Or maybe . . . maybe I'm really tired and confused . . . and maybe these are all crazy thoughts. Shhh!

I hear thunder. I hear rain and wind and the wrath of the ocean. Outside my bedroom window, gray storm clouds gather in the morning sky but the ground is dry.

Friday, December 31

I bought a cowboy hat today. Fortunately, the salesman was quite knowledgeable about hats. If he wasn't, he sure had me fooled. I had no idea that buying a cowboy hat was so complicated. So many things to consider at the same time! Jesus Christ, I'm glad that I'm not a hat salesman. LOL.

It's black, of course. And I got a pair of black boots to go with it. Took me a nice hot shower, put on a splash of cologne, and then put on some Tim McGraw. I listened to "The Cowboy in Me" over and over again and put on the new duds with a sleek black western shirt and a pair of Wranglers.

I wore the shirt wide open to display my hairy chest. Over my chest, I put on my favorite talisman, the one with the red teardrop bead and an oval mirror at the base. I held the talisman out in front of me, and the mirror caught the light as it spun around.

Something about the pattern of the beads looks different than I remember.

The patterns . . . the patterns are repeating. That's it! The answer was right before my eyes the whole time, but I was too blind to see: There's a cross in the center of Everything!

The patterns are repeating more rapidly now. The time is getting near. Soon I must make a copy of my book. I must prepare a package for mailing. I must not use the post office. I must use Federal Express. The journal is the key. I must get my journal to Ken Wilber. He can be trusted. So much depends upon it.

I went to dinner with Mike at the Broadway Grill and then we headed to The Cuff.

"Happy New Year!" Mike said in a toast.

"Happy New Year to you, too! And Happy Bridge of Light."

"Bridge of Light?" said Mike.

"Yeah, that's the new name for the holiday I've been working on. Used to be Yuletide. Remember? It will be a New Year's celebration instead of a party on the solstice."

Mike replied, "Yes, I remember, but I don't get it."

"Well, I originally conceived of Yuletide as a celebration of queer identity. But with Bridge of Light, I'm beginning to see it as something much more. It could still be a celebration of queer identity, but I see it as a new global cultural tradition to celebrate the full equality of all people, the next wave in the evolution of all liberation movements in the modern era: a way of helping to bring about radical equality in all nations by making manifest in an embodied form the evolving collective consciousness of the World Soul."

"Slow down, Joe!" said Mike.

"You're right."

I could tell from Mike's expression that he didn't think the Bridge of Light idea was the greatest thing since assless chaps.

"Let's change the subject. We should enjoy ourselves tonight, Mike. I'm going to be moving. I don't know exactly when or where, but it will happen soon."

As the dinner conversation moved on, my thoughts silently turned back to Bridge of Light. I see myself on the top of a water tower, standing at the edge of a precipice. I bring my fists together in front of my belly and then raise them overhead in the shape of a rainbow arch. Then I say, in many different languages: *This is my body! This is my blood! Do this in memory of me.*

The DJ played Madonna, Seal, Prince, George Michael, and all the other classics. LOL.

I caught my look in the mirror at the far end of the dance floor. My black hat was hot! I liked it and the boots and the duds and the talisman and . . . I just smiled and looked myself in the eyes and held my own gaze. For so many years I never used to be able to look at myself that way.

The DJ started the countdown to the New Year. 10-9-8-7-6-5-4-3-2-1. And everyone wished everyone else happiness. I got a kiss and a huge bear hug from Mike.

"Take your shirts off! Everybody take your shirt off!" screamed the DJ. Mike took off his. I kept mine on but popped open another button or two. LOL.

The ecstatic energy of the dancing brought blood to my head. I dissolved into the pulses of the music, the rhythmic motion of the crowd, and the heat of physical desire. Of course, the whisky sours and a shot of something called a Cowboy Cocksucker were also doing their thing. LOL. Cowboy Cocksucker with spurs. LOL.

Each moment came as pure enjoyment. I heard the voice of the Vipassana teacher in my head. These thoughts seemed to bring me more deeply into the present moment. Each thought came as if it were a . . . a whisper guiding me into the Now.

"Be with the sensation in your falling foot on the floor . . . Feel the sensation . . . Concentrate on it . . . What does each part of your foot feel? What is the sensation of the sock against your skin? Can you feel your boot?" My feet fell on the dance floor one after the other, and each step seemed to bring me higher.

Mantras! That's the word I was looking for, I think. Mantras. The whispers came to my mind like mantras. Maaaaaantras. LOL.

I am One with the music . . . I am One with the beat . . . I am One with the black hat . . . I am one with the ground beneath my feet . . . I am One with the angels . . . I am One with the devils . . . I am One with the boys down on Castro Street . . . I am One with All that arises . . . This is what God feels like when he dances in a gay bar . . . I am One with All that arises . . . This is what God feels like when he flirts with a young thing . . . I am One with All that arises . . . This is how God gets a hard-on . . . I am One with All that arises . . . Oh baby, I want to be one with him . . . I *am* One with him! . . . LOL . . . This is how God looks when he appears as a man—a horny, happy, drunk, gay man . . . I am One with All that arises. LOL.

Postscript

THUNDER EXPLODES in the air, then LIGHTNING ILLUMINATES a parking lot. It's raining fiercely. Eerie shadows fall on the pavement, giving the scene a surreal, otherworldly air.

It's a FedEx Kinko's storefront near the University of Washington, midnight. We are looking through the front window of a shop open 24 hours a day. Inside the store, a man wearing a black cowboy hat puts a manuscript into a manila envelope. The cover page reads "SOULFULLY GAY BY JOE PEREZ."

The man scribbles on the envelope with magic marker: "URGENT!" and "FOR KEN WILBER'S EYES ONLY." He nests the envelope in another one and attaches an address label. WE DO NOT SEE HIS FACE OR HANDS.

A blonde woman takes his package and rings up his order. He pays cash. Woman: "Your change."

The man zips up his black leather jacket then turns and runs out of the store. He speeds off in a blue car parked out front.

The car cruises wildly down virtually deserted streets, switches lanes abruptly, bumps over medians, and erratically weaves to and fro. The steering is probably too precise to be the job of a drunk. And at times the ride is cautious and deliberate—this is no mere prank or joyride.

The man's face remains hidden by shadows. He opens a window to keep the windshield from fogging up, but it's no use. The visibility is zero, but he speeds. He passes numerous street signs. One sign says Highway 99 and another says West Seattle Bridge.

THE CAR SAILS OFF THE ROAD AND TEARS INTO A FENCE separating the highway from a precipice. It dangles precariously over the edge.

FADE TO BLACK

References

I list here only the major works that have been of use in the making of this book. This list is by no means a complete record of all the works and sources I have consulted.

Allen, Jay. "Ascending the Ladder, Dancing on the Rungs." 22 Jan. 2004, Kensho Godchaser, www.kenshogodchaser.com. (Accessed 23 Jan. 2004.)

Arnot, Robert. *The Biology of Success.* Boston: Little, Brown and Co., 2000.

Associated Press. "Gay couple denied communion in northern Minnesota church." 9 May 2004, GrandForksHerald.com, www.grandforks.com. (Accessed 9 May 2004.)

Bly, Robert. *Iron John: A Book about Men.* Reading, Mass.: Perseus Books, 1990.

———. *A Little Book on the Human Shadow.* San Francisco: HarperSanFrancisco, 1998.

Boisvert, Donald L. *Out on Holy Ground: Meditations on Gay Men's Spirituality.* Cleveland: The Pilgrim Press, 2000.

Covey, Stephen. *The Seven Habits of Highly Effective People.* New York: Free Press, 1990.

Cresap, Kelly M. *Pop Trickster Fool: Warhol Performs Naïveté.* Urbana: University of Illinois Press, 2004.

De la Huerta, Christian. *Coming Out Spiritually: The Next Step.* New York: Tarcher/Putnam, 1999.

Deida, David. *Intimate Communion: Awakening Your Sexual Essence*. Deerfield Beach, Fla.: Heath Communications, 1995.

———. "Ken Wilber Is a Fraud." Deida.com, http://www.deida.com. (Accessed 30 Mar. 2004.)

———. *The Way of the Superior Man: A Spiritual Guide to Mastering the Challenges of Women, Work, and Sexual Desire*. Austin: Plexus, 1997.

dr_rieux. "UU Atheists: An Endangered (and Embattled) Species?" 4 June 2004. Unitarian Universalists' Journal, www.livejournal.com/community/unitarians/220502.html. (Accessed 17 June 2004.)

Edelstein, Amy. "Gay/Straight, Man/Woman, Self/Other: What Would the Buddha Have Had to Say about Gay Liberation? An interview with José Cabezón." *What Is Enlightenment?* Fall-Winter 1999. http://www.wie.org.

"Exclusive: Imam Accused of Gay Hatred." *Herald Sun*. 7 Dec. 2003. heraldsun.news.com.au. (Accessed 7 Dec. 2003.)

Forrest, Steven. *The Inner Sky: How to Make Wiser Choices for a More Fulfilling Life*. San Diego: ACS Publications, 1988.

Fuller, Robert. *Spiritual, but Not Religious: Understanding Unchurched America*. New York: Oxford University Press, 2001.

Garber, Jeffrey S. "Among Gays Who Belong to a Religion, Few Are Practicing." The Gay/Lesbian Consumer Online Census. 12 Nov. 2003. www.glcensus.org.

"Gay-hating Philly minister convicted of soliciting sex from male teenager." *The Advocate*. 16 Jan. 2004. www.advocate.com. (Accessed 16 Jan. 2004.)

Gilligan, Carol. *In a Different Voice: Psychological Theory and Women's Development*. Cambridge: Harvard University Press, 1982.

Green, Jeff. *Pluto: The Evolutionary Journey of the Soul*. St. Paul: Llewelyn Publications, 2003.

Hart, William. *The Art of Living: Vipassana Meditation as Taught by S. N. Goenka*. San Francisco: HarperCollins, 1987.

Harvey, Andrew. *The Essential Gay Mystics*. Edison, N.J.: Castle Books, 1997.

Hegel, G. W. F. *Phenomenology of Spirit*. New York: Oxford University Press, 1977.

Homans, Peter. *The Ability to Mourn: Disillusionment and the Social Origins of Psychoanalysis*. Chicago: University of Chicago Press, 1990.

Imani, Ko. *Shirt of Flame: The Secret Gay Art of War*. Ypsilanti, Mich.: Goko Media, 2003.

James, William. *The Varieties of Religious Experience: A Study in Human Nature*. New York: Macmillan Publishing Co., 1961.

Jennings, Theodore W., Jr. *The Man Jesus Loved: Homoerotic Narratives from the New Testament*. Cleveland: Pilgrim Press, 2003.

Johnson, Toby. *Gay Perspective: Things Our Homosexuality Tells Us about the Nature of God and the Universe*. Los Angeles: Alyson Books, 2003.

Judge, Mark Gauvreau. "Bring back hate: It's a lost virtue in lost times." *New York Press*, vol. 16, issue 37 (10 Dec. 2003.) http://www.nypress.com.

Jung, Carl Gustav. *Modern Man in Search of a Soul.* New York: Harvest Books, 1955.

Keepin, Will, and Roger Walsh. "Is Our Fate in the Stars?" Institute of Noetic Sciences. Autumn 1997. http://www.noetic.org.

Kort, Joe. *Ten Smart Things Gay Men Can Do to Improve Their Lives.* Los Angeles: Alyson Books, 2003.

Kramer, Joseph. *Fire on the Mountain: Male Genital Massage.* The New School of Erotic Touch. Oakland, CA. DVD.

Kramer, Larry. *The Tragedy of Today's Gays.* New York: Penguin Books, 2005.

Küng, Hans. *Does God Exist? An Answer for Today.* New York: Vintage Books, 1981.

———. *On Being a Christian.* New York: Doubleday, 1984.

Lerner, Michael. *Spirit Matters.* Charlottesville, Virg.: Hampton Roads, 2002.

Liu, Timothy. *Burnt Offerings.* Port Townsend, Wash.: Copper Canyon Press, 1995.

Marion, Jim. *Putting on the Mind of Christ: The Inner Work of Christian Spirituality.* Charlottesville, Virg.: Hampton Roads, 2000.

Mattingly, Terry. "Coming soon to a theater near you: Hollywood Heaven lite." 14 Mar. 2004, GetReligion, http://www.getreligion.org.

———. "Liturgical Dances with Wolves: 10 Years as an Episcopalian: A Progress Report (1993.)" Prof. Terry Mattingly's Home Page, http://tmatt.gospelcom.net.

———. "Star Wars, Wolves, Gaia and that GetReligion bias." 30 Sept. 2004, GetReligion, http://www.getreligion.org.

McNeil, John. *Taking a Chance on God: Liberating Theology for Gays, Lesbians, and Their Lovers, Families, and Friends.* Boston: Beacon Press, 1988.

Metcalf, Linda Trichter, and Tobin Simon. *Writing the Mind Alive: The Proprioceptive Method for Finding Your Authentic Voice.* New York: Ballantine Books, 2002.

Mondimore, Francis Mark. *A Natural History of Homosexuality.* Baltimore: Johns Hopkins University Press, 1996.

Moore, Thomas. *Care of the Soul: A Guide for Cultivating Depth and Sacredness in Everyday Life.* New York: HarperCollins, 1992.

Moore, Robert, and Douglas Gilette. *King Warrior Magician Lover: Rediscovering the Archetypes of the Mature Masculine.* San Francisco: HarperSanFrancisco, 1991.

Morrison, David. *Beyond Gay.* Huntington, Ind: Our Sunday Visitor, 1999.

Nietzsche, Friedrich. *Untimely Meditations.* Cambridge: Cambridge University Press, 1983.

Nimmons, David. *The Soul Beneath the Skin: The Unseen Hearts and Habits of Gay Men.* New York: St. Martin's Press, 2002.

Rauch, Jonathan. *Gay Marriage: Why It Is Good for Gays, Good for Straights, and Good for America.* New York: Times Books, 2004.

Shea, Mark. "And in our Feast of St. Narcissus Dept." 19 Mar. 2004, Catholic and Enjoying It!, http://markshea.blogspot.com.

———. "Soulful Blogger Spews Highly Acidic Evolved Consciousness All Over the Screen." 11 May 2004, Catholic and Enjoying It!, http://markshea.blogspot.com.

———. "Theory and Practice." 25 Nov. 2003, Catholic and Enjoying It!, http://markshea.blogspot.com.

Solomon, Robert C., In the Spirit of Hegel: A Study of G.W.F. Hegel's Phenomenology of Spirit. New York: Oxford University Press, 1983.

Sullivan, Andrew. "A mandate for culture war." 3 Nov. 2004, The Daily Dish, http://www.andrewsullivan.com.

———. "Federalism works." 3 Nov. 2004, The Daily Dish, http://www.andrewsullivan.com.

———. "Out rage." 28 Sept. 2004, The New Republic Online, http://www.tnr.com.

———. Virtually Normal: An Argument about Homosexuality. New York: Alfred A. Knopf, 1995.

The Editors of The Stranger, "The Urban Archipelago." 11 Nov. 2004, The Stranger, http://www.thestranger.com.

Thompson, Mark. Gay Soul: Finding the Heart of Gay Spirit and Nature with Sixteen Writers, Healers, Teachers, and Visionaries. New York: HarperCollins, 1994.

Trujillo, Petirrojo. "Thoughts from a confused reader." 29 Dec. 2003. Trujillo's Xanga Site, http://www.xanga.com/Trujillo.

Tolkien, J. R. R. The Lord of the Rings. New York: Houghton Mifflin Company, 1998.

Waskow, Arthur. Godwrestling. New York: Schocken Books, 1987.

Wilber, Ken. Boomeritis: A Novel That Will Set You Free. Boston: Shambhala Publications, 2002.

———. "Excerpt G: Toward A Comprehensive Theory of Subtle Energies." www.kenwilber.com. (Accessed Oct. 2004.)

———. The Eye of Spirit: An Integral Vision for a World Gone Slightly Mad. Boston: Shambhala Publications, 1998.

———. Kosmic Consciousness. Boulder: Sounds True, 2000. Audio.

———. One Taste: Daily Reflections on Integral Spirituality. Boston: Shambhala Publications, 2000.

———. Sex, Ecology, Spirituality: The Spirit of Evolution. Boston: Shambhala Publications, 2000.

———. A Theory of Everything: An Integral Vision for Business, Politics, Science and Spirituality. Boston: Shambhala Publications, 2000.

Index